A New Deal for South Dakota

This publication is funded, in part, by the Great Plains
Education Foundation, Inc., Aberdeen, S.Dak.

Library of Congress Cataloging-in-Publication data is available.

Printed in the United States of America

The paper in this book meets the guidelines for permanence
and durability of the Committee on Production Guidelines
for Book Longevity of the Council on Library Resources.

Please visit our website at sdhspress.com

20 19 18 17 16   1 2 3 4 5

Cover illustration:
Workers constructed sidewalks in Volga, South Dakota,
under the auspices of the WPA, ca. 1938.
South Dakota State Historical Society

Designed and typeset by Judy Gilats

A New Deal for South Dakota

Drought, Depression, and Relief, 1920–1941

R. ALTON LEE

South Dakota Historical Society Press

PIERRE

For Ralph and Alice Lee

who raised six children

during these terrible times

Contents

Preface

LIFE PROVED FULL OF TRIBULATIONS for those hardy souls who moved west after the Civil War to settle the Great Plains. They needed fortitude, patience, and stamina if they were to acquire their share of the American Dream because they soon encountered a capitalist system that was not only uncontrolled but, instead, was fortified by the power of government, leading to exploitation of the poorer classes, both laborers and those who worked the land. In Dakota Territory, farmers finally rose in revolt, formed the Populist party, and fruitlessly tried to redress their grievances.

The failed Populist movement, however, sowed the seeds for later reform. South Dakotans were on the cutting edge of the Progressive changes, only to lapse into a period of conservatism and reaction, along with the rest of the nation, during the Great Crusade and the 1920s. These hard-working, self-reliant people had their mettle tested during this period with declining markets and crop prices, but their lives came completely undone when the capitalist system, again uncontrolled and unregulated, created the greatest depression the modern world had yet endured.

These tough farmers faced this economic blow, as well as the setbacks Mother Nature delivered: grasshoppers, droughts, and unprecedented dust storms that stripped away the top soil that was millions of years in the making. Most of South Dakota lies in an area that receives fewer than twenty inches of rainfall annually. From 1890 to 1935, however, precipitation was below average for half of those years. Drought, even more than economic depression, was the primary reason South Dakotans were desperate for relief in the Dirty Thirties. The years 1930 to 1934 saw the longest period of drought in the state since weather bureau records began. The combination of weather and economic conditions sent farmers and ranchers, along with thousands of other South Dakotans, to seek relief. They were forced to turn to the federal government, which they saw as having aligned with the capitalists who had exploited them—an indignity that tested their central political and economic mores. The most distressing statistic to come out of this situation is that, at the height of the relief load, 39 percent of the people in South Dakota were on relief rolls, compared to the national average of 13 percent.[1]

This "Greatest Generation," as native South Dakotan Tom Brokaw has hailed them, was severely tried. Their children were hungry, their cattle starving, their crops were drying up and blowing away—events that eventually overcame their pride, and they sought outside help. This is the story of those depression years in South Dakota that preceded World War II, which, while it restored the American economy, also tested the endurance of the country and the state of South Dakota.

In addition to Catherine McNicol Stock's fine scholarly study of the depression years in North and South Dakota, *Main Street in Crisis*, Paula Nelson has written *The Prairie Winnows Out Its Own*, which appeared in 1996—an excellent social and cultural analysis of the depression years in West River country, South Dakota. By contrast, my approach in this book is to emphasize the economic and political aspects of the New Deal from two perspectives: South Dakota's elected officials who administered President Roosevelt's many relief programs, and the state's citizens themselves.

The staffs of a number of libraries and archives assisted in this study. To begin at home, I must acknowledge the help of the staff at Hale Library at Kansas State University. Gene Morris of that magnificent research facility, Archives 2, was of great help in finding sources for me in the National Archives, as were Jake Ersland and Barbara Larsen in the regional archives of Kansas City. Dan Daily of the University of South Dakota archives was most helpful. Ken Stewart, Matthew Reitzel, and Virginia Hanson of the South Dakota State Historical Society were indispensable for those archives. Frank Nelson of the library in White City, Kansas; Melissa Lineman of the public library in Manhattan, Kansas; and a former hunting companion, Joe Edelen, and Stephen K. Johnson of the I. D. Weeks Library at the University of South Dakota were vital in handling the necessary interlibrary loans for me. Finally, my thanks to my wife Marilyn, who read and commented on the manuscript, and to Janet Daley Jury, who did an outstanding job in editing the final draft.

Unfortunately for this historian, South Dakota governors Tom Berry, Leslie Jensen, and Harlan J. Bushfield left no papers of any significance. Governor Jensen left one folder with some letters in the state archives at Pierre, but none of them pertains to the depression; Bushfield left two boxes in the archives at the University of South Dakota, devoted primarily to his party leadership and inaugural addresses. Michael Kennedy, another key player in the relief programs implemented in South Dakota, also left no papers.

My particular interest in this period of depression and the war years that followed comes because these were my formative childhood years. Born in 1931, I did not experience the negative effects of the 1930s because I was too young to be aware of the economic privation. My parents and older sisters had known the earlier prosperity in the 1920s and recognized that the penny allowance I received on Saturday nights when the family went to town was a pittance. I did not know this. For me, a penny bought a week's worth of hard candy. It was not until 1942, when my wages for odd jobs rocketed from ten cents to twenty-five cents per hour, that I saw the difference and felt suddenly rich!

My parents never recovered from the ordeal of making a living for a family of eight during those difficult times. For the next three decades, my father continued to warn me that the nation would soon endure another Great Depression and we must be prepared. I wrote this book to bring a historical perspective to the experiences of my parents, who knew the difference between prosperity and depression, and I dedicate it to them.

A New Deal for South Dakota

1 Before the New Deal

Miles and miles and miles of flat brown country. Snowdrifts here and there. Russian thistles rolling across the roads. Unpainted buildings going to seed. Hardly a straw stack or haystack for miles. What a country—to keep out of.

Lorena Hickok to Harry L. Hopkins
on Winner, South Dakota[1]

DURING WORLD WAR I, the government encouraged farmers to plant from "fence to fence" to produce for the fighting forces and to supply a seemingly insatiable European market. "Food Will Win the War" was the rallying cry, so farmers turned out livestock and cereals to their limit and beyond, and prices continued to spiral upward. Some of the increased production came from techniques that were more efficient; a good deal came from thirty million acres of sod formerly used for livestock production that were plowed under in South Dakota and elsewhere on the Great Plains and planted to wheat.

This agrarian prosperity continued after the war ended until European agricultural production was restored, and the normal flow of grain resumed from Canada, Australia, and Argentina to European markets. Wheat prices began to decline in 1920, and South Dakota farmers soon found themselves in a depression. Small farmers, who had overexpanded their tillage, were hardest hit and found it difficult to adjust. Increasing technology in the form of improved machinery and the widespread introduction of tractors made ag-riculture more efficient, but it exacerbated the crisis as farmers now faced the cost of accelerating mechanization. New scientific farming methods and the latest findings of the county agents were another challenge. With all this, the average farmer could handle 138 acres in South Dakota, but the continued output of surpluses of corn, wheat, hogs, and milk drove down their market prices dras-tically.[2] Another factor in the economic plight of farmers was the high protective tariff implemented during the 1920s.[3]

Presidents Warren Harding, Calvin Coolidge, and Herbert Hoover had all enjoyed the fiscal advice of Secretary of the Trea-sury Andrew Mellon, banker and multimillionaire head of the Alcoa Corporation. He recommended keeping taxes low on large incomes and maintaining a high tariff to protect American manufacturers from foreign competition. There were no controls over the easy credit available for speculation on the wild bull market on the New York Stock Exchange. Buyers purchased more and more stocks on less and less margin until 24 October 1929, when the market crashed under this pressure. In the next three years, the value of stocks de-clined from almost $90 billion to less than $20 billion. This gigan-tic paper loss did not cause the Great Depression, but it proved to be a trigger, resulting in a catastrophe for the world's leading cap-italist system and only a little less so for American farmers. South Dakota, fundamentally an agrarian state, suffered terribly.[4]

While wages rose slightly during the twenties, the fiscal policies implemented during the decade brought stagnating incomes for the middle class. On the other hand, from 1923 to 1929, the top 400,000 people who reported incomes of more than $10,000 increased their income by 76.6 percent; the top 40,000 by 129.5 percent; the top 4,000 by 207.5 percent; and the income of the 400 "real rulers" of America increased by 234.5 percent. An article in *The American Mercury* noted, "The bigger the ownership the better it did."[5]

Even conservative bankers indulged in stock market hysteria, and they suffered accordingly, with 5,000 banks failing across the nation during the three-year financial debacle after the 1929 crash. Corporate income fell from $2.5 billion in profits in 1930 to net zero in 1931 and to $3.5 billion in net losses in 1932. Unemployment rocketed to 25 percent, perhaps as high as 33 percent—no one is certain because the government did not keep accurate records at that time. The price of wheat dropped from one dollar to thirty-eight cents, corn to thirty-two cents, and hogs to six cents. Gross farm income, already low, declined another 60 percent during this chaos. After 1920, rural incomes were about half the size of incomes in the manufacturing sector.[6]

The depression's most devastating effect hit farmers and the small town business owners whose existence depended on them for their commerce—more than half of the American population. This depression was far more devastating than the Panic of 1893 or any other similar episode that Americans had yet witnessed.[7] Following the stock market crash, Mother Nature struck blows in rapid succession. The drought in 1930 was so severe that "it literally tore, cracked, and ruined the earth." Unbearable heat and awesome swarms of grasshoppers destroyed the crops. One South Dakota rancher recalled, "It started to get dry in 1930 . . . and every year it got worse." Between 1927 and 1938 there were two relatively wet years, but the rest were dry, with 1934 and 1936 being the driest residents had ever endured. Wells, springs, small streams, and even lakes dried up. Chinook winds followed the cold, snowy winters. They brought such a quick thaw that the moisture ran off without even penetrating the thirsty soil. A few spring showers and a few drops of rain in the hot summer followed, but moisture often arrived when the crops were no longer salvageable. If crops survived in one of these better summers, plagues of grasshoppers that hatched quickly in the dry, windy weather devoured everything in sight. Once the crops were gone, they ate up the meager family gardens. Once the land was barren, the dust storms began.[8] Prices dropped for crops, and, as farmers suffered, they bought less while unemployment spread. South Dakota towns depended on farmers, and when they had no money to make purchases, storekeepers had to cut back inventories.[9]

Homemakers tried to make do with sewing underwear from flour sacks. Farmers fed their livestock with Russian thistles. They found that if they cut them green and stacked them, they made "fair feed." However, the cattle developed sore mouths and diarrhea, forcing one to stay "ten feet behind when bringing home the milk cows." Professionals, even teachers, did not always receive their salary in cash. They lived on chickens and eggs and received their pay in warrants or scrip that merchants discounted. Selling one's real estate was difficult; in fact, in many cases one could not give it away. One man complained bitterly that "the fellow who never did have anything anyway—can get plenty of help . . . [but] the fellow who has kept out of debt must now get into debt to get any help from the government."[10]

During the 1920s, the national average per capita income for the decade hovered around $750, but for farmers it was $250.[11] While the annual farm income declined, the importance of the income farm wives brought to the family increased. Commonly called "pin money," in fact, the value of women's supplemental income became more significant to families. Studies by historians Dorothy Schwieder and Barbara Handy-Marchello, among others, have revealed how important women's contributions were to the family farm, sometimes making the difference between starvation and sustenance, foreclosure or survival.[12]

Farmwomen had traditionally planted large gardens and canned large amounts of fruit and vegetables. Letters to the *Dakota Farmer* indicate this aspect of farm life played an increased role during the depression years. Not only did the farmwife increase her production for the family table, but in some cases, she produced extra food for cash sales. Some women reported canning fifty quarts each of several vegetables annually. In Schwieder's study, a Lawrence County farmwife indicated she had canned this quantity and "put away" 1,400 pounds of potatoes, along with a bushel of onions. With five milk cows and some chickens, she estimated her grocery bill at two dollars weekly.[13]

Women also made a significant contribution with poultry and eggs. Many hatched their own chicks, both with setting hens and with incubators. Some women produced two or three batches yearly. Throughout the 1930s, "many women raised flocks larger than 399 chickens." Between 1932 and 1941, South Dakota women averaged production of 523 million eggs annually and sold 72 percent of them. Turkey production also thrived on these farms.

Women shared the milking duties and were largely responsible for the separation of cream from the milk. Butter making was a related task. They used the butter at home and sold it to town families and to merchants in a barter system. The farmwife "traded" eggs and butter to the grocer for items that needed to be purchased, such as condiments and clothing. Letters to the *Dakota Farmer* indicated that poultry, eggs, and dairy products were "absolutely essential for feeding and clothing farm families."[14] Farmwives during the depression also stopped purchasing many of their household supplies and either made them at home or found substitutes. They used fine ashes for scouring or cleaning and made their own soap. Many sent in recipes for homemade toothpaste, furniture polish, fly paper, fly spray, hand lotion, and stove cleaner.

In addition, rural women in the early part of the twentieth century faced physically demanding and time-consuming chores to keep the household running. To do the weekly washing, a farmwife pumped water from an outside well, hauled it into the house, and heated it on a wood or coal stove. She ironed and cleaned house with only the simple and traditional tools available without electricity. She baked and cooked for her family and whatever hired hands might be working on the farm, and in her spare time, she raised a large garden (when rains came) and did an immense amount of canning. These chores were daily, in addition to the farm work she provided when her husband was unusually busy, during the calving season, for example, and through the threshing season.

National home economist Day Monroe reported that South Dakota farmwomen, through cash income, bartering, or trading farm
products for family necessities, might realize half the annual farm
income of $634. While letter after letter written to the *Dakota
Farmer* during the Great Depression reflected the accepted view of
farming as "essentially a male occupation," women's supportive
work was essential for the family.[15]

Almost all the South Dakota farmers raised grain and livestock,
cultivating approximately 200 acres. The remaining acreage was
devoted to horses and mules, cattle, hogs, sheep, and chickens.
Raising hogs was their most profitable endeavor. Typical of the
area, farm tenancy averaged 41.5 percent. These farmers neglected
to keep adequate records but most failed to clear $500 annually.
Tax burdens were excessive as rural South Dakotans sought to improve their roads and schools to satisfy the needs of expanded use
of gasoline-powered vehicles. In the late 1920s, about 66 of every
1,000 farms in South Dakota were sold for taxes. These sales increased rapidly from 1928 to 1932, and in 1933, there were 103.1
farms per 1,000 changing ownership, with 25.1 percent of these
coming from default on taxes.

In 1890, 55 percent of farms in Potter County had no indebtedness; by 1930, this had dropped to 27 percent. Southeastern South
Dakota had the lowest tax delinquency in the state while some
West River counties had delinquency rates of 40 percent or higher.
A precipitation map superimposed over a tax delinquency map
shows that counties with the least precipitation had the greatest
tax delinquency rate. The farm crisis was not of one variety but "a
whole series of integrated problems."[16]

Many farmers had overexpanded, and their expectations had
"ballooned," but "both plummeting land values and anemic commodity prices had deprived them" of a standard of living comparable to the urban middle class. As a result, many took out second
mortgages and became ever more deeply mired in debt. With their
increasing grain surpluses, high farm debts, and declining land

values, South Dakota farmers were "ill-prepared to face the Great Depression" when it hit.[17]

In this chaotic situation, farmers were willing to follow leaders who offered ready panaceas or proposed chimerical ideas to solve their situation. The first U.S. senator from South Dakota, Richard F. Pettigrew, was one such politician. Senator Pettigrew, conservative Republican turned Silver Republican (in favor of moving from a gold standard to silver) turned Populist-cum-Democrat, and finally a Socialist, followed a number of popular paths depending on the current political winds. At the end of his career, ready to incur the wrath of national authority, he eventually supported the Farmer-Labor movement. When that group met in Chicago in July 1923, the former South Dakota senator welcomed them with a speech praising the Soviet system. "All power to the men who do the work and create the wealth," he urged; "Don't buy the mines and railroads, take them." He died shortly thereafter.[18]

At about the same time, a powerful political movement with strong Socialist tendencies was sweeping the Dakotas. A. C. Townley, a North Dakota farm organizer, made rapid headway with his Nonpartisan League (NPL) movement, beginning in 1915. Townley viewed railroads, banks, machinery "trusts," and lawyers as the farmers' major enemies and promoted the political concept that their salvation lay in entering the political arena by capturing primary elections for their candidates on a nonpartisan basis. These Socialists pursued a program of government-owned mills and elevators and a rural credits plan to make agrarian loans at low interest rates. Townley discovered farmers liked his ideas but disliked the "red card" membership of the Socialist party. They were willing to support his Socialist plans by voting for nonpartisan candidates who promised to promote the Socialist goals of government-owned resources important to farmers.[19]

These concepts were quickly exported into neighboring South Dakota and Minnesota. In the latter, the movement eventually emerged as the Farmer-Labor party during the depression decade.

A friend of two-term South Dakota Governor Peter Norbeck (1917–1921) warned him that the NPL was invading his state like "a swarm of grasshoppers." Norbeck was a liberal Republican and a supporter of Theodore Roosevelt's policies. Most importantly, he was a relentless promoter of his farmers and wanted desperately to help them out of their economic morass without resorting to socialism.[20]

Norbeck had espoused progressive Republican views in his campaign for the governorship in 1916. He saw no problem with extending the powers of the state government if that authority were used to help his embattled farmers. After winning the election, Norbeck proposed and the legislature approved a rural credits program similar to that in North Dakota in an effort to combat current high interest rates. In contrast to the conservative Republican government in North Dakota before the election of 1918, his legislature was controlled by progressive Republicans, and they had no hesitation in endorsing Norbeck's constitutional amendments to extend governmental powers into new areas. These included creating a post for a commissioner to control abuses in marketing; establishing a workmen's compensation law; creating a state highway department; and appointing committees to investigate the possibility of operating a coal mine and a cement plant, and also building mills and grain elevators, similar to those activities taking place in North Dakota. South Dakota eventually owned a cement plant that prospered and a coal mine that suffered from inefficient management. When mining had nearly depleted the coal, the mine was sold at a loss of nearly $175,000.[21]

George N. Peek, a farm economist who became president of the Moline Plow Company in Illinois, observed, "You can't sell a plow to a busted farmer," and led the campaign at this time to enact the McNary-Haugen Farm Relief bill. This program sought to remove surpluses from the market to force an increase in domestic prices, and farm leaders in South Dakota desperately pinned their hopes on this assistance. Introduced in 1924, the measure finally passed

Congress in 1927 only to have President Calvin Coolidge veto it. Congress passed it again the following year with another Coolidge veto. He explained that the national government could not interfere with economic forces to help farmers, although it was helping business with high tariffs, low taxes, and other policies.[22]

In South Dakota, the two governors who served during President Hoover's term were from different parties but took very similar approaches to the impending disaster that the depression was fast becoming. The state's first eleven governors were Republicans (Andrew Lee was officially listed as a Populist), and the party had held sway in South Dakota politics for years. In the election of 1926, however, for the first time, voters elected a Democrat. William J. Bulow defeated the incumbent Carl Gunderson, and held the position for two terms, 1927–1931. Bulow proved to be a "conservative old line" Democrat who made few people unhappy. Despite the economic woes that loomed, Bulow viewed his second administration "as a sort of era of good feeling." In 1930, he decided to forego another gubernatorial race and ran instead for the U.S. Senate seat held by William H. McMaster, a Republican and former governor. He won by the narrow margin of 6,000 votes and went on to serve two terms.

With the governor's seat open, the Democrats nominated D. A. McCullough, while five candidates were involved in the Republican primary. Gladys Pyle received 33,000 votes, Gunderson 31,000, Brooke Howell 22,000, Carl Trygstad 21,000, and Warren E. Green 8,000. Because no candidate won the required 35 percent, the delegates to the state convention held a runoff, during which one of the candidates withdrew in favor of Green, who then won on the twelfth ballot. In a modest campaign, Green, a former state senator, subsequently defeated McCullough by 15,000 votes in the general election. A conservative self-styled "dirt farmer" of Hamlin County, Governor Green continued Bulow's fiscal policies during the emerging depression.[23]

The Green family had moved from Vermont to Wisconsin to Iowa and, after the Civil War, to South Dakota, where Green farmed in Hamlin County. By the time he became governor, he and his wife owned five quarters of land and sixty Hereford cattle. Advocating a conservative course of action for South Dakota, Green was plagued with patronage problems after his party came to power, and he made thousands of enemies by saying "no." His proposed budget cut the one Bulow had proposed by $500,000 and the legislature reduced this by an additional $200,000, compensating with a slash in state employee salaries. When North Dakota's capitol building was destroyed by a fire in December 1930, the South Dakota legislature quickly determined to protect its own state records and authorized an annex costing $270,000. To pay for this, Green attempted to cut state expenditures further by reducing college and university salaries by 10 percent.[24] Problems were multiplying exponentially for the state and the nation.

President Herbert Hoover tried to help farmers by persuading Congress to establish the Federal Farm Board in 1929. The board was to promote the marketing of farm commodities through cooperatives and stabilization corporations. The law provided for a revolving fund of $500 million for loans to these agencies. After spending $180 million of this had been spent and the Grain Stabilization Board had accumulated 257,000,000 bushels of wheat without any appreciable effect on prices, this purchasing program was dropped. The solution to the problem of surpluses remained out of reach. The Federal Farm Board had spent $345 million by 1933, and its attempts to "urge" farmers to cut production were a miserable failure. Force was required for the recalcitrant.[25]

South Dakota's percentage of population engaged in agriculture was the fourth largest in the Union. The paucity of other natural resources, such as timber, petroleum, coal, and waterpower, compounded the problem. Due to the lack of natural resources and subsequent lack of industries, when crops failed, there was little to which farmers could turn for a livelihood. Their suffering also affected the small towns whose merchants were dependent on them as their most numerous and reliable customers. For the first time most of the merchants had to announce a "cash only" policy. "We trust in the Lord," their signs read, "cash only to all others." Bonds for city improvements languished as town taxpayers were unwilling to commit themselves in the depressed economic conditions. The economic downturn forced banks to merge or close, taking depositors' savings down with them. It drove county and other local units of government to curtail services. School officials "struggled to hold costs down," cut salaries, and often resorted to paying teachers in scrip (redeemable with local merchants); merchants became increasingly skeptical of accepting it, as the scrip was not an acceptable currency to pay for replenishing their inventory. In farm country, when farmers hurt, everyone hurts.[26]

With real estate values in a sharp decline and the farmers' outgo, in terms of fixed charges, including taxes and debts, remaining stationary, the result was a sharp rise in tax delinquency. Farm foreclosures, which reached a high in 1924–1925, were again on the increase in 1932. Some 34,419 farm foreclosures occurred from 1921 to 1932, with one-third of them in the last two years. Farm tenancy rose from 34.9 percent in 1920 to 44.6 percent by 1930 and provided many reasons for a farm revolt.[27]

Farmers who were strapped for cash sought loans to keep their operations going. To receive loans for reseeding, farmers had to describe the land to be seeded and how the loan was to be repaid. The county auditor received this information, and each county had a loan committee to oversee the process. To receive any kind of assistance, South Dakotans had to demonstrate that family resources were exhausted or real property was mortgaged before receiving relief. When the Hoover administration acknowledged the responsibility of the national government in this economic crisis, it marked a turning point in the role the federal government was to play.

Late in President Hoover's term, Congress authorized his Reconstruction Finance Corporation (RFC) to loan $300 million to states for relief work. Most authorities assumed, correctly, that the loans would never be repaid. The needy also began receiving surplus commodities from the Federal Surplus Relief Corporation (FSRC). Among other programs, the RFC set up a feed and grain loan program that helped farmers remain on their land. This approach would work in a short-term crisis, but the Great Depression was not temporary. As it continued, farmers incurred further debts, which Mother Nature prevented them from repaying by destroying their crops.[28]

The RFC was revolutionary for South Dakota. To take advantage of RFC loans, Governor Green established a required State Relief Committee. Members included Attorney General Merrill Q. Sharpe, Henry McGrath of Aberdeen, W. C. Lusk of Yankton, B. C. Yates of Lead, and R. F. Looby of Artesian. In mid-November 1932, Roy L. Emry, state relief director, telegraphed county commissioners in fifty-seven counties who had relief projects currently functioning that they must halve their programs until a new plan of relief was constructed. Emry, at the time, was in Washington, D.C., to learn about the new federal plan to help relief with RFC funding. At this point South Dakota had received $368,000 in RFC loans, in addition to $50,000 for the Mount Rushmore project, and these funds were being used primarily for road building and water improvements.[29]

One week later, Roland Hayes of the RFC held a conference in Pierre to instruct the governor and other state officials on the new program. Green was able to telegraph county officials that they should resume work relief with loans ranging from $1,000 to $5,000. Work relief supervisors and county commissioners were warned not to exceed their allotments and to give the work "only to the destitute needy families." Hayes then returned to Washington with South Dakota's request for an additional loan of $436,000 from the RFC and information to substantiate the need for increased funding.

The new plan called for shifting administration of the funds from the county commissioners to "individual administrators" in

Beadle, Davison, Codington, "and possibly other counties." Workers would be compensated with food, clothing, and fuel, but not in cash, and the funds would be used "entirely for destitution relief and not for unemployment relief." RFC loans for South Dakota were cut from Hayes's recommendation of $436,000 to $290,000. Emry lamented the fact that the amount was "not as large as we had hoped to get" but the state could now "meet relief needs up to the first of the year."[30]

As conditions worsened, the rumblings of a farm revolt could be heard across the Midwest. The agrarian movements took various forms and had a variety of leaders. Milo Reno, president of the Iowa Farmers' Union from 1921 through 1930, became the leader of a populist organization known as the Farmers' Holiday Association (FHA), established in 1932. In addition to currency inflation and agricultural production and price controls, Reno and his supporters were promoting farm strikes in the Midwest to call attention to the plight of Great Plains farmers.[31]

Beginning with a "cow war" in Iowa, Reno goaded farmers into taking direct action through his FHA. Dairy farmers began blockading the highways into Sioux City, Iowa, by leaving boards with protruding nails in them and dumping the milk of those who tried to run the gauntlet. In the autumn of 1932, and again in 1933, they blockaded highways into market cities such as Sioux City, Madison, Yankton, and Sioux Falls, demanding the withholding of crops until the cost-of-production issue was settled. In Moville, Iowa, and Jefferson, South Dakota, angry farmers halted freight trains hauling farm produce into Sioux City. Fifty farmers at Jefferson were placing torpedoes on railroad tracks, waving red lanterns to halt trains. This, of course, was a direct interdiction of the flow of interstate commerce that quickly caught the attention of federal officials who brought this activity to an immediate halt. These agrarians also insisted the Frazier-Lemke Farm Mortgage Moratorium Act, languishing in Congress, be enacted to refinance farm mortgages. Further, they revived the old Populist demand to expand the amount of currency in circulation.[32] Farmers in the wheat, corn, and hog belts of eastern South Dakota were particularly active in the boycott movement. In a brief holding action in Watertown, events got out of control, resulting in the shooting death of one person.

Emil Loriks, a wealthy farmer from Oldham, South Dakota, and a leader of the state's FHA from 1927 to 1932, had "logged thousands of miles" in organizing support. He urged moderation at all times and found his cooperative approach to be particularly appealing to South Dakota business leaders. Two hundred of the 1,200 people that launched the Holiday movement in Minnehaha County were business owners. Historian John E. Miller discovered that they and lawyers often played key leadership roles in farm organizations and as organizers. Loriks found that "the residents of towns and cities are backing the movement better than the farmers in many instances." He noted that merchants and business owners in Howard and De Smet had joined the Holiday movement 100 percent but more important, all had paid their fifty-cent dues.[33]

While Governor Green was sympathetic to Farm Holiday goals, he sought peaceful means to achieve them. He addressed a Holiday meeting in Huron in August 1932 and "indicated his approval of a holding action," but insisted on using his gubernatorial authority to keep highways open. He received approval from the FHA board to hold a meeting of governors and farm leaders from fifteen states in Sioux City on 9 September to formulate "an orderly, practical, legal, and nonviolent plan" to increase farm prices. There were many South Dakotans among the five thousand in attendance who listened to Farm Holiday spokesmen threatening a farm revolution if their demands were not met.[34]

The governors rejected the cost-of-production concept, the Frazier-Lemke farm bill, and the strategy of withholding produce from markets. Attorney General Sharpe opined there was no legal basis for states to embargo goods crossing their borders; in fact, he advised governors that this would contravene the power of the national government to control interstate commerce. Instead, the governors submitted "a tepid set of resolutions" for President Hoover's consideration. The Holiday leaders then proceeded with plans for a voluntary withholding of livestock and grain, and the governor gave this action "his full support." As a result, grain receipts fell at Rapid City and Huron for a couple of days, and hog sales at Sioux Falls, the state's primary hog market, were cut in half, but generally the state remained calm. Most farmers were resolved to wait and evaluate the Roosevelt farm plan.[35]

Communists and other radicals, however, were not idle during this crisis. The Communist front for farmers, the United Farmers League (UFL), was very active in North Dakota, as well as in Roberts and Brown Counties in northeastern South Dakota, where the cities of Frederick and Sisseton are located. This area had formed the basis for support of liberal politics since Populist days and continuing through Socialist organizing and to the NPL failure to conquer South Dakota politics. John Miller notes, "These locations were also the home to the most prosperous farmers working in the highest valued land in the state and, in general, they suffered less from drought and depression than did farmers further west."[36]

Clarence Sharp, who sold the Socialist newspaper *Appeal to Reason* on the streets of Bristol, South Dakota, in the first decade of the twentieth century and was currently an implement dealer, supported the NPL and joined the Communist Party "in 1930 or 1931," according to historian William Pratt. He became South Dakota chair of the Communist Party, USA (CPUSA) in 1932 and was soon busy organizing branches and recruiting members. He found most success in the northeast corner of the state and brought Knute Walstad and his son Julius, farmers in Roberts County, into the fold, who proceeded to support CPUSA member William Z. Foster for president in the 1932 campaign. Pratt notes that the area "was ripe for Communist organizing," and there may have been 100 members there by 1933. Sharp also recruited successfully in West River country among former Socialists and members of the NPL.

In 1931, another Communist Party leader, Ella Reeve "Mother"

Bloor, and her North Dakota recruits organized a "drought relief caravan" to exchange coal mined in North Dakota for wheat grown in northeast South Dakota. Trucks drove through North Dakota to Frederick, South Dakota, in August 1931 then hauled grain back for sale in North Dakota.[37]

In Wilmot in Roberts County, former members of the Ku Klux Klan joined the CPUSA and were in the forefront of radical agitation. In Milbank, a forced sale of a farmer's chattels attracted "a large number" of United Farmers League (UFL) members who attempted to prevent a deputy sheriff from holding an auction. He pointed his gun at someone and it discharged. The crowd disarmed the deputies and conducted a "Sears-Roebuck" sale, also known as a "penny auction," where the neighbors bought equipment and livestock for a penny or a nickel and returned them to the owner. The state brought an injunction against the UFL and "some ninety individuals," prosecuting fifteen of them for this violence. After a dramatic trial in Sisseton, a local jury acquitted them.[38] In another example of violence, in February 1933, Keats Markell and his two sons tried to run a highway blockade near Sioux City and all three received buckshot wounds. Conditions were deteriorating rapidly, requiring cohesive legislative action that the divisive legislature was unable to provide.[39] Pratt estimates that there were 300 to 500 members of CPUSA in South Dakota, but their numbers declined after 1934 when the Agricultural Adjustment Act (AAA) program was proving successful.[40] These assaults by conservatives and reactionaries stoked the early flames of anti-Communism that Karl Mundt was able to exploit in his election of 1938 and thereafter.[41]

In an address at the annual state attorneys' meeting in 1932, Attorney General M. Q. Sharpe described what this topsy-turvy world order was doing to South Dakotans. He deplored the "vote-buying statesmanship of the 20th century" that he said was weakening public morale. He lamented that "shyster politicians, lavish use of public funds for pensions, bonuses and public works had encouraged a tendency to lean on and live off the government." He deplored the effect of the "beneficiaries of mothers' pensions and poor relief funds cavorting around in automobiles, attending movie picture shows and enjoying a better state of affluence than the average citizen enjoys." Sharpe and other conservatives found this new attitude of indolence and dependence on the state for support to be degrading and a regrettable development for American society.[42]

The help from Mothers' Pensions to which Sharpe referred was the major contemporary support for needy children in these trying times. This program dated from the Progressive period when reformers were attacking child labor abuses. They discovered that available charitable sources were insufficient to sustain children who had no father to support the family. A coalition headed by federated women's associations managed to overcome intense opposition to providing for these pension funds. Between 1911 and 1913, twenty states established such a program. By 1935, only Georgia and South Carolina had failed to do so. The South Dakota legislature was on the cutting edge of this movement, enacting a fund in 1911.[43]

The South Dakota program made a cash allowance for children of poor women who had been widowed, divorced, or abandoned. Judges of county courts determined the amounts, usually using the average costs of "institutionalizing" the children in orphanages or poor houses as a basis for payments. In South Dakota in 1931, the average grant per month per family was $21.78, about in the middle of a list of forty-three states. After a judge awarded the status of "worthy poor" and decided upon the stipend, based on need, the father's status, and the suitability of the home, an official periodically visited the family to determine if the conditions of the award were being maintained. The sums were generally inadequate, forcing the mothers to supplement this income by taking in laundry or engaging in some other kind of domestic work.

American relief laws had been based on English poor laws that assumed the poor were responsible for their condition and that "they had to be forced to overcome their laziness and go to work." If relief became necessary, it was the responsibility of local government or private charity. As historian William Bremer asserted, often the destitute were subject to means tests and "direct relief was given in kind, so that others prescribed what the unemployed should eat or wear."[44] County commissioners appointed a "Poor Agent" in charge of overseeing the county dole, grocery list, trade in kind, or whatever system they used to feed the hungry. Mothers' Pensions were later supplanted by Works Progress Administration (WPA) programs for women, which helped relieve the financial pressure on county budgets, followed by Social Security's Aid to Dependent Children (ADC). The Children's Bureau in the Department of Labor sought to monitor the earlier program, but later the State Bureau of Social Services took responsibility for it.[45]

The Great Depression challenged these concepts and showed Americans that poverty "could be caused by brutal economic circumstances, not just weak character." The widespread economic crisis demonstrated that local government and private charity were inadequate, and the situation required national action. Such federal assistance would not "sully" the character of the poor.[46]

The Great Depression also revealed the truth that all the Great Plains states whose economies were primarily agricultural and whose populations were largely rural were not created equal. Neighboring states—Kansas, Nebraska, and even North Dakota— were more advanced industrially than South Dakota. Their economies were rooted in the production of grain and livestock, but, in addition, Kansas held extensive oil and gas deposits, Nebraska had its meatpacking industry, and North Dakota possessed processing plants for its agricultural production. In contrast, South Dakota's economy was fully dependent on agriculture with only a smattering of extractive work and a tourism industry in its infancy.

At the same time, South Dakota faced droughts and grasshopper plagues even more severe than in neighboring states. These conditions dealt significant blows to an already aggrieved economy, which, in combination with the economic conditions, placed almost 40 percent of the state's population in a crisis condition.[47]

In late 1931, Secretary of Agriculture Arthur M. Hyde wrote in a letter to President Herbert Hoover, "Tens of thousands of farm families have had their savings swept away and even their subsistence threatened." The following year, Edward A. O'Neal, president of the conservative Farm Bureau Federation, warned Congress, "Unless something is done for the American farmer we will have revolution in the countryside in less than twelve months."[48]

President Herbert Hoover strove diligently but fruitlessly to stem these economic tides. When he ran for reelection in 1932, the economic life of the country was already draining away, and continuing the policies of his Republican predecessors did not staunch the flow. American voters were looking for change in 1932 and found it in Franklin Delano Roosevelt's (FDR) campaign promises of a New Deal.

The depression was nearing its nadir by the election of 1932. With unemployment and destitution rampant, the voters turned to Franklin D. Roosevelt, whose presidential campaign appealed to the "forgotten man on the bottom of the economic pyramid." Onefourth of farmers had lost their farms before Hoover left office, and most of those who maintained possession of their land were having a difficult time surviving. South Dakotans blamed the president and his lack of interest in agrarian concerns.[49]

An unsuccessful Democratic candidate for the vice presidency in 1920, Roosevelt developed poliomyelitis the next year that left him permanently paralyzed from the waist down. Nevertheless, he kept his name and political future alive, placing Alfred ("Al") E. Smith's name in nomination for the presidency in 1924 at the Democratic convention to run against President Calvin Coolidge. Four years later, Smith lost to Herbert Hoover, while FDR became the governor of New York. When the Great Depression struck, Governor Roosevelt instituted a feasible state program to combat adverse economic conditions and won a second term two years later by a wide margin. By 1932, he was ready to challenge Smith, who continued to seek his turn in the White House.[50]

Roosevelt's promise of a "New Deal" resonated with farmers. During a coast-to-coast campaign tour, the New Yorker appealed to farmers in a major speech in Topeka, Kansas, in which he promoted a domestic allotment plan. The brainchild of a Montana economist, M. L. Wilson, the domestic allotment plan operated on the idea that agriculture had to adjust production to demand or, according to the current philosophy, follow a program of "planned scarcity." In contrast, Hoover spoke to farmers about keeping the tariff high to protect their products. If the Democrats were to enact their promise of a low tariff, Hoover asserted, "grass would grow in the streets of a hundred cities, a thousand towns, the weeds will overrun a million farms." Roosevelt's ready response was that was exactly what was happening with the current Republican tariff, the highest in American history.

In 1932, all eyes were on the presidential race between Franklin D. Roosevelt and the incumbent Herbert C. Hoover. In South Dakota, which was traditionally a bulwark for Republicans, historian Herbert S. Schell noted, "the smaller margin of victory for Republican state candidates in 1930 and an increase in the number of Democratic legislators clearly portended unrest among the voters." The unrest was apparent among the Republicans where fissures again broke open. Green's supporters denounced the use of taxes to promote Black Hills tourist attractions during difficult economic times and were convinced the Mount Rushmore carving was never-ending, frivolous, and needlessly costly. Norbeck defended the development of the Black Hills as vital to the state's future and won his primary.[51]

On the Democratic side, Emil Loriks declined the urgings that he run for governor. Fearing that an election run would only prove to be an opportunity to mortgage his farm in a losing effort, he misjudged the mood of the country and his state. The futile efforts of President Hoover to combat the depressed conditions heralded

1932 as a Democratic year. The ongoing economic crises of adverse weather and continued depression are revealed in the real estate statistics of the time.

By 1932, the average value of South Dakota farmland had dropped from $71.39 in 1921, to $35.24 in 1930. It would continue to decline to $18.65 in 1935. Wheat brought 50 cents, corn 30 cents, and hogs $2.68 per hundredweight. These factors increased the farmers' debt burden, and in 1931–1932 some 7 million acres, or 19.6 percent of the farmland in the state, suffered foreclosure. This produced "public outcry for relief" on property taxes.[52]

The Democrats drew up a platform calling for reduction in state expenditures and a revision of the tax code to place it on "the ability to pay." The major farm organizations, the Farmers Union, the Farm Bureau, and the Grange, agreed on a plan of action for farm programs on the state and national levels, a graduated income tax, and a severance tax on gold. They chose Tom Berry, a cattleman from Belvedere, as their candidate for governor.

Berry had been born in Paddock, Nebraska, married a schoolteacher named Lorena McLain, and homesteaded in Mellette County, South Dakota. Over the years they built up a prosperous ranch of 30,000 acres, raising Hereford cattle and superior saddle horses under the XX brand. The father of four children, he served three terms in the South Dakota House of Representatives and on the Custer State Park Board until Governor Warren E. Green replaced him with a Republican. The two men now faced off for the governor's chair.

South Dakota Superintendent of Banks Fred R. Smith became an issue in the 1932 campaign. Attorney General Sharpe investigated the state's financial institutions and disclosed Smith's misappropriation of funds. When he was arrested, he admitted to the embezzlement of $1.2 million from closed banks whose assets had been "placed in a state bank operated by members of his family." He pled guilty and received a seven-year prison term in 1931. Governor Green had previously praised Smith publicly, then Smith confessed, making himself *persona non grata* politically, and the Republicans tried to turn the issue back on the Democrats. They argued that the Democrats had reappointed him to office, blaming Berry with "guilt by association." Excitement over this disclosure had not dissipated when the state was struck with grasshopper invasions, drought, and crop failures. A decade of economic disasters left the state ill-prepared for these additional distresses.[53]

Berry was a "ruggedly handsome" fellow with a droll sense of humor. With a paucity of funds, Berry used his western wit to good effect in the campaign.[54] For example, in one of his speeches, he insisted there was "so much nepotism in Pierre that they could have a father and son banquet every night." Berry made up for a lack of campaign funds by energetically campaigning, often delivering twenty talks a day. His wit, down-to-earth explanation of problems, and proposed solutions proved most effective in wooing South Dakota voters."[55] Senator Bulow "enthusiastically joined the campaign," traveling with Berry and appearing at a large rally with him in the Sioux Falls Coliseum. Former governor Carl Gunderson also endorsed Berry as he "vehemently disagreed" with a number of Governor Green's policies and wanted a change in leadership in Pierre.

As early as mid-July the *Argus-Leader* reported the campaign of 1932 as heating up. Both parties were ignoring the political issue of prohibition and stressing the sick economy. Democrats described Hoover's plan of recovery as "hesitant and blundering, and in the interests of the rich and powerful." In turn, Republicans pictured Roosevelt as "weak, vague and given to radical predictions." Governor Green offered this Hooveresque statement on the campaign trail: "People will soon lose their fear of the future when they see a fine improvement made possible by a fine crop."[56] Both candidates insisted they would cut state expenses more deeply than the other, symbolized by Berry with the axe he carried on the campaign trail. He promised to revise taxes, saying he preferred an income tax "similar to those in more than 30 other states in the Union."

As of 30 October the GOP had spent $1,454,179, compared to the Democrats' miserly $5,000.

Roosevelt swamped Hoover in the November election, winning 42 states, or 472 to 59 votes in the Electoral College, easily carrying the anti-Hoover farm vote. In South Dakota, Roosevelt won over the traditionally Republican agrarian vote, gaining 185,000 votes to Hoover's 100,000. His lopsided victory changed the political landscape of South Dakota as well, bringing Democrats to power in the executive and legislative branches of state government. Despite this great difference in campaign spending, Democrats won the governorship and both seats in the U.S. House of Representatives, electing Tom Berry, Fred H. Hildebrandt, and Theodore B. Werner, respectively. Berry received 63.6 percent of the vote on the platform, "Use the Axe." Only Republican Senator Norbeck was able to retain his seat in the Democratic sweep, to continue his work next to Senator William Bulow, a Democrat and former South Dakota governor who had won his seat in 1930.[57] As Norbeck expressed it, "The President is so immensely popular over the country that the Republicans here are on their knees and the Democrats have their hats off."[58]

2 The New Deal Comes to South Dakota and the Nation

> If the President ever becomes dictator, I've got a grand idea for him.
> He can label this country out here "Siberia' and send all his exiles
> here. It is the "Siberia" of the United States. A more hopeless place
> I never saw.
>
> Lorena Hickok to Harry L. Hopkins[1]

BETWEEN THE ELECTION and Roosevelt's inauguration on 4 March 1933, several governors responded to the economic crisis by declaring bank holidays in their states to prevent the complete collapse of the banking system, closing banks in thirty-two states. From 1920 to 1934, the number of state banks in South Dakota declined from 557 to 148, while the national banks in the state dropped from 135 to 64. In other words, 71 percent of the banks in South Dakota failed in this fourteen-year span. Acting under the World War I Trading with the Enemy Act, President Roosevelt declared a national banking holiday after his inauguration until Congress could act, and he gave his advisors five days to draft a banking bill for the solons to consider.[2]

He called a special session of Congress, which met on Thursday, 9 March, in a crisis, even warlike, atmosphere. With a great unanimous shout, thirty-eight minutes after its introduction, the House of Representatives approved his banking bill, sight unseen, and the Senate endorsed it that afternoon. On Sunday evening, the president addressed the nation in his first "fireside chat" over the radio to an estimated sixty million listeners, explaining what was happening in the nation's capital. With passage of the Emergency Banking Relief Act, he assured listeners in his magnetic, soothing voice, "When your bank reopens its doors, you will know it is safe to redeposit your money." As political humorist Will Rogers said, FDR explained banking in a way that even bankers could understand. People immediately began to redeposit and that financial crisis slowly faded. Presidential advisor Raymond C. Moley's assessment was that "capitalism was saved in eight days" with this action. This fireside chat proved so successful that Roosevelt successfully delivered a number of them during his presidency on important national issues.[3]

On 10 March the president sent a budget message to Congress asking for broad economic powers, including the reduction of federal salaries, which they granted through the Government Economy Act. Passage of the Beer and Wine Revenue Act followed, which provided for sale of beer and light wines to raise badly needed revenue, even though the 21st Amendment repealing prohibition did not pass until the end of 1933.

During these Hundred Days (actually 105 days), a compliant Congress enacted most of the first New Deal programs. Willing to experiment with remedies, Roosevelt felt strongly that the leadership had to be proactive to combat the national attitude of extreme pessimism that the depression caused. His leadership was a great relief to most Americans because of the widespread, erroneous belief that Hoover had done nothing to alleviate the crisis.[4]

In addition to the three acts already mentioned, FDR persuaded Congress to pass the Federal Emergency Relief Act (FERA), which authorized the Reconstruction Finance Corporation (RFC), a Hoover measure, to assist states in their relief plans for the unemployed. South Dakota, like many states, used this opportunity to build a modern highway system, while FERA sent hundreds of millions of dollars to states in financial assistance, benefiting stricken farm families. Another relief program that had long-term, positive consequences for South Dakota was the Reforestation Relief Act, which established one of Roosevelt's favorite depression measures: the Civilian Conservation Corps (CCC). In the eight years of the CCC's existence, it provided more than six million dollars in earnings to 26,500 South Dakotans between the ages of eighteen and twenty-five and left a legacy of buildings and improvements to the state's parks and infrastructure.

Of critical interest to the agricultural states was what plan the Roosevelt administration would produce to help destitute farmers. One indicator was the campaign speech Roosevelt had made in Topeka, proposing a system of domestic allotment. Bruited about by New Deal planners, the plan asked agriculture to adjust production to demand.[5]

While many in the Farm Holiday movement agreed to give Roosevelt time to develop his farm plan, Milo Reno, for one, anticipated correctly that the American Farm Bureau Federation and the Grange would dominate Roosevelt's thinking in producing his policy. Reno held no brief for the domestic allotment approach and had little faith in Secretary of Agriculture Henry A. Wallace because he might have "absorbed some of the academic idiocy" of the thinking at Iowa State Agricultural College in Ames.[6]

Senator Peter Norbeck had long supported the McNary-Haugen Farm Relief Bill, but he also endorsed restriction of production and government benefit payments. As early as 1923, Norbeck had pushed the domestic allotment idea, but by the late 1920s he had abandoned the possibility of reducing American production to American consumption. In June 1932, Norbeck had introduced a modified domestic allotment bill but it had no possibility of success until after the election. The country was awaiting the new agriculture and relief programs and hoping for the positive outcomes they might provide.

On 16 March, the administration introduced a bill embodying the principle of domestic allotment in the House of Representatives with FDR's assurance that it paved "a new and untrod path."

It was the first effort of Congress to control supply and demand of farm commodities, and passage of the Agricultural Adjustment Act (AAA) became a walk on a rough and difficult road for the administration. As with the other Hundred Days legislation, the House gave the bill perfunctory scrutiny. After a brief hearing, the agricultural committee approved it with a three-to-one majority, and it came to the House floor under rules that forbade amendments and limited the debate to four hours. The Senate proved to be not so compliant and added two obstacles to the bill: the cost of production formula, supported by the Farmers Union, that the secretary of agriculture *could* employ to support farm prices, and several currency-expansion amendments attached to the farm credit sections.[7]

Leading the charge for the AAA was Secretary of Agriculture Henry A. Wallace. He and his father, Henry C. Wallace, were well known in farm circles because of their journal, *Wallaces' Farmer*, but also because the senior Wallace had also served as secretary of agriculture in the 1920s. Many farmers supported the new secretary of agriculture, but they wanted strong executive action during the rapidly deteriorating emergency. Wallace supported the parity concept that farmers should command the same purchasing power that they had in the golden years of agriculture in 1909–1914. He understood that if cost of production were included in the plan, domestic allotment could not function. In addition, he opposed any effort to include the World War I concept of price-fixing in the new farm bill. Wallace's position was that this idea was easy to apply in 1917 because demand at that time far exceeded supply. In 1932, the primary requirement was to reduce surpluses.[8]

In his book *Agricultural Prices*, Wallace had insisted that a free market on agricultural products hurt prices for producers. If farmers ever were to "receive fair prices," they would first have to control their production and limit surpluses. Citing Joseph's biblical interpretation of the Pharaoh's dream of seven fat years followed by seven lean years, Wallace would later argue that farm surpluses should be stored to meet the needs of lean production, or American policy should encompass an "ever-normal granary," which became the foundation of American agricultural policy for many years.[9]

Three major farm organizations were influential in lobbying the Senate: the American Farm Bureau Federation (Farm Bureau), with 1,125,000 members; the National Grange, which favored the export debenture plan; and the Farmers Union, with perhaps a half-million members. The fiery Farmers Union president John A. Simpson of Oklahoma testified at length during the congressional hearings and voiced his opinion that there were two basic systems under which men lived. The capitalist system was "the devil's making," he insisted, because "it has as its foundation principle, selfishness, greed, avarice; it leads to theft, robbery, murder, suicide and war." The cooperative system, however, "is based upon service instead of profit." Simpson asserted, "No man who is a Christian has a right to want more than the average could have."[10]

Nationally, the Farmers Union was split ideologically between those who promoted cooperatives and those who sought support from legislative programs in Washington. In South Dakota, Loriks and the Farmers Union pressed for a guarantee of cost of production, a plan that might produce more income but that failed to address the real problem of overproduction, or surpluses. He believed that cooperatives were the "engines of democracy."[11] President Hoover wanted to help farmers but opposed the McNary-Haugen bill because of its government controls. The New Deal subsidy programs, on the other hand, appealed to the wing of the Farmers Union that supported the federal program of emergency seed loans. This division of leadership and policies meant that the Farmers Union in some states was hostile to the New Deal, and in other states, favored it.

Simpson and the Farmers Union wanted Wallace to determine the amount of production necessary for consumption in the United States and the cost of this production, including wages and interest on investment. Production above this amount should be stored on the farm and not sold. He found a champion in Senator George W. Norris from Nebraska. Wallace admitted to the Senate Agricultural Committee that Simpson was "philosophically and fundamentally sound" but it would be almost impossible to determine prices accurately under this proposal.

The Norris-Simpson amendment proved to be the key issue in the Senate debates that followed. Simpson and his supporters remained adamant despite opposition from loyal Democrats, and a last-minute message from Wallace proved futile. The Senate accepted this demand from farmers by vote of 47 to 41, passing a cost-of-production amendment and presenting the president with his first reversal by the Hundred Days session.[12]

The House of Representatives rejected the cost of production amendment. In the House-Senate conference discussion, it was resurrected, of course, and the conference reported a disagreement. The House again defeated the idea 283 to 109. Senator Norris had to advise his colleagues to retreat from the amendment because the House would never accept it, as agrarian interests had much less influence there than they possessed in the upper chamber with its state equality. Other senators foresaw the possibility of a nationwide farm strike if cost of production was not included, and Norris reversed himself, requesting the Senate to refuse to yield. His colleagues, however, voted 48 to 43 against the concept, laying the amendment to rest in Congress.[13]

At the height of debate, word of the "Bradley episode" reached Washington. In Le Mars, Iowa, Judge Charles C. Bradley was hearing foreclosure litigation when a group of farmers pulled him off the bench and onto the lawn, where he refused to swear he would not hear another foreclosure case. They then drove him out of town, pulled down his trousers, and put a noose around his neck. They finally satisfied themselves with emptying a hubcap full of grease on his head and left him on the roadside. Word of this mob action "increased the sense of urgency in Washington."[14]

An administration-sponsored supplement on farm credits gave

the New Dealers a series of inflation riders for later use. These provided for expansion of federal loan facilities, scaled-down interest rates, and refinancing of farm mortgages with fiat money. Finally, the bill authorized the administration to decrease the amount of gold in the American dollar to create a cheap dollar for inflationary purposes, a route FDR was eager to explore.[15]

Congress passed the Agricultural Adjustment Act on May 12, after almost two months of intense debate. It specified seven basic commodities that were in surplus—wheat, corn, hogs, cotton, rice, tobacco, and milk—and provided that, in return for voluntary reduced production of these crops, farmers would receive parity payments. Funds for these payments were to be derived from a processor's tax, which would then be passed on to consumers. This was late in the growing season, and millions of acres of wheat and cotton had to be plowed under, which enraged many citizens. Pigs and hogs were also destroyed, but as much meat as possible was salvaged for relief distribution by welfare agencies. An aide to Harry L. Hopkins observed that allotment checks did "a lot" to calm down farmers in the region.[16]

Farm journals, many of whose editors supported the new program, continued publication without making ardent commitments of approval. This failure to "stand up and be counted" on policy matters stemmed from fear of alienating their readers because "many farmers had no love for production controls and thousands more" continued to demand cost of production. Most farmers would never have accepted reduction of production "without attractive cash inducements" and agreed to the concept only as an emergency measure.[17]

The Farm Bureau eventually committed itself to the new plan, as did the National Grange with somewhat less enthusiasm. The Farmers Union adamantly declined to accept the domestic allotment concept and continued to advocate Simpson's ideas. Simpson himself, though, made no further attempt to oppose the AAA administration.[18]

The administration had much smoother sailing with other New Deal programs. Congress created the truly revolutionary Tennessee Valley Authority (TVA), which sought to provide electrical power and a range of other economic benefits to Tennessee and neighboring states. Other important pieces of legislation included the Federal Securities Act; the Wagner-Peyser Act; Homeowners Refinancing Act; Banking Act of 1933, which included banking reforms and established the Federal Deposit Insurance Corporation (FDIC); and, finally, the National Industrial Recovery Act (NIRA), which established the National Recovery Administration (NRA) and the Public Works Administration (PWA).

In his optimism, Roosevelt initially described the National Recovery Act as Congress's "supreme legislative achievement," an assessment he would soon reject as criticism of the ill-fated program mounted. Nevertheless, Title II of this law created the PWA, which poured billions of dollars into the states' infrastructures and provided employment to millions. Eighty percent of the funding to the PWA went toward purchasing materials for projects, and the labor to construct them gave employment to millions.

New Deal programs were rooted in America's federal system of government. The recovery plans emanated from Washington, D.C., but required implementation from the state capitals like Pierre. This meant poverty-stricken local governments had to raise precious matching funds to participate in these programs or lose the funding. The money was one problem; finding competent administrators for the entirely new system of offering relief in modern society was another. South Dakota needed much help from the federal government on both fronts.[19]

This study attempts to view the New Deal from the perspective of South Dakotans in order to understand more clearly the complexity of this revolutionary phenomenon. The New Deal imposed a distant bureaucracy on South Dakotans that appeared heartless and uncaring, a relentless and indifferent tyranny. One choice that eased the implementation of the New Deal in South Dakota was the empathetic nature of the man Roosevelt put in charge of federal relief: Harry L. Hopkins.

Hopkins was a rather odd former New York state social worker who proved to be a great fit for the position of FERA director. He was deeply committed to assisting helpless people and was innovative in getting help quickly where it was most needed, while remaining nonpartisan. By February 1934, his FERA, Civil Works Administration (CWA), and the CCC reached almost 8 million families, or 28 million people.[20]

Hopkins, originally from Iowa, did not belong to a church, "had been divorced and analyzed, liked race horses and women, was given to profanity and wisecracking, and had little patience with moralists." As he talked to reporters "through thick curls of cigarette smoke . . . his eyes darting and suspicious, his manner brusque, almost iconoclastic, almost deliberately rude and outspoken . . . ," he was virtually unknown in Washington, but by Roosevelt's second term "he would be the most powerful man in the administration." With his office in the Reconstruction Finance Corporation hallway, "he spent over five million dollars in his first two hours" in office.[21]

Hopkins insisted the millions on work relief were victims of economic collapse, "fine people, the workers, a cross section of America's payrolls."[22] To many individualistic South Dakotans, such as M. Q. Sharpe, however, they were morally degenerate, lazy cheats. Unaccustomed to needing relief programs or facing such a desperate all-encompassing economic situation such as this, the average, proud, self-reliant South Dakotan was filled with disbelief and dejection. They found it difficult to distinguish between the degrading dole and the CWA "shovel-leaner" who was willing to accept the taxpayers' charity. The receiver had created his situation by being incapable of managing his affairs, a person who had lost all initiative, they insisted.[23]

In the 1930s, most South Dakotans were one generation away from their pioneering ancestors. Even though their children were hungry and needed to be clothed, they resented accepting charity from strangers in the despised East. Regardless of the circumstances that led to their predicament, they felt some shame for being unable to provide for their families, as well as suppressed anger. This emotional component is an important corollary with the conservative nature of South Dakota politics.

Thought they elected Democrats to state offices and voted for President Roosevelt, they paradoxically blamed them—consciously or unconsciously—for this personal shame. This adverse experience would produce statewide political consequences, but, as Eleanor Roosevelt noted, "businessmen who ordinarily would have scorned government assistance were begging the government to find solutions for their problems."[24]

The South Dakota delegation to Congress generally supported President Roosevelt's plans for dealing with the Great Depression. Senator Norbeck, who referred to himself as a "Theodore Roosevelt Republican," supported the First New Deal, although he opposed the speedy passage of the bank bill, and heartily endorsed the investigation and regulation of the securities industry. Serving on the Banking and Currency Committee, he was influential in producing the Federal Securities Act and the Securities and Exchange Commission. He was impressed with the New Dealer's willingness to experiment. FDR had "turned out so much better" than he had hoped that the Republican senator "occasionally" found himself "singing faint praises."[25]

Senator William J. Bulow actively supported FDR's program, although he expressed his conservatism thereafter. Congressman Fred H. Hildebrandt was known for his ability to provide jobs in depression-ravaged South Dakota "for his family." The more conservative Congressman Werner endorsed most of the First New Deal, but opposed FDR on the Economy Act and later New Deal measures.[26]

As governor, Tom Berry sought to turn South Dakota's agrarian discontent into support for President Roosevelt's farm program.[27] He proved to be more concerned than his predecessors about helping his constituents in this crisis and was innovative in getting help where it was most needed. Berry used his personality effectively, both in obtaining funding and in promoting New Deal programs in the state.[28] When he took office in January 1933, more than 65,500 South Dakotans were on relief and soon FERA monies became available for help. Leaving his sons in charge of the ranch, Berry moved to Pierre where he could work on the gubernatorial job full time.

In the legislature, for the first time in state history, Democrats controlled the state senate 29 to 15, compared with the previous Republican majority of 31 to14. They dominated the state house 68 to 34, in contrast to the earlier Republican majority of 79 to 24. This meant, of course, they would control committees in both houses. Berry was most concerned over patronage, and, recalling his lack of campaign money, assessed his appointees 10 percent of their salaries to build a slush fund for future campaigning. He appointed political allies to office and denied appointment to progressive Democrats.[29] Emil Loriks became chair of the all-important appropriations committee. Oscar Fosheim, with whom Loriks would later team up on the gold ore tax, had been elected to the house. Farming elements dominated the legislature, with ninety-three of the lawmakers coming from the agrarian community. This Democratic legislature readily supported Berry's austerity program.

On opening day of the state legislature, Governor Berry was "cheered enthusiastically" as he addressed the joint session with a message calling for the reverse of all on which he had campaigned. He proposed a general sales tax, a regressive measure that he had opposed during the campaign. Further, he recommended dismantling a series of programs won by the Populists and Progressives over the years: the Railroad Commission, the hail insurance fund, the state coal mine, and the direct primary. He believed the latter cost a lot of money and made no significant contribution to political life. Berry's rugged individualistic philosophy was far stronger than any sense of reform or progressive ideas. Voters soon chose sides on their governor. "Either he was a powerhouse politician" or "a western rube, a man of rude manners, incapable of subtlety or progressive thought."[30]

South Dakota's constitution required a balanced budget, which forced the liberals in the legislature to slash expenses even further than the conservative governor had recommended. As one of his patronage appointments, Berry rewarded the man he had defeated in the Democratic primary, Lorenzo E. Corey, with appointment as state finance and tax director. The administration proposed a gross income (gross receipts) tax of 1 percent on salaries or sales to relieve the burdensome, and increasingly uncollectable, property tax. The estimate was that this would produce $10 million in revenue annually. Farm progressives, though, continued to press for a net income tax plan.[31]

Farm groups immediately rose in opposition to Berry's regressive policies. The Farmers' Union, the Farm Bureau, and the Grange all endorsed a graduated net income tax, debt burden relief, and drastic cuts in the state budget—items heartily endorsed by Loriks, Fosheim, and Lieutenant Governor Hans A. Ustrud. The legislature debated the gross income tax, including a requirement to reconsider it in two years if enacted. A Republican senator chortled that when every taxpayer had to file a report on gross receipts every quarter, "he will curse the Democratic party." Controversy immediately broke out over the issue, and opponents rushed a test case to the state supreme court. By a three-to-two vote, the court held the issue to be nonreferrable, and the administration had one day to get the tax and its required supporters "up to speed."

The gross income tax was close to a general sales tax, a concept all agrarian progressives abhorred because of the fear of shifting the tax burden to "groceries, implements, and seed bills." They managed to amend the bill to include a graduated scale. Wages and salaries under $2,000 were taxed at the 1 percent rate; between $2,000 and $5,000, the rate would rise to 1.5 percent and would increase to 2 percent in excess of $5,000. Payers would remit payments quarterly, using forms available at county court houses. Revenues were estimated at $10 million initially before the supreme court opinions were delivered, and this income would eliminate the need for the four-mill state property tax levy and also reduce local school district property levies by one-third.[32]

Farmers continued to oppose the gross income tax because they would be taxed on their transactions even if they resulted in a loss, and they adamantly supported a net income tax concept. Ustrud unfailingly insisted that Berry support this, but the governor adamantly declined to accept any substantive changes to his tax. In meetings to debate the issue, Berry would airily wave aside any questions he received and answer them as "immaterial." Finally, he asked farmer representatives, "Who do you represent anyhow? I doubt if you represent 10% of the farmers of this state while I represent all of them." The governor ruthlessly used his powers of patronage to push through his tax program. Ustrud described his process, with some hyperbole: "Never in the history of the state has the abuse of patronage and intimidation and coercion on the part of the executive been so openly and flagrantly misused as in the passage of this gross income tax bill."[33]

Taxpayers were soon faced with "wordy and legalistic definitions" of the tax published in the tax department's instructions and procedures. A woman from Sioux Falls reported her income for a quarter and paid her tax with two three-cent postage stamps. The department used a three-cent stamp to return her stamps with instructions that she should submit a check or money order for her payment. The state's leading newspaper suggested that this seemed a waste because the tax department either had, or would soon have, use for "a considerable quantity of stamps."[34]

Even with the new tax, there would still be insufficient revenues, so Berry called a special session to consider placing the liquor laws under the administration of the department of agriculture and placing a tax on beer and wine. After the U.S. Congress authorized the distribution of beer and wine in March 1933, following ratification of the 22nd Amendment, this became a significant source of revenue for many governmental units. When the state legislature assembled, a number of other measures were introduced, including one by Loriks providing for a net income tax. Only the liquor bill passed, and this tax issue widened the chasm between Berry and the progressive Democrats.[35]

In another test case, the South Dakota Supreme Court held that part of the gross income tax dealing with interstate commerce was unconstitutional, and this decision cut the expected annual revenues in half to $5 million. With the state teetering on the edge of bankruptcy, the governor persuaded the legislature to end the tax exemption on farm gasoline and to divert half of the four-cent tax for highways from the gasoline tax fund in order to pay on the Rural Credits debt. Loriks and his supporters wanted to use those two cents to lower property taxes, but the Berry administration carried the day. Berry signed the measure, and Minneapolis banks advanced the state the necessary funds to meet the bonds falling due that same day. South Dakota's credit rating was temporarily saved once again.[36]

Loriks was successful in obtaining some tax relief for farmers. On his recommendation, the legislature cut the interest rate on delinquent taxes from 10 to 8 percent, abolished compounding the interest, and extended the time for redeeming tax deeds from two to four years. Knowing the vote would be close on the interest rate, Loriks got Senator Hans Urdahl out of his sick bed in Lake County and into a taxi to Pierre, where he gave his supportive speech, then back to his bed. The bill passed by one vote.[37]

The issue of debtors and declining tax collections was an especially bitter one for this legislature. Governor Berry failed to mention to them the growth of farm mortgage foreclosures, while nearby governors were actively fighting against the foreclosures. Governor Floyd B. Olson of Minnesota was declaring a mortgage moratorium in his state at the same time, and Governor William Langer was calling out the North Dakota National Guard to enforce his moratorium on all kinds of debts. The South Dakota legislature enacted debtor relief laws, but provided a mortgage moratorium law that allowed one year for redemption and permitted delinquent taxpayers to combine their back taxes for ten years and pay them off in ten annual installments without accumulated interest. The state's primary election law survived with the lieutenant governor's tie-breaking vote.[38]

The state legislature proved to be deeply divided, though, and was never able to agree upon an agricultural policy, even though farmers and ranchers completely dominated the session. Unaccustomed to governing, the Democrats largely failed in their first opportunity to achieve a winning coalition and resolve economic problems. This represented a dismal lack of leadership on Berry's part. In the end, while the New Dealers clearly emerged as a liberal national bloc, in South Dakota they remained undistinguishable from the Republicans, failing to offer a progressive alternative. Berry was unable to unite the various factions of his dominant party.[39]

In his implementation of the New Deal programs coming out of Washington, D.C., however, Berry had more success. He enjoyed a good relationship with President Roosevelt, culminating with being invited to deliver a seconding speech to FDR's nomination for president in 1936. He found a friend in Hopkins, head of the Federal Emergency Relief Administration, which provided for direct grants, not loans, to state relief agencies that would increase their spending efforts.

Roy Emry, appointed by the former governor, continued in his role of director of relief, while Governor Berry named Michael A. Kennedy of Pierre as the chief statistician for South Dakota's relief efforts. A native South Dakotan, Kennedy came from an old stock Catholic family in Fort Pierre, attended the public schools there, and worked in a lumberyard until World War I, when he spent several months overseas. Returning home, he married and accepted a job as secretary to the growing South Dakota State Highway

Commission, where he made a reputation as an efficient administrator, very familiar with the political situation in his state. Kennedy would later assume control over relief in the state and served as the state administrator for the Works Progress Administration when it was established in 1935. He carried out both programs magnificently throughout the decade of the 1930s.

Federal relief came quickly and generously. During April 1933, counties were given the munificent sum of $202,800 in FERA funds. The following month they received an additional $122,000, with Sioux Falls granted an extra $15,000 because of its relatively large urban population. The counties of Armstrong, Campbell, Hamlin, McPherson, and Washington did not ask for funding in May. Beadle, Brown, Codington, Davison, Pennington, and Yankton counties, again with their more numerous populations, received the largest apportionments. Officials were directed to use these funds "for the same purpose and in the same manner" as those from the RFC.[40]

One of the first things state FERA officials did, in October 1933, was to conduct a census on unemployment relief. FERA field statistician R. O. Carte viewed the reports from South Dakota with suspicion because Kennedy, while new to his position, "was well acquainted with the type of workers each political subdivision has to offer." Carte and Kennedy "rearranged" the bookkeeping so there would no longer be overlapping of work. At this time every eighth family was on public relief rolls. Most of them were large families, with 60 percent containing three to six members; 156 of them had twelve or more. Males "considerably" outnumbered females in the state and this was reflected in the relief rolls, which showed 51,249 males and 46,764 females. Only in the 18-to-24 age bracket did females slightly outnumber males. Forty-three percent or 46,414 were children under the age of seventeen and half of these were grammar school age.[41]

Many of these proud and independent Dakotans had little choice but to seek this outside help, though, when it could be found. Urbanites, who had endured relief problems earlier, benefited from trained social workers and established organized welfare agencies. In rural states, while the Red Cross was present to help starving people and livestock, philanthropic organizations were scarce, and welfare funds from counties were almost nonexistent. Nevertheless, county commissioners made roadwork available for the truly needy and attempted to coordinate the efforts of charity organizations with county and state work. Private groups, such as the American Legion Auxiliaries, held parties and bake sales for local welfare. Red Cross rules for feed distribution warned local committees to grind the wheat destined for livestock to prevent farm families from using it for seed to sell on the local market.[42]

The New Deal "profoundly altered" the policies and activities of the Red Cross. "The alphabet soup" agencies of FERA, CCC, and CWA "lessened the pressure on these private agencies to feed and clothe the unemployed and their families." Hopkins and Washington bureaucrats, of course, did not seek to exclude these voluntary bodies, but "the government bypassed the Red Cross when it distributed surplus commodities" to drought victims, and the Red Cross increasingly focused on disaster relief, such as flood or tornado victims. This type of work demonstrated that private relief was still required, and the organization carried on its work in close cooperation with the government. But the Great Depression definitely changed the focus on individual relief.[43]

Franklin D. Roosevelt's commitment to make the national government an agency to provide massive relief for starving Americans was a major turning point. At this juncture, one-sixth of the nation's population was on some kind of relief. The passage of the AAA did not solve the rural ordeal as Roosevelt and Wallace had hoped, however. Shortly after its enactment, a sharp advance occurred in farm prices. From mid-March to mid-July, they rose from 50 percent of the 1909 to 1914 base to 76 percent, a very rapid rate exceeded only by that in the spring of 1917 when the U.S. entered World War I. This produced quiescence among farm radicals. By August, however, the rural honeymoon ended when farm prices declined to 70 percent of parity and the price of goods that farmers purchased began to rise sharply. Agrarians decided that the success of the NRA with its codes was responsible for the rise in consumer prices, and there was considerable unrest in rural areas. Accompanying the subsequent protests came an increasing demand for the traditional farm panacea of inflation.[44]

The Roosevelt administration refused at first to yield to these pressures for inflation but began a counter-offensive of purchasing $75 million of surplus farm commodities for relief purposes. This also served as a response to the general public protest to the idea of destruction under the "planned scarcity" of the AAA. The demand for inflation was accompanied by a strident revival of the concept of cost of production. The first overt action in the Wheat Belt came in mid-October, when North Dakota Governor William Langer instituted an embargo on the shipment of wheat outside his state. FDR immediately phoned Henry Morgenthau, Jr., head of the Farm Credit Administration (FCA), with the plaintive request that his agency buy twenty-five million bushels of wheat for Hopkins and FERA to bolster the price of the cereal. Morgenthau bought seven million bushels and the price rose nearly twenty cents. He purchased a total of sixteen million bushels and held the price above the mid-October low.[45]

Milo Reno now demanded an NRA code for agriculture that would fix prices for farm products at a cost-of-production level. When this code was not forthcoming, he called a farm strike for 19 October, and Roosevelt countered with his fourth fireside chat to the nation. While he admitted in the address that farm prices had not risen sufficiently, he agreed with Henry A. Wallace that the best solution was reduction of surpluses. At this point FDR decided to yield to the inflationary forces and began his program of purchasing gold at inflationary prices.

National attention shifted on 1 November 1933 to the arrival of five governors from Midwest, including Berry and William Langer, to the nation's capital to discuss their relief needs with the president.

They had a three-hour session with Roosevelt, followed by an additional hour-long talk. Berry hit it off well with the president when the latter offered him $100,000 in aid if he would "go home."

"Are you trying to buy me lunch?" Berry responded. "We want a full meal."

At this meeting, Governor Berry reiterated his consistent support for the administration. "I think he is doing everything he can for us," Berry said of Roosevelt. "I know he wants to help. He may not have the right program for some things but he's sincere." The rancher-governor came home with assurances of one million dollars in relief assistance. Thereafter FDR referred to him as "cowboy" and the two got along famously.[46]

With this attitude of good will dominating the meeting, Roosevelt was able to stall the governors, and, by November, the AAA subsidy checks of approximately 29 cents a bushel began arriving in South Dakota, which deflated criticism. Problems in securing farmers' signatures to join the program and verifying compliance with acreage reductions delayed the checks. Also in November, the administration began buying three million hogs for relief purposes and liberalizing the corn loans, raising the price of hogs by ten cents. The administration thus resolved the farm rebellion that FDR had foreseen if he had not acted positively and immediately. It did not halt the relief crisis, however, that was gripping increasing numbers of farmers who were losing their land and livelihood and needed some kind of assistance to feed their families.

3 Work for the Unemployed, Food for the Hungry

Most of the men who used to work in the shops have been out of work
for two or three years! They haven't even enough money to get out of
Mobridge! And so there it sits—with the west wind howling down its
wide, empty streets. Everyone just stays at home and mopes.
Lorena Hickok to Harry L. Hopkins[1]

PASSAGE OF THE FIRST Agricultural Adjustment Act (AAA),
with its subsidies, crop reductions, commodity loan payments, and slight monetary inflation "took the sting out of rural
radicalism." It felt good to have the cash from the subsidy payments
and be able to treat the family to ice cream cones again. The public
strongly disapproved of the concept of destroying surpluses in time
of need, but the AAA "brought needed economic assistance," and
this was what aggrieved farmers were demanding.[2]

Adam Cohen points out that enactment of the AAA also indicated that the federal government "would start taking more responsibility for the nation's economic condition." New Deal administrator Adolph A. Berle noted, "The federal government was there
to keep order, to do certain reform work, assist from time to time,
but the normal process of laissez-faire economics were supposed
to provide the results."[3] Roosevelt insisted that when communities
and states could no longer meet the needs of the unemployed, as
was happening everywhere, "it becomes the positive duty of the
federal government to step in to help." Modern society, acting

through government, he insisted, "owes the definite obligation to prevent the starvation or the dire want of its fellow men and women who try to maintain themselves and cannot."[4]

The corn/hog and cattle programs were of great importance to South Dakota, but it was pigs that first got the AAA into a public relations ruckus. Hog prices had dropped to $2.95 per hundredweight, the lowest since 1878. That division of the AAA labored for weeks to negotiate an industry-wide contract, with hog prices declining and hog numbers increasing all the while. It was not until the middle of July, however, that farm groups met in Des Moines, Iowa, the heart of corn and hog country. Almost half of the representatives who attended opposed controls on corn production. The threat of great overproduction of hogs, though, with the result that slaughter numbers were high and hog prices were plummeting, forced a decision. The AAA finally responded in mid-August with a purchase program of more than 6 million hogs at prices ranging from $6 to $9.50 per hundredweight, with "piggy" (pregnant) sows fetching a bonus of $4. Those pigs large enough to be processed were turned over to relief agencies, but packers were reported unprepared for this deluge of pork.[5]

The destruction of hogs brought "charges of criminal insanity and warnings of divine retaliation. People ranging from the naive and humanitarian to the lunatic fringe" expressed their opposition to the slaughtering of "expectant mothers," and the superstitious warned that this action would summon "the wrath of a vengeful God upon a sinful nation." Clarence Darrow, the famous defense attorney from Chicago, decried the action of killing little pigs and throwing them out "on the prairie to decay while millions are hungry." Darrow viewed the problem as "a sick society which saw a maldistribution of products rather than underpaid farmers."[6]

The Federal Surplus Relief Corporation (FSRC) emerged from the AAA slaughtering program, a result that most people applauded. The agency procured agricultural surpluses and transported them to state relief agencies for distribution. This was a great solace to

Henry A. Wallace, who rejoiced that, at last, the New Deal had "a mechanism through which the surplus could reach the hungry." He was also pleased that this permitted the AAA to continue its surplus-reduction programs. The FSRC bought or received from the AAA programs "such diverse products as butter, cheese, apples, sugar, syrup, potatoes, flour, coal, blankets, and cotton." Eventually the AAA returned "to the Federal Farm Board policy of buying surpluses to affect prices but with the humanitarian and politically significant safety valve of distribution to the needy."[7]

Harry L. Hopkins was put in charge of the FSRC, in addition to his duties as head of Federal Emergency Relief Administration (FERA) where most of the farm products were sent. FSRC lasted two years and, generally, Hopkins's relations with Wallace were cordial. Relief officials sought to use FSRC as a relief agency, while the AAA viewed it as "a helpful adjunct to its surplus control operations." State and local relief agencies were often "inefficient, wasteful, and reflected local biases." To overcome this problem, the FSRC required groups who wanted to receive free food to develop effective means of distribution.[8]

The commissary method was one such procedure where a local family designated as needy could come to a distribution center and receive an allotment. Hopkins described this method as "degrading," however, and the FSRC developed a new system with a central warehouse from which trucks could deliver food to the needy. Obviously, the foods in this distribution did not constitute a balanced diet, but it did introduce people to foods with which, in some cases, they were unacquainted. A story made the rounds that one woman cooked a grapefruit in every way she knew and complained that her family still refused to eat it.[9]

In 1935, FSRC was replaced with the Federal Surplus Commodities Corporation (FSCC), administered by the department of agriculture. The FSCC continued to distribute surpluses, aided by the newly created school lunch program that was initially established as a service to affluent families but was later used to increase the amount of surplus food distributed to needy children. By the mid-1930s, the Red Cross, the Parent Teacher Associations (PTA), and other civic groups sought to expand the school lunch concept to achieve a more balanced diet for children. The long-lived food stamp program was introduced as well, designed to help reduce food surpluses by permitting persons on relief to purchase weekly stamps for each family member that were redeemable in designated surplus commodities. The latter could have been revolutionary, except that Wallace curtailed its scope to one of assistance to the crop-reduction goal of his department, with expansion of objectives coming much later.[10]

Hog farmers soon discovered that processors covered the cost of the tax by reducing the price they paid producers by an equivalent amount—a result the opposite of that intended by supporters of the AAA. Farmers were convinced, rightly so, that they were paying the processing tax, and their protests eventually led to judicial scrutiny in the U.S. Supreme Court in 1936. One highly influential merchant from Yankton, South Dakota, agreed with the hog farmers and, he played a significant role in securing "railroad carloads of food and livestock feed" for drought victims in Arkansas, Nebraska, and South Dakota in 1932.[11]

Deloss Butler ("D. B.") Gurney was president of Gurney Seed and Nursery Company and also the owner of the WNAX radio station. The station boasted the highest towers in the Midwest, which assured the company a five-state range for its broadcasts. A prominent Republican figure, Gurney and his radio station helped promote the relief effort. After the 1936 court decision voided the AAA, he was also active in helping farmers to recover their hog processing tax refunds.

According to Senator Bulow, Governor Tom Berry deserved credit for initiating the AAA's cattle-buying program. Only six months into Berry's first term, another severe drought struck the state, and he found himself turning to the national government for help.[12] In August 1933, Berry, his relief director W. L. Eales, and

Arthur Mullen, Democratic national committeeman from Nebraska and a boyhood friend of the governor, met with the president. Berry armed himself with pictures of the grasshopper and drought damage in South Dakota and showed them to President Franklin D. Roosevelt. FDR found the pictures shocking and asked how much would be required to alleviate the cattlemen's problem. Berry responded with the figure $25 million. The president countered with $15 million. "That would be fine, Mr. President," Berry shot back, "but I just don't know where I would get the other $10 million."

Roosevelt arranged for him to meet the next day with Wallace, Hopkins, and Henry Morgenthau, Jr., and recommended they send three men to verify his pictures. Berry reported that, in their discussion, Roosevelt had suggested taking drought-stricken western South Dakota out of cultivation and returning the area to livestock grazing.[13] FDR's proposal was much like the one the Poppers, a pair of Rutgers geographers, recommended fifty years later when they suggested this same thirty million acres be returned to grass, its natural state, and make the High Plains a "Buffalo Commons."[14]

The following day Berry and Eales conferred with Wallace and some of the relief administrators to discuss other requirements. After talking to FERA officials, the men expressed confidence that the relief needs of the state "would be adequately met." Half the five million dollars FERA currently had available could be allotted on a "discretionary basis," and Berry felt sure that South Dakota's drought and grasshopper "emergencies were sufficient grounds for Hopkins to allot money from that source."

On 13 September, President Roosevelt made $60 million available to the Dakotas, the Texas Panhandle, the Rio Grande region, and other areas suffering from drought, as emergency aid through the FERA, Farm Credit Administration (FCA), and public works. On 14 September, Berry could assure his farmers they would be "taken care of this winter."[15] The state received some $23 million for the project, with FDR's condition to Berry that "you yourself be the relief administrator of South Dakota."[16]

Berry was the only governor in the nation to serve as his own relief administrator for his first year in office, as he had promised President Roosevelt, and he was highly effective in this role in obtaining funds for his constituents. As he traveled to Washington to seek aid, he quickly made his presence known. "Dressed in his grey or tan western-cut suit, multicolored shirt, shiny brown or tan boots and large cowboy Stetson, he stood out in a city dominated by dark suits, white shirts, and conservative neckties." He succeeded quite well in his endeavors "to get more aid for the people," and, convincing both Roosevelt and Hopkins that South Dakota's extreme weather conditions placed the state in a unique situation, he was able to receive more than his share of funding in many cases.[17]

Widespread drought solved the wheat surplus in 1933; in 1934 and 1935, farmers took some 30 million acres out of production and the price of wheat rose to one dollar in 1936. AAA administrators sought compliance by keeping controls at the local level as much as possible, with a committee established in every county to determine the acreage allowed on each farm in their area.[18]

FERA helped the urban unemployed and their families, as it did the rural poor, but some of the latter faced the harsh impossibility of feeding their children. As the grasshoppers and droughts arrived, not only crops but also the vegetable gardens failed. For those who lost their farms, this slight opportunity was unavailable, and the empathetic Roosevelt sought to help them. Through FERA, Hopkins established a relief program for farmers that he saw as common sense bureaucracy to reduce some of their unemployment. Ralph Hansmeier of Webster, South Dakota, for instance, was a large operator, farmed some 3,000 acres, owned his own elevator, and employed twenty men. He applied for a $5,000 federal loan, offering 7,000 bushels of wheat, 3,000 bushels of seed barley, 20,000 pounds of sweet clover seed, and a half-section of land as security. His application was rejected because he owned his own elevator and this made his warehouse receipts for his grain unacceptable. As a result, he had to fire twelve men and cut the wages of the remaining eight. His loan could have kept these twelve families off relief.[19]

To assist stock growers, the FERA established the 4-4-2 limit for relief assistance—a maximum of four horses, four cows, two brood sows, and twenty chickens—to qualify for livestock food assistance. Berry heard from some needy farmers who had already sold off 50 percent of their stock; their concern was that with the low price of cattle, reducing the herd to only four head would bankrupt them and they would be "on relief for years to come." Conditions would worsen for stock growers when severe drought hit the state in 1934 and again in 1936.[20]

Lorena Hickok was a newspaperwoman and a close friend of First Lady Eleanor Roosevelt, whom Hopkins sent out to tour the most impoverished areas of the country and report her findings directly to him. She grew up "about fifty miles" west of Huron and penned some penetrating comments of her experiences in South Dakota. She reported that Berry was adamant but quiet about his opposition to the limit of four cows. He believed ten should be the maximum but agreed this number would have been difficult to establish at first and it also made farmers "hustle for feed more than they would have otherwise." Most needed a minimum of ten, he insisted, to survive. "These farmers are nothing but children," he insisted, "and you don't want to spoil a child. But you don't want to starve him either." Berry did not criticize the policy publicly, Hickok assured Hopkins, because "he is afraid you will think him ungrateful and honestly feels that you have done magnificently by South Dakota."[21]

Other "money-producing" AAA programs were enticing to South Dakota livestock producers, but it was the weather conditions that caused them to accept Berry's purchase program. In eight months in 1934, the Drought Relief Service (DRS) purchased more than nine million head of cattle that were judged unable to withstand a trip to market. The DRS paid between four and twelve dollars for diseased animals and twelve to twenty dollars for healthy ones. The

$111 million was divided between a purchase payment and a bene-fit payment reserved for the producer.[22] State Extension Director A. M. Eberle of the South Dakota Agricultural College (SDAC) in Brookings was placed in charge of the cattle-buying program. He announced that $7.5 million would come into the state as a result of the federal purchase plan.

Michael A. Kennedy explained that relief workers would kill and bury the cattle too weak to endure shipping. Animals that would not withstand shipping would be gathered at processing points. Thirty-four veterinarians from South Dakota and neighboring states would examine and make the determination of which ani-mals were fit for human consumption. Soon the DRS was reported to have purchased 18,500 head of cattle in the state through the corn/hog buying plan and wheat supports by the end of the year. If Mother Nature would cooperate, the agrarians might survive.[23]

The cattlemen, of course, sought to sell their poorest stock at the highest prices. For many South Dakotans, this entailed all their cattle. The cows were described as "gaunt, scrawny, bony looking in various degrees of standing almost lifeless, with their heads down and their tails between their legs." These were in the best condi-tion of any around and would end up in surplus relief inventories; the remainder, the condemned, were usually burned or buried on the prairie. Almost 80 percent of South Dakota cattlemen partici-pated, and many of them, of course, believed this average price of ten to twelve dollars was inadequate. When they turned to Senator Peter Norbeck for his help in raising the established price schedule, he responded that the taxpayers might resent this. In addition, he reminded his listeners, the payments were "partly in the nature of a gift from the treasury," and perhaps they should not "look a gift horse in the mouth."[24]

In 1934, Secretary of Agriculture Wallace journeyed to Sylvan Lake to hear the concerns of disgruntled cattlemen. He informed them they had an opportunity to "turn the present drought calam-ity into a future blessing" in "eliminating second-grade animals" by selling them through the national government's cattle-buying program. He followed this up with a trip to the state capital, where he informed bankers of the cattle-buying program, which he described as "eminently wise and fair." Bankers, however, considered the purchase plan to be "unfair to mortgage holders." It is difficult to understand how they came to this conclusion unless they were referring to chattel mortgages, as any assistance to their farmers would also help them.[25]

A problem also arose when the FSRC wanted to use the beef to distribute to the needy and to provide processing jobs for the unemployed. As they did with the hog-buying program, the FSRC opened processors and canneries in many places, staffed by reliefers, which meatpackers condemned as "a menace to the public." In competing interests, the AAA wanted to complete the processing quickly and save as much of the feed as possible for the surviving cattle, while relief officials wanted to use the hides for shoes and clothing for the needy, and the Tanners' Council complained of the government encroaching on their territory. Criticisms came from all sides, especially from the public, that again, "good food" was being destroyed in the midst of great want, overlooking the fact that it was a huge exaggeration to label these gaunt, emaciated cattle as "food."[26]

Hopkins disliked the original dispersal of relief funds as a dole system whereby FERA funds were spent on "make work" projects, such as raking leaves or digging postholes that would never be used. The men, in turn, received grocery orders for this "work." Hopkins believed this labor was demoralizing to men, that they lost their pride and work ethic in this system. He preferred programs with a purpose, projects that helped restore their dignity after suffering the degradation of chronic unemployment and assistance.

FERA officials began discussing serious planning for relief projects for the coming winter. "As bitter winds heralded" the approach of the cold season, "officials hurried to list projects on which thousands and thousands of men could be put to work quickly." Hopkins, with $400 million to spend in the next four months, took the lead in these discussions, and out of them came the concept of the Civil Works Administration (CWA) for the winter months of 1933–1934 to provide work relief with goals of real benefit. A forerunner of the Works Progress Administration (WPA), the program was also a cross between small-scale planning of Public Works Administration (PWA) public works and large-scale WPA work relief—a Hopkins hybrid or bridge between his FERA and the later WPA.[27]

To put the CWA machinery in motion, Hopkins called a meeting of governors and their relief administrators in Washington. Berry attended, along with Ben Lawske of the Sioux Falls Chamber of Commerce and the city's mayor. It was an eye-opening experience for the local politicos. "The governor swings a big stick down there," observed Lawske. The mayor added, "This fellow Berry is all right. He calls a spade a spade and talks to those people down there just like they were cowboys." The city officials proudly announced that the CWA would bring $60,000 monthly to Sioux Falls, with a weekly income of fifteen dollars for 1,000 unemployed men who were currently on county relief.[28]

The CWA abolished the "means test," whereby a man was denied work relief if a member of the family was already employed. In announcing this new largess, President Roosevelt expressed the desire that job applicants would not be asked if they were "a republican, democrat, socialist, or anything else."[29] The new approach required time to make the transition from grocery orders to cash payments, but instructions were telegraphed to local relief offices to change immediately. Beginning 20 November the CWA would transfer two million men nationally from work relief to paying them a minimum of fifty cents an hour for a thirty-hour work week. At the same time, Berry wired his office in Pierre from Washington that CWA officials had accepted South Dakota's water conservation program and road building for its work relief projects, if they proved feasible. Despite the approaching South Dakota winter, D. W. Loucks, state engineer, assured federal officials that "with average weather it would be possible to work on dams throughout the winter in dry soil." Current county relief committees would be designated as civil works committees, and investigators would be retained to check on eligibility of applicants for CWA jobs. This cash infusion for workers was an immense benefit to the state, especially during the harsh winter.[30]

FERA had scarcely begun its humanitarian work when its practices came under attack. R. J. Reinholtz, Paul Barrager, and D. G. Brown of Aberdeen erroneously wrote to Secretary of Labor Frances Perkins, instead of Hopkins, to complain that 500 area men were being worked nine hours daily at twenty cents per hour. With no assistance for rent, many were being evicted from their homes, they were receiving inadequate medical attention, and failure of the small grain crops due to drought was depriving them of this meager supplement to their income. Much of this, perhaps, was due to inadequate social training of the county staff.[31]

The department of labor forwarded these charges to FERA, whose secretary passed them on to the secretary of the South Dakota State Relief Committee for his reaction. He responded that "for quite a number of months" they had endured criticism from Brown County, occasioned by "a bunch of Communists that are eternally stirring up trouble" with the people on relief. This county was the stronghold of Father Robert Haire, a politically active Catholic priest in Aberdeen during the Populist uprising, and home to many Socialists and other liberals from that epoch. "The less we recognize these people's complaints," he continued unsympathetically, "the less trouble we are going to have."[32]

Nellie Carrier of Aberdeen added her voice to these criticisms. The Associated Press (AP) news service carried reports that the FERA minimum wage would be fourteen dollars weekly but these men in Aberdeen, most of whom were former railroad workers, received seven to ten dollars weekly and that was not in cash but in produce from the county commissioners. Why should these laborers "be forced into a virtual peonage in the guise of relief?" she asked. George E. Pieffle, director of the local relief office, responded to this complaint by blaming the unrest on "the Communist elements headed by a certain Marguerite Hunt of California and Paul Seidler reported to be from Chicago."[33]

County commissioners across the state, dominated by Republicans, held their annual meeting in Mitchell and complained of Democrats wasting money on unnecessary overhead. Berry immediately responded, explaining that federal officials stipulated how many administrators to hire for their programs. When he became governor, the state relief committee was composed of seven Republicans. He had retained four of them and replaced three with Democrats. Berry was pleased that he had been able to get "Washington officials interested in South Dakota's economic situation," but never expected the Republicans to make a partisan issue over the resulting funding he was bringing home.[34]

Ella Walstead was a member of a farm delegation who met with Hopkins and Lawrence Westbrook, director of FERA's rural rehabilitation program, to complain that South Dakota farm families on relief received only two to five dollars weekly. Westbrook assured her that an average of thirty-five dollars monthly was being sent to the state for this purpose, but promised to investigate. Kennedy denied Walstead's charge by announcing that the "approximately 59,000 families" averaged $5.75 weekly during March 1935. Kennedy reminded Westbrook that his figure included costs for "administration, medical care, dormitories, and other phases of the relief program."[35]Another delegate from North Dakota complained that 20 percent of the horses in his district were starving to death while FERA had 500 tons of hay in storage there.

In addition, there were the usual complaints of favoritism on relief work. A committee of the United Workers League, "the largest labor organization" in Minnehaha County, wrote the president, complaining that married men received two shifts of work monthly at $7.50 per shift, and single men received one shift monthly. The committee insisted, "a great disparity exists in the amount of relief received by different individuals in the same financial circumstances." Some people in relatively good financial condition were receiving "steady work," and some in "bad" circumstances were denied "the right to work at all."[36]

The conservative Farm Bureau, which normally supported Republicans, added its voice of criticism to these dissidents. The group's president, H. B. Text of Frederick, charged the Berry administration with "permitting partisan politics into the relief program." Berry, of course, denied this accusation, and Text assured South Dakota citizens that the Farm Bureau adhered to nonpartisan politics and would continue to do so. Yet this organization repeatedly accused the administration of "the practice that now seems to be almost universal of placing [Democratic] members of the legislature on the state and federal payrolls," as though this were an unheard of and indefensible political practice.[37]

Actually, South Dakotans had little to criticize on overall New Deal expenditures in the state. At the end of 1933, the AP compiled some figures of assistance for South Dakota. Not including the Civilian Conservation Corps (CCC), the state received more than $31 million in 1933 and was expecting another award of $26 million in 1934. These figures did not include the money spent on cattle and hog buying programs nor the money received from FSCP. Money had been allotted for PWA projects, but no PWA funds had actually arrived at year's end. In addition, the FCA reported loans of $10,992,574; the Homeowners' Loan Corporation (HOLC) made 336 loans totaling $734,080, while 1,400 loans aggregating $2,121,088 had been approved and were "awaiting closing." State banks received $1.5 million in Reconstruction Finance Corporation (RFC) loans and another $263,500 on assets of closed banks that would be used to repay depositor losses. These sums did not include AAA wheat allotment checks of $5,229,000 that would come in 1934. The state had also received 949 carloads of corn, 118 carloads of oats, and 12 carloads of wheat as surplus food worth an estimated $600,000. Officials had begun the New Deal in South Dakota as very generous benefactors. Assistant State Relief

Administrator E. J. B. Longrie later noted that RFC loans would be repaid out of the funds due the state "under the federal road building program."[38]

R. O. Carte, chief statistician for FERA, paid his first visit to the FERA branch office in Pierre and met with Eales and Longrie, the Pierre office's chief statistician. He was annoyed with their book-keeping system, seeing "much lost motion" through their double accounting systems. He believed he would "have a considerable amount of work to do here." A week later he reported that he had faith in Chief Statistician Kennedy in learning his job correctly, but the current setup of "voluntary" county chairmen and county relief workers with no formal training would result in their submitted reports being "nothing more than mere guesswork." Director Eales, he reported, "strikes me as being a very cold-blooded man with [regard to] relations to the personnel." Among other problems, he was "no believer in vacations, etc."[39]

Eales soon wrote Hopkins that South Dakota farmers found direct relief, or what they called the dole, to be degrading. The CWA work was insufficient for them to support their families, and he asked permission to place farmers on CWA work projects earning a maximum of fifty dollars monthly and a thirty-dollar minimum if they also were on the stock-feed program. Drought conditions became so desperate that some counties were unable to assist relief programs in any way. When Miner County commissioners resolved not to assist relief programs at all, Eales shut down their CWA projects. This brought a prompt rescinding of their resolution not to pay CWA administrative costs.[40]

To cut costs, the CWA issued orders that, beginning 15 February 1934, employees would cease receiving surplus commodities. Eales received permission from Aubrey Williams of the FERA to exempt CWA farmer-workers who were receiving only fifteen hours of work weekly. To do otherwise would require them to sell off their live-stock "at whatever they can get," and currently the price "hardly pays the freight charges." South Dakotans, he observed, must save their herds in order to function once again when the state's weather "comes back to normal conditions."[41]

Several relief problems seemed to be converging all at once, so Regional Representative T. J. Edmonds called a conference of FERA officials at Sioux Falls. He reported to Hopkins that they had discussed the problem of transients that were currently an increasing concern in some counties. Nationwide economic conditions caused hundreds of thousands of Americans to roam the country in search of work, assistance, or a panacea of any sort. Young and old, male and female, black and white, these hobos rode the rails, including many that ran through South Dakota, creating an additional burden on the almost nonexistent local relief sources. They often realized too late that they had chosen the wrong direction to travel, as this was the state least capable of offering them succor.

William J. Plunkert of the national FERA office wrote a paper entitled "The Transient Problem," in which he promoted a plan that not only would feed and shelter these people but also would try to educate and rehabilitate them. By the fall of 1934, this program had registered 300,000 transients in the 600 camps throughout the country, and the FERA was spending between four and five million dollars monthly on them. They received free board, lodging, clothing, medical care, and transportation, plus one dollar weekly in pay. In turn, they were expected to work five hours a day and six days per week. One journalist reported a high turnover, with many of the unattached men traveling from camp to camp. He also reported his opinion that the camps failed to rehabilitate the men. For some of them, alcohol was their downfall; for others it was a necessity to keep one step ahead of the law; and for many it was simply wanderlust, a fruitless search for some meaning in their lives.[42]

Eventually, FERA established shelters for transients in Huron, Aberdeen, Mobridge, and Rapid City. Transients were processed at these centers and, if desired, could receive help at a nearby camp where they could find work on farms or in forestry and logging operations for their room and board, in addition to recreational and educational facilities. The camps offered facilities for 700 men. A key feature of these camps, as in the CCC, was the opportunity to receive vocational training. Enrollees could also participate in baseball, volleyball, boxing, and horseshoes, with silent movies offered each week. The South Dakota Peace Makers Association (sheriffs and police) estimated that their transient problem had been reduced "nearly a hundred percent" by this program. As a result, there were fewer men on the move, less petty thievery, and fewer asking citizens for "a cup of coffee," which also implied some accompanying food.[43]

The transient camp at Huron, formerly a Mennonite colony, became involved in the canning program for slaughtered cattle. These FSCR cattle were processed at the Armour Packing Plant there. The plant retained the hides and offal, including vital organs, as a price for doing the processing. The plant processed about 30 carcasses daily, or about 4,500 cans containing twenty ounces of meat, and weighing about two pounds each. At the workroom at the fairgrounds, the women were taught sewing. The transients engaged in truck farming and raising subsistence cattle and chickens, as well as canning meat. The county relief minister had to deal constantly "with Communists and other groups that turn the heat on him." He received $100 monthly, "which is considered by some in the community as being too much."[44]

The canning plant in Rapid City employed about 300 men, operating in shifts. State cannery supervisor Mary A. Dolve and Eberle, state head of the AAA, both from SDAC, inspected a number of sites in the area and decided to locate the cannery at the Indian School. The plant was expected to process five to six thousand cans daily. With the operation running twenty-four hours a day and six days a week, with 150 men per shift, the plant was expected to "absorb most of the relief workers here [in the Rapid City vicinity]."[45]

The transient camp in the Black Hills assumed an additional task. A "cyclone" [tornado] in the area the previous year had taken a heavy toll on timber in the Rockford district. Transients were set to work cutting fuel wood and sawing lumber from fallen timber. The state had been issued permits for 37,000 cords of fuel wood and 2,000,000 board feet of "saw timber" for relief purposes. Officials leased "small portable saw mills with a capacity of 10 to 15 thousand board feet of lumber per day" from local operators. The fuel wood was shipped to "various relief centers throughout the state."[46]

Eleanor Roosevelt was concerned about the situation of unemployed women, both widows and single women who were without means of support, and she put pressure on Hopkins to create a women's division within FERA. To head this agency, Hopkins named Ellen S. Woodward of Mississippi, who became known as Roosevelt's most important non-Cabinet female appointee. Woodward was "a politically astute and competent administrator with a humane and progressive outlook toward social betterment." She organized projects such as Collection (of toys, clothing, and books), Repair (books, garments, and furniture), Sewing, and Home Economics (canning and school lunches). When Franklin Roosevelt later created the WPA, this women's division assumed a greatly expanded role.[47]

Delegates to the Sioux Falls meeting discussed the centers for transients. Eales was "not yet sold on the transient problem but he has the Army spirit and will take orders," Edmonds reported. He added that Eales did not "get along at all with Collins, the State Reemployment man," and the mayor of Sioux Falls wanted very much to resolve this conflict. The delegates agreed to consolidate the offices of county commissioners of relief, the county welfare boards, the social workers, and all city, county, private, federal, and CWA activities into one office under one supervisor. Because the state's attorney general had ruled that counties could not pay administrative costs for supervising relief work, Eales ordered the state to pay these salaries.[48]

In the political arena, Edmonds reported meeting with U. S. D. Cherry, Senator Norbeck's Democratic opponent, and W. S. Cook, minister to Venezuela under Harding and Hoover. They "spoke highly" of Norbeck and Berry and agreed that Eales was "straight on political matters but that the administrative job was probably too big for him." They also asserted that the governor's secretary and a handful of Democratic politicians were "playing politics so hard that they were injuring the Governor." Edmonds further reported that Eales was "in very bad" with Robertson, the governor's secretary, "and some of the other State House officials." He would soon be replaced.[49]

He also came under fire for maladministration of relief. Sponsored by a mass meeting of the Beadle County Farmers Union, a committee representing farmers, laborers, and unemployed petitioned Berry and Hopkins, insisting that Eales's administrative requirements "were marked by too much red tape and delay" and they wanted him to be reprimanded. They asked Eales to resign his position if he failed to comply "with the honest demands of the people for relief."[50]

The complaints had an immediate and positive effect. Three days later Eales concluded that the problem was poor organization and faulty information, and he announced a new state structure for relief administration. The state's five divisions would be divided into sixteen regions with a supervisor in each. After "several days of instruction," the supervisors were sent to their respective regions with orders to consult their office records, correct "any improper handling of relief work," and remove those ineligible for relief from the rolls and add those "in actual need." They were told to recommend replacement of officials who were "not functioning properly." Eales declared that neither the federal nor state administrations wanted anyone to suffer "from lack of food, clothing or fuel" but "we are not a Christmas tree." Everyone who was "destitute and eligible for relief" should receive it "regardless of color, creed, or political persuasion," but the supervisors should eliminate all who were not eligible from the rolls.[51]

Meanwhile, Morgenthau, chair of the Federal Farm Board, and his assistant, Cornell University president W. I. Myers, were working on a plan to overhaul the obsolete farm credit agencies. President

Roosevelt could consolidate some of the scattered units by executive order. They planned to make the seed and feed loans, totaling $90 million in 1933, available through existing farm credit agencies "to obtain capital from the sale of securities in the same manner used by the federal farm loan board." The two also hoped to obtain a government guarantee of bonds, if possible, "to reduce the rate of interest" which, in turn, would lower "the interest rates to farmers."[52]

On 25 January 1934 Governor Berry asked Hopkins for an additional grant of $1.5 million to cover relief needs for February, and he authorized $500,000. In the middle of February, Berry renewed his plea for an additional one million as the $500,000 had already been expended. He reminded Hopkins that crop conditions in South Dakota had been "so bad for the past two or three years" that, as a result, "fully fifty percent of our people are destitute."

"You have been very good indeed to my people," the governor assured him, "for which I thank you," but without the additional money, "we will not be able to function." How could a compassionate bureaucrat respond to this plea except to wire back that the FERA was making $288,000 in funds available immediately and an additional $210,000 to take care of the situation through the middle of March?[53]

Hopkins decided to terminate the CWA program when Congress enacted the Civil Works Emergency Act on 15 February 1934 that authorized $950 million for FERA until the end of 1935. Hopkins sent Eales the following rules changes in relief: drop 20,000 from the CWA payrolls of 44,000, effective 23 February, and terminate employees "needing the work least" and in those communities where seasonal work or industrial employment were greatest. There was no industrial employment in South Dakota. Workers remaining should be paid "the prevailing rate of wage" but not less than thirty cents per hour. Workers would be investigated as to needs, and hours of employment would be flexible, not set, to allow each worker to meet his "weekly or monthly investigated needs."[54]

Ten days later Eales reported to Hopkins that a "slight" error had been made in the statistics the state had reported. South Dakota had listed 42,000 employees as working on CWA projects on 1 March 1934. This number included 22,908 drivers of teams of horses and 136 drivers of trucks. The latter numbers should not have been included with the 44,170. Later CWA officials asked Eales how many teams were employed, and he responded 22,000. The Washington office then combined the two reports to come up with 64,000 employees. Both Eales and Berry tried unsuccessfully to contact Hopkins several times and finally explained the error to Edmonds. Eales gave assurances they intended no deception.[55]

Upon termination of the CWA program, Hopkins excitedly described its history. "We were told that we couldn't put 4,000,000 men to work," he exulted, and "later we were told we couldn't demobilize them. We put them to work and we demobilized them." Meanwhile, "we built playgrounds, roads and schools, and undertook great drainage projects that did more to contain malaria than has been done in 25 years." Unfinished projects, he ordered, must be completed by 1 May.[56]

The end of CWA in the spring of 1934 created problems in placing these people on some type of relief work. A group representing both farmers and laborers met in Huron on 17 March 1934, protesting the "new relief setup." Representatives from the Central Labor Union and the Beadle County Farmers Union demanded a minimum of twelve dollars weekly for work relief that would support families of unemployed. E. T. Gitchell, mayor of Huron, submitted a resolution of their board of commissioners to Senator Bulow to the effect that the drought accentuated the area unemployment problem and requested the senator use his influence to secure "an adequate or greater wage scale" than that currently in effect. Hopkins received another complaint from the city of Mitchell that the South Dakota Relief Administration was not implementing his relief plans correctly. The State Federation of Labor understood that FERA insisted the "prevailing rate of wages" would be determined by a local committee. Instead, the state relief office arbitrarily set a scale of 50 cents for mechanics and thirty-five cents for unskilled labor. Weekly hours were to be set at twenty-four in urban areas and fifteen in rural zones. Instead, workers received two eight-hour days weekly or those with a large family could work three eight-hour days.[57]

Late in 1934, Hopkins concluded he should abandon FERA's thirty-cent minimum wage and establish a prevailing rate concept of the area where the work was being done. This rate would be determined by local committees representing labor, business, and the local relief administration. Harry Byrne, then state relief director, announced that the new policy "would have no effect" on South Dakota workers, as this was about what they were currently receiving. A short time later it was reported that relief and the CWA program in South Dakota had grown into the state's "largest single public enterprise" with 700 supervising employees. At that point the CWA was paying its 37,500 employees over $500,000 weekly. The state paid only the field and office personnel. The average monthly benefit of those families on relief came to $28.37.[58]

The abrupt abandonment of the CWA was of concern to Hopkins because, among other things, this left a number of airports uncompleted in South Dakota. By this time, Berry had replaced the incompetent Eales with Republican H. M. Cass, and the latter had a long telephone conversation with Hopkins about this dilemma. Cass reported that they would need about $30,000 to complete work on dams and about $120,000 for livestock feed. He optimistically believed they could complete the airports and dams by "the first of July."

That same day Berry wrote to Edmonds that Mother Nature was wreaking havoc on South Dakota farmers. Because of the continued drought, only 22 percent had repaid their government loans of 1932, and this had declined to 2.5 percent in 1933. As a result, most farmers in the state could not qualify for an FCA loan. The governor hoped to set these people up with "a few head of livestock" and chickens and encourage them to plant forage crops, such as amber cane, Sudan, and millet. He added that amber cane was "a drought and grasshopper resisting crop which makes excellent food for milk cows." Because of the dust storms, he noted, the fences are "almost buried, just the tops of the posts sticking out—and the country looks like a desert."[59]

Berry followed up on the airport construction problem by noting that there were twenty-four projects begun by CWA that were currently uncompleted. The FERA had committed $183,741 to this project and local committees had "obligated" themselves to furnish the necessary $58,135 to complete the jobs. But they were encountering a new problem—horse fatigue. Hickok had noted the previous year that horses in the Huron area were in terrible shape due to the scarcity of feed for livestock.

> A farmer will show up in the morning and hitch his team to a road grader. They will work willingly and fairly well through the morning. By noon they are tired out. By night they are completely exhausted. They don't come back the next day. They die right in the barnyards, from starvation. There have been cases where half-starved horses have dropped in the harness, right on the road job.

The governor asked Hopkins if it were possible to get $5,000 from FERA to purchase some necessary materials and for machinery where it was needed "due to lack of teams of horses."[60]

Again Hopkins came through for South Dakotans. He wired Berry on 26 April 1934 that he was making available to the state $1,314,000 for general relief and work programs; $25,000 for transient relief; $8,027 for expenses for local relief offices, and $6,135 for student aid. This money must "cover all obligations through the month of May." He directed Berry, "File application immediately" for this money.[61]

Hickok's role as observer in the Midwest led to another relief program. On one occasion she toured the Huron area that had been devastated by grasshoppers. The "miles and miles" of fields she drove through looked as though they had just been plowed. The hordes of grasshoppers had simply cleared off the vegetation, roots and all. The area was "just black earth." The plague of locusts had eaten off the bark of "scraggly trees," and women were afraid to hang out their washing for they even ate clothing off the lines.[62]

Nature at this time added even further insult to the desperate economic situation with awesome dust storms. Hickok described one near Huron, which was already an area of "desolation, discomfort, and misery" before the storm began. She wrote:

> It blew the night before. The next morning the sky was clear but you couldn't see the sun. There was a clear brown haze—only right above was the sky clear and the wind was blowing a gale. It kept on blowing, harder and harder. And the haze kept mounting in the sky. By the time we had finished breakfast and were ready to start out, about 9, the sun was only a lighter spot in the dust that filled the sky like a brown fog. We drove only a few miles and had to turn back. It got worse and worse—rapidly. You couldn't see a foot in front of the car by the time we got back! It was like driving through a fog, only worse for there was that damnable wind.[63]

These and other physical phenomena led Roosevelt to observe in July 1934 that Great Plains farmers faced special problems of high winds, soil erosion, and drought. On 21 July he issued an executive order to spend $15 million of a $525 million drought relief fund for a Great Plains Shelterbelt Project. His proposal included an area a hundred miles wide from the Canadian border to the Texas Panhandle, covering twenty million acres of land with the planting of 1,820,000 trees.[64]

Immediate criticism arose. Jonathan Mitchell, a political analyst, wrote for the *New Republic* that this represented "a desirable, if minor, step toward the civilized use of our land." He added that the idea would work in "moderately moist areas," but could not prevent dust storms such as that in 1934. He thought dust storms could best be prevented by turning western lands back to grazing.

The shelterbelts would not increase humidity or rainfall. There would be no lumber to harvest from them as the high winds would stunt the growth of the trees and they would not flourish on the Great Plains.[65]

Two Eastern professors, one from Yale and the other from Syracuse, insisted the project was "unscientific" and would "aggravate the evils" it was intended to correct. The Great Plains did not have the proper climate for crop production or forestry, and should be used only for cattle grazing. The government, they insisted, should fund further forestry experiments before beginning any such extensive program.[66]

The comptroller general added his voice of pessimism by ruling that the president could spend only one million of his proposed fifteen million dollars because his program was "only an indirect relief measure and only Congress could decide on its funding." Roosevelt responded that he would ask Congress for funding for his idea. Congress, however, was not forthcoming in meeting his request until February 1936 when $1,180,000 was approved for further investigations of the concept and to distribute free trees if farmers would plant them.[67]

Despite insufficient Congressional support, FDR managed to keep the shelterbelt concept alive through use of emergency WPA funds from 1937 through 1940. When he asked Director of the Budget Harold Smith to include the program in the Emergency Relief Appropriation Act of 1941, Smith responded that he believed the project should be transferred from the Forestry Service to the Soil Conservation Service. Acting on this advice, the transfer was made, and eventually this reforestation work was done by the states, local agencies, and individual farmers. In 1944, *Business Week* rejoiced that the project had spent only fourteen million instead of the seventy-five million dollars Roosevelt had envisioned. This was one of the least successful New Deal programs and was damaged by the unfavorable publicity it received.[68]

In an Orwellian twist on the traditional labor maxim that strikes should occur in times of prosperity when labor was scarce, the depression years were filled with strikes across the nation for better wages and working conditions. This strife accelerated after the enactment during the Second New Deal of the Wagner Act that guaranteed workers the right to organize and bargain collectively, but strikes also occurred before this landmark in 1935. The strike against John Morrell & Co., a meat-packing company in Sioux Falls, occurred before the "first" sit-down strike in Flint, Michigan.

Working conditions at Morrell were deteriorating, with one worker quoted as saying, "it was about the poorest-paying place in town."[69] There was no job security, and hours were being cut. With the encouragement of New Dealers and the passage of the NRA that guaranteed workers the right to organize and to bargain collectively, those supporting a union began meeting surreptitiously and organized a local of the Amalgamated Meat Cutters and Butcher Workmen of North America. This development alarmed the company, which determined to crush the fledgling union immediately. Every foreman carried dismissal cards and, if one thought two men were talking union, he would use the dismissal card without questioning.[70]

Layoffs increased, and the company announced a reduction of 108 men in March 1935. Labor difficulties at Sioux Falls's "largest industry" had periodically broken out in the past and this time seniority rights was the issue: the union wanted it based departmentally, while management interpreted it as plant-wide. Union members determined to strike to force recognition, and the workers began a sit-down strike on 9 March 1935. Expecting it to be of short duration, they were surprised to see it stretching into the night and beyond.

Although no violence occurred, at the request of Minnehaha County Sheriff Melvin C. Sells, Governor Berry sent in the national guard, becoming the first governor in South Dakota history to call out the troops during a strike. Berry called strike leader Sam Twedell on the plant telephone and asked him to call off the walkout. The union men were certain Sioux Falls business owners were making the governor's decisions, and Twedell informed him the strikers would not leave until the troops were gone. The two men agreed that if the governor would withdraw the national guard, the strikers would "vacate the plant and establish the picket lines outside." Berry then withdrew the guard in the early morning hours, and the strikers, including fifty women, evacuated the plant.[71] After one full day of no violence, martial law orders were rescinded.[72]

After the sit-down strike ended, some 300 union members staged a picket line outside the plant, armed with "staves, canes, and sawed-off rake handles," and forming "at least two lines of defense" on routes leading to the plant. Governor Berry again established martial law and quickly dispatched the national guard troops a second time, shutting down the plant for two days and breaking the strike.

The company agreed to negotiations with the workers, but they fired twenty-nine union men involved in the strike, but interestingly, not Sam Twedell. Mayor A. N. Graff and Sheriff Sells were sharply criticized for failing to promote arbitration and for their request for martial law. Also at issue was the failure of the discharged union officials to gain reinstatement. The union struck again in July with some fifty employees being taunted for refusing to join the pickets. An assistant foreman was "roughed up" by the pickets, which included fourteen women, who booed and jeered the non-strikers as "scabs." The sheriff and the Sioux Falls police chief, armed only with nightsticks and a reserve of tear gas bombs, escorted the "scabs" to work through the throng of 2,000 strikers. During this confrontation, several were injured with head lacerations and broken ribs and arms. Strikers denied the assertion of William H. T. Foster, Morrell Co. plant secretary, that Communists were supporting the strike. The company saw no reason for importing strike-breakers as "there are plenty of former Morrell employees right here in the city who would like to go to work."[73]

Strike fever spread to Sioux Falls relief workers the following month. Several hundred men walked out, demanding fifty cents an hour and a thirty-hour per week minimum for married men with families. City police regarded this as "a governmental affair" and refused to enter the dispute. Strikers promised no violence and apparently never questioned the oddity of striking a relief job generously provided by the national government. Meanwhile, violence broke out in the Morrell strike when five non-union men went to work under police escort. In this situation, William Green, president of the American Federation of Labor (AFL), sent his representative, Paul Smith, to try to prevent the meat-packers strike from widening into a general strike.[74]

When more than a hundred sheriffs, deputies, and local police had gathered in the strike area and 760 non-union men were working in the plant, relief strikers attempted to broaden their movement by visiting the future Lincoln County project, then under construction, to try persuading the dam workers to join their walkout. When this request was declined, the strikers decided to picket the dam site.[75]

In the meantime, the union organized an effective nationwide boycott of Morrell products, and the company offered to reinstate all men, except the twenty-nine. Meanwhile, increasing numbers of workers returned to the plant, especially those with families, and soon the plant was buzzing with 1,000 men and women. When the fired workers protested, the National Industrial Recovery Act's (NIRA) labor board decided that the workers had been unfairly discriminated against, but a short time later, the Supreme Court ruled against the constitutionality of the NIRA, making any decision by the labor board moot. Union forces continued to picket, and from then until the end of the strike in 1937, "a series of disagreements, fights, and general unruliness prevailed."[76]

Before this, one last clash occurred in April 1936 when stones were thrown at non-union personnel as they came to work. The police arrested Twedell and used tear gas to disperse the pickets. Prolonged conferences took place in the following twelve months.

By early 1937, the Supreme Court had sustained the Wagner Labor Relations Act and the National Labor Relations Board (NLRB) was functioning. Also, as part of this law, the U.S. Conciliation Service served to bring the two sides to a labor dispute and, in this case, Robert E. Mythen mediated a settlement. This, and the effective boycott, brought the company to the bargaining table. Both sides could claim victory as the company claimed they increased their net profits over the previous year. The union won, but at a very high cost to its people, as usually happened in disputes such as this.[77]

The challenges of the Dirty Thirties forced thousands of South Dakotans to relinquish their farms and seek other alternatives for making a living. Wallace continued to emphasize this problem, pointing out that farm owners were being rapidly transformed into tenants. A survey conducted in 1936 demonstrated that 83 percent of the people interviewed supported some kind of program that would assist tenants in buying the farms they were working, especially as many of the mortgage holders wanted to be freed from supervising their lessees. FDR established a Special Committee on Farm Tenancy, which held a series of public meetings. Tenants could get help from Federal Farm Loan Banks but they needed more—the ability to secure a decent family living. New Dealers resolved this dilemma with the Resettlement Administration (RA), established by executive order in April 1935.[78]

Roosevelt placed one of his trusted advisors, Rexford Tugwell, in charge of the RA, a multipurpose program to resettle the poor, those who needed housing, and farmers without farms, and retiring vulnerable land from farming. The Division of Substantive Homesteads, a concept rooted in rural utopias of the nineteenth century, was designed to help impoverished farm families not assisted by the AAA. The agency was authorized to resettle destitute or low-income families displaced by floods, soil erosion, or stream pollution. The RA also constructed suburban communities for low-income urban workers called "Greenbelt" towns, such as Greenbelt (near Washington, D.C.), Greenhills (near Cincinnati), and Greendale (near Milwaukee). The RA had a total of 9.7 million acres of farmland under operation by April 1936.[79]

The RA announced in mid-1936 that it would buy more than 900,000 acres in drought-stricken South Dakota at a cost of $3,370,000. Much of this was unproductive land that the government would convert to "grazing ranges, Indian pastures, and recreational areas." Lands in Pennington, Custer, Fall River, Lyman, Stanley, Jones, Dewey, and Sully counties were to be converted to pastures. Those to be turned over to the BIA lay in Washabaugh, Shannon, Todd, Hyde, Hughes, Lyman, Buffalo, Stanley, and Dewey counties.[80]

Congress refused to make the RA a legal entity, and in 1937, Roosevelt merged it with other farm lending institutions into the Farm Security Administration. Congress approved this with the Bankhead-Jones Act that year that authorized low interest loans repayable in small installments over a forty-year period. It also authorized rehabilitation loans for operating expenses and educational assistance and aided migrant workers with sanitary camps and medical services. As Theodore Salutos notes, however, "tenancy had not been created overnight and was not going to be eliminated overnight."[81]

4 Building Public Projects: The PWA and the CCC

> The establishment of a Public Works Administration with an appro-
> priation of $3,300,000,000 satisfied the public works advocates.
> Arthur Schlesinger[1]

TITLE II OF THE National Industrial Recovery Act established the Public Works Administration (PWA) to help state
and local governmental units build public works and infrastructure
through a fund of $3.3 billion to "prime the pump" in stimulating
employment and business activity. During its existence, the PWA
spent $4.25 billion on some 34,000 public projects, such as build-
ings and roads, using labor from the reemployment bureau after
1935. The PWA became a key factor in constructing public works
in South Dakota that both stimulated the state's economy and left
many projects of lasting value.[2]

President Franklin D. Roosevelt appointed Harold L. Ickes
as head of PWA. His administration stood in stark contrast to
Harry L. Hopkins's CWA. The latter poured money, not recklessly
but with some abandon, into putting millions of unemployed to
work in the first year of the New Deal, and distributing more than
two billion dollars in Federal Emergency Relief Act (FERA) and
Civil Works Administration (CWA) funds. Ickes, on the other hand,
"was trickling money into the nation's coffers at such a slow pace
that it provided no significant uplift to the economy." As the *New*

Republic described it, Ickes "couldn't spend any public money without an acute personal soul crisis and what amounted to a grand jury investigation."

To his critics, Hopkins was characterized by "profligacy in the use of public funds and, according to his critics, by that curious category of relief boondoggling," which means "useless and meaningless activity." The conservative columnist George Socolsky wanted an investigation of Hopkins's spending on relief, believing it was impossible to spend money on "the scale that these agencies have without tar sticking to the clothes of the spenders."[3]

To qualify for help from the PWA, the civic institution or group involved had to provide the materials—which was not always easy in financially devastated South Dakota—and the PWA would supply the labor. The PWA got off to a slow start, partly because of the over-cautious Ickes, and partly because it was difficult to stimulate city voters to approve bonds to pay for the materials or to borrow from FERA until it became known the "loan" would not have to be repaid.[4] Locally, Dakotans failed to criticize PWA for its spending because they had to vote funds to participate in the program.

Ickes defended the slow pace of PWA. After only a hundred days, he argued, the agency had allocated $1,709,000,000 "against difficulties almost insurmountable" to get the program underway. But by February 1934 Ickes announced he had too many "backlog" projects to approve any new ones, and under intense pressure, he allocated $2,450,000 for forty-six small programs in nineteen states. Brookings, South Dakota, for instance, was awarded an $8,000 swimming pool, and Groton and Corona received school building funding from the PWA at this time.[5]

As early as June 1933, South Dakota cities, counties, and school districts began developing plans. S. H. Collins of Aberdeen, secretary to the state public works committee, reported a total of $17.5 million in state requests to the PWA. Sioux Falls alone asked for $2.3 million for its schools, a city hall, a swimming pool, a bridge viaduct, and a sewage plant addition. Aberdeen came in second with a $1,360,000 request for a library addition, an auditorium, sewers, and water expansion.[6]

Six weeks later the state PWA advisory board approved expansion of water and sewage projects for Chamberlain, Mitchell, Rapid City, Aberdeen, and Hot Springs, and a schoolhouse at Corona for a total of $1.5 million. The beer tax passed by the state legislature during the special session called by Governor Tom Berry in 1933 was forecast to produce one million dollars annually and would promote PWA projects because the legislature agreed to distribute half the revenue on the state level for highway construction and the other half to counties for PWA projects.[7]

Larger cities, such as Huron, received approval of a big PWA project of $1.3 million, but small towns also were beneficiaries of smaller programs. Groton, Redfield, and Corona received approval for schoolhouses, and Milbank garnered a dam and water system. Clear Lake extended its water system, as did Alpena, Volga, Frankfort, and Mellette. Roberts County built a courthouse and made jail repairs, and Sisseton improved its streets. Many small towns across the state built water and sewage systems for the first time in their history.[8]

Sioux Falls voters approved a $1,175,000 bond issue for a winter construction program of a half-million dollars for school improvements, $210,000 for sewage improvements, $30,000 for an east side storm sewer addition, and $35,000 for park improvements. That October, W. L. Eales announced a PWA program to employ farmers from twenty-two counties that had been hard hit by drought and grasshoppers, and he and Berry promised to request an expansion of this effort from the federal agency. Destitute farmers, in turn, maintained a steady barrage of criticism, not against the program but directed at the hapless Secretary of Interior.[9]

Before the elections in the fall of 1934, the PWA was reported to be seeking a "huge appropriation" to create jobs. How much would depend, of course, on how much private industry would spend in funds for materials. Roosevelt and his advisors maintained private investment was still failing to employ "four or five million willing workers," and if private sources continued to fail to fill the gap the "government must try to do it." The *Argus-Leader* reported PWA officials were "preparing to lay before Congress a list of operations which might be launched quickly if its coffers, once brimming with $3.7 billion, are replenished." In turn, state PWA engineers were asked to submit new projects that would qualify, in particular, requests for aid in constructing roads and bridges. "Well informed persons" suggested the amount to be requested ran into "the millions and perhaps billions."[10]

Three months later Sioux Falls mayor A. N. Graff spent a week in D.C. conferring with national officials. He thereafter announced an additional grant of $53,400 "to assure completion" of the new city hall. This would increase the cost of this center to $385,000, of which city taxpayers would furnish $265,000, which still would be "well within the $300,000 bond issue authorized two years ago." The new cost would include installing new jail equipment, elevators, "completion of the entire third floor, and purchase of necessary storage vaults and new furniture." The mayor also requested release of "an installment of $72,000" from Ickes to complete the sewage plant addition.[11]

Within days, Sioux Falls received word that PWA had approved its request for the new unit at Washington High School. In addition, the city commission awarded contracts for completion of the new city hall and a storm system for the east side, but in May they requested $28,442 additional money to complete the projects. In addition, the city was awarded $15,000 to pave Phillips Avenue, bonds to become available after 1 July. Ickes and Hopkins were said "to be working even more closely together in an effort to get many people off direct relief and onto made jobs." W. F. Cochrane, state Works Progress Administration (WPA) engineer, asked the South Dakota State Planning Board to assist in its canvassing of each town, school district, and county board for a project inventory.[12]

Planning was a major objective of the New Deal and, although this concept was a tough sell to South Dakota farmers, local New

Dealers sought to comply with national demands. This idea was rooted in the notion that lack of planning produced the terrible conditions of drought and depression, and the solution was to plan for the future land use and preclude the problem. The National Resources Committee in Washington asked states to create planning boards to assist their efforts in planning work projects. In the next two years, forty-six state planning boards were set up, with South Dakota being among the first. In February 1934 Berry named a "temporary State Planning Board of eleven members."[13] On 30 March 1935, after the state legislature gave the board legal status, Berry named the following men to staggered terms, ranging from two to six years:

W. R. Ronald (chair), Mitchell
S. H. Collins (secretary), Aberdeen
Robert D. Lusk (vice-chair), Huron
Judge J. R. Cash, Bonesteel
Dr. James C. Clark, Sioux Falls
I. D. Weeks, Vermillion
Nick Caspers, Rapid City
Dr. P. B. Jenkins, Pierre
Theodore Reise, Mitchell
Charles Trimmer, Pierre
Charles Entsminger, Chamberlain[14]

The State Planning Board was headquartered at the state agricultural college in Brookings with Walter Slocum of Hot Springs employed as general office manager. He supervised twenty-eight full-time employees, with Fred Bingham in charge of a branch office in Pierre. These field workers gathered information requested by the state subcommittees. The data they worked with included taxation, finance, economic statistics, population, and demographic trends, and similar information to assist counties and other governmental units in planning relief projects.[15]

The board made an important survey of land ownership in the state, reporting that 66.7 percent was owned by individuals, 11.5 percent were Indian lands, and 10.8 percent were public lands. Another study involved surveying Brookings and Hamlin counties and found that there were large numbers of "stranded rural families in small towns and villages." These people had once lived on farms but now had "neither capital nor machinery" with which to return to agricultural production. There was little or no prospect "of their future employment" in the towns where they had resettled and "some form of rehabilitation" was necessary for them to reestablish themselves. The report expressed belief that this problem "should be of concern" to the county planning boards. The WPA would soon employ many of these people and planning for this eventuality must be undertaken.[16]

Ronald reported that the planning board had achieved "great progress" in planning future PWA projects with county committees. This was part of the Roosevelt administration's intentions to have "in readiness sufficient projects to provide work" by 1 July 1935 for those currently on relief, prior to the passage of the huge work relief bill in Congress. The county committees were composed of mayors in each incorporated city and three farmers, a truly grass-roots involvement to plan for needy community projects and to proffer advice to W. F. Cochrane.[17]

Robert D. Lusk, vice chair of the state planning board and PWA legal advisor, was attending a conference on rivers and harbors in Washington and said that the planning board "would attempt to point the federal work relief program in South Dakota to meet its agricultural problems." Rural rehabilitation, he indicated, would constitute "one of the chief goals" in any work relief program. The president, of course, would turn this huge appropriation into WPA programs, with objectives differing from those of the PWA.[18]

In March, South Dakota government officials submitted 2,402 work relief projects estimated to cost $107 million. In cooperation with the state planning board, 155 plans for water works were proposed at an estimated cost of $2.4 million; 109 sewers at $2.6 million; 821 streets and highways for $48.5 million; 273 school buildings at $7.7 million; 253 "other" buildings for $6.25 million; 36 utilities at $10.3 million; 18 airports at $303,000; 6 city grade crossings for $800,000; 241 recreational facilities at $1.2 million; 272 drainage, irrigation, and reclamation projects at $24 million; and 78 "miscellaneous" projects for $2 million. This survey merely reflected a wish list and made no attempt to evaluate their feasibility.[19]

In 1936, the planning board reported a summary of total expenditures of FERA, the Reconstruction Finance Corporation (RFC), the PWA, and the CWA for 1931–1934. These amounts ranged from over $2.8 million for Minnehaha County to a few thousand dollars in Shannon County, with a statewide total of $45,925,051. Brown County came in second with $2.6 million.[20] The planning committee admitted, however, that "communities must be sold on the idea that returns over a period will be highest for the community as a whole if land is put to use for which it is best adapted." Many farmers thought this was obvious and a waste of taxpayer money. When the Beadle County board resigned as a body in 1937, it was the end of New Deal planning for South Dakota.[21]

President Roosevelt was insistent that Congress pass a program to put some of the millions of unemployed young people to work on the nation's parks and forests. On the last day of March 1933 Congress enacted the Civilian Conservation Corps (CCC) to make his dream come true. Roosevelt envisioned enrolling young men ages eighteen to twenty-five, and who were single, except those who were veterans, whose families were on welfare. They would be paid a dollar a day plus subsistence if they would send twenty-five dollars home each month. The plan was to set up housing in 200-man camps in national and state parks. The CCC would be administered cooperatively: the Department of Labor would enroll the men, the Department of War would operate the camps, the Department of Agriculture would supervise the conservation projects, and the Department of Interior would oversee the work in parks.[22]

The program would thus function cooperatively, both as an agency and as a unit acting for both the national and state governments. South Dakota's leading politicians "appear to have been enthusiastic about the CCC from the beginning." Senator Peter Norbeck and congressmen Hildebrandt and Werner supported it, as did Berry and his relief administrator Roy L. Emry. Leaders of farm organizations also were "favorably inclined as they believed its work might be directed, at least in part, in relieving farm problems."[23]

While Congress was considering the measure, William Green, president of the American Federation of Labor (AFL), objected strongly to legislation designed to benefit one certain group of workers. To mollify his supporters, Roosevelt appointed AFL vice president Robert Fechner as director. Many people resisted the idea of the army supervising the program because this smacked too much of totalitarianism and its regimentation of youth that was occurring in Europe at the time. The army likewise resented the assignment and undertook its responsibility "with undisguised reluctance."

A caseworker investigated each young man who made an application to the CCC to determine his eligibility. Once approved, the recruit had to pass a physical examination and then went to an army post for two weeks of "reconditioning," which many of the boys sorely needed, and then was assigned to a camp. Three of every five enrollees in South Dakota were assigned to the Black Hills.[24]

The *Argus-Leader*, although hostile to New Deal spending in general, noted that "these raids upon the United States treasury are offensive to us," but the state must "resort to such tactics as a matter of self-protection." Some six weeks later the editor had changed his mind about the New Deal and reported that in the coming year, the New Deal "would pump some one hundred million dollars" into the state and this amount was "something of consequence." At this point, neither the editor nor anyone else had any concept of how much enduring work the young men would contribute to the state.[25]

Most participants later spoke glowingly and fondly of their CCC experience.[26]

Roy Emry announced in mid-April 1933 that state quotas would be based on population and the state could expect "approximately 1,500 men initially." All their work in the state, he announced, would take place in the Black Hills and Harney National Forest, the Sioux National Forest of Harding County, Custer State Park, and the schools and public lands in the Black Hills. The men would work on reforestation and building roads, trails, and fire lanes. There would also be "some soil erosion and flood control work" in the national forests. Emry was stunned when 6,000 men immediately applied for these 1,500 jobs, most of them coming from southeastern South Dakota.[27]

Emry and representatives from the Forest Service met in Rapid City to make plans for the camps. They decided to locate eight of them in the Black Hills National Forest with starters at Mystic, Warren-Lamb lumber camp no. 15, Horse Creek, Estes, Pactola, Roubaix, and Rochford. The Harney National Forest would receive camps at Hill City, Silver City, Custer, and "south of Custer toward Hot Springs." As the work progressed, Emry announced, they would move the camps "from place to place." The men would receive their "conditioning" at nearby Fort Meade. Colonel W. R. Pope, in command there, said provision was being made at the fort to handle a thousand men at one time.[28]

South Dakota was eventually allotted thirteen camps and 3,600 men, the largest per capita quota in the nation. Camp construction began immediately in West River counties and the Department of Labor delegated authority to enroll men to the State Emergency Relief Commission. While more than two-thirds of South Dakota's population was rural, over one-half of the CCC enrollees came from small villages rather than rural homes. Camps in sparsely populated areas received enrollees from more populated states in the East to fill their quotas. "An average of 20 percent of those who served in South Dakota came from out-of-state."[29]

World War I veterans of any age were eligible if they were on relief, and the Corps very successfully utilized local experienced men (LEMs). They were assigned to certain camps to "lend experience and maturity" to projects. Official files indicate that LEMs "contributed a great deal to the success of the camps and when it was suggested" in 1937 that their use "might be curtailed, there was a great outcry of protest."[30]

In May 1933, Relief Director Eales announced that recreational facilities had been provided for these thirteen camps. Each would have athletic equipment, a radio, a traveling library of some 200 books and current popular magazines and newspapers, writing equipment, and religious services. They were contemplating camp exchanges, similar to army post exchanges, where the men could purchase toilet articles, candy, and cigarettes with what few funds they had left each month. Not more than 5 percent of the men would be paid forty-five dollars monthly for leadership positions and no more than 8 percent would receive thirty-six dollars per month for minor executive jobs. Camp penalties could include admonition, suspension of privileges, specified work duties, and deduction not to exceed three days' cash allowances.[31]

Dorothy Hubbard Schwieder reported on the CCC camp at Presho, South Dakota. "Camp officials needed food for the camp," she noted, and "the workers themselves patronized local businesses." The camp was active during the summers of 1934–1936 and provided recreation for the townspeople with the dances attracting locals, "particularly young women."[32] The camps not only provided entertainment for the men in the evenings after work, they also offered "home improvement" courses for them to complete their high school program and to enroll in college-level classes, or to take courses in training for a vocation and otherwise acquire a skill for future employment. Training in typing, carpentry, and auto mechanics was available, to make enrollees more employable. Their entry-level college courses led many to enroll in a college after completing their CCC enlistment.[33]

The CCC began its work in forests, culling out dead trees, planting new ones, building hiking trails, and checking ponds. After the dust storms of 1934 devastated the country from east to west, the CCC began teaching farmers how to terrace the land and the art of contour plowing. One year later, another expansion occurred in the wake of "an outdoor recreation renaissance" in the nation that was placing greater emphasis on improvement of national and state parks to enhance their recreation features, a relatively cheap form of public entertainment.[34]

The camp at Mystic was built in 1933 and remained in good condition for the 177 men housed there four years later. The recreational hall contained a piano, pool table, ping-pong, and checkers. The men had transportation to town twice weekly for movies. Sixty percent of them were enrolled in elementary school courses and 40 percent studied at the high school level. In addition, 40 percent of them were in some type of vocational work, such as carpentry, auto mechanics, and acetylene welding. The men, 164 from Nebraska and 13 South Dakotans, built roads and made timber improvements over an area twenty-five miles long and nine miles wide.[35]

Men at Camp F-14 near Custer worked on timber improvement and forest fire prevention in Harney National Forest. Herbert A. Martin, the camp educational advisor, not only offered the usual curriculum of studies, but he also organized a glee club and an orchestra. Camp F-20 near Sturgis engaged in similar work in the Black Hills National Forest. Adrian W. Kreir's program offered "an excellent educational and recreational program that included sports and publication of a monthly newspaper." On the other hand, Camp F-15 near Rapid City was not as well administered. Enrollees there complained of bad food, as well as filth and poor leadership from Second Lieutenant Fred Adams who was finally reassigned and replaced by a more competent officer.[36]

Enlistees in SC-5 near Alcester worked on private lands, improving erosion control and moisture conservation through terracing and building check dams, under the command of Captain John W.

Walker and with the supervision of John W. Sponseller and ten men of the U.S. Soil Conservation Service. Camp DBR-2, north of Belle Fourche, did repair work on Orman Dam and its 650 miles of irrigation ditches. When first organized, the men slept in army tents but they built barracks before winter arrived. Men at the same camp worked at a factory in Newell, making tile for the various irrigation projects.[37]

By mid-September 1933, all of the camps were able to report great progress. They had thinned 6,127 acres of timber, constructed 21.5 miles of roads, built 8.5 miles of telephone lines, cleaned up five miles of roadside and 1,493 acres of land, built two buildings and 14 bridges, provided waste disposal for four campsites, cut 4,775 fence posts and built 38 miles of fences, constructed nine reservoirs, completed 3,275 acres and 96 miles of land and timber surveys, and provided 15,600 acres of rodent control. Colonel Allen S. Peck believed that the nation's taxpayers had received "full value for their money" from these men.[38]

The CCC at Rockerville in the Black Hills received an interesting assignment in May 1934. The Army Air Corps and the National Geographic Society planned a stratospheric balloon launch near Rapid City in response to the flights of Auguste Piccard of Switzerland. One hundred CCC workers built a road to a huge bowl "surrounded by 400 foot walls," at the launch site that became known as the Stratobowl. Supplies of hydrogen tanks were hauled to the area by Army trucks whose "hard tires" were being replaced with "pneumatic tires for the hauling work." Rapid City businessmen were cooperating with the project by pledging $1,154 of the necessary $2,000 needed for support. The balloon reached a record-breaking height of 13.71 miles, propelling Rapid City into the national spotlight.[39]

These camps were inspected periodically, and in two cases, wood-burning heating stoves were discovered to have bad cracks that presented a serious danger to the young men. An investigation by the CCC and the army found that the problem was not the fault of stove maker, Excelsior Stove Company of Quincy and the Lincoln Foundry of Bellville, Illinois, but rather it was caused by the wood used in some of the Dakota camps. They used "dry seasoned pitch pine, supplemented by green pitch pine which produces intense heat almost instantaneously." When "pitch pockets" were encountered, the "reaction is comparable to a blast furnace" until the pitch was consumed. In other camps, similar stoves failed to crack because oak and spruce wood were used as fuel. Hereafter, camps in Minnesota and the Dakotas would use the "improvised oil barrel type heater" instead of those that burned "all types of fuel."[40]

In another instance, the inspector gave the camp in Union County a good report on 27 January 1939, but a week later serious trouble occurred. A group of Kansas men who were stationed there requested a group discharge. Fifty of the crew of sixty-six returned to camp from work at 10:30 am, with sixteen protesting the stoppage and the remaining fifty refusing to return to work. It was a cold, clear day with no wind. A fire was kept going to warm the men periodically, but the entire group continued to huddle around it instead of rotating turns there and at work. Brigadier General George P. Tyner ordered them back to work, telling them to be on the work truck "or else." Twenty-six of them got on the truck, but twenty-four refused, complaining that their crew leader had "cursed them out" that morning. The unsympathetic general discharged the recalcitrants the following morning when they again refused to go to work. The men were from large towns or cities in Kansas, and the report observed that the "discharge rate has been exceedingly high on all enrollees of Kansas origins when they are transferred outside their state of origin." The chief complaint of these big-city boys centered on being stationed in an area where the nearest town was Alcester, which offered few recreational advantages.[41]

Members of the veterans' camp in Meade County on highways 14 and 16 just east of Rapid City reported a special problem. The men had to turn over three-fourths of their pay each month to their families on relief. Several counties were reluctant to accept the added responsibility of medical expenses and other costs of supporting these veterans' families, and they moved them to Meade County where the CCC veterans' camp was located. In some cases the veterans involved were "not even advised of the impending arrival" of their families, who were "literally dumped off a truck on the doorstep of [their] barracks." As a result, 150 children became unexpected wards of that county. In those families with two children, the twenty-five dollars per month could not cover more than "the bare necessities." Where there were three or more children, there had to be some funding for additional food, clothing, health care, and costs of schooling. The county appealed to Senator Norbeck for help, and he passed the problem on to Robert Fechner. The administrator wrote to the Veterans Administration, and a representative from that agency met with one of Fechner's men to try to resolve the problem.[42]

State Auditor George O'Neil, himself a veteran, was particularly concerned over the plight of these families, and he reported a final resolution of this dilemma after a conference with Berry and Eales. The conferees discovered that CWA men also suffered from the same problem of supporting their families with their meager monthly salary. While they earned twice as much as CCC men, or sixty dollars monthly, "their work may be stopped at any time" and they had to try to save "for a rainy day." O'Neil met with the local chamber of commerce and county commissioners and the resolution consisted of investigating "meritorious cases," and where there was "satisfactory showing of need," the difference between the two categories of income would be supplied "out of federal funds." Attempts would also be made to unite the families "preferably as near to the camps where the men are located as possible."[43]

Occasionally the camps developed great rapport with the nearby communities. "Despite the extreme cold and inclement weather," the CCC men went to Hot Springs in January 1935 to attend a special party in their honor. The Custer and Wind Cave camps played a basketball game that afternoon, followed by a six o'clock dinner and smoker for the officers and their wives. The city merchants wanted to show the CCC men "a good time and to make their lives more pleasant." They promised a "big sports day program" for the men "next spring."[44]

In March 1935, CCC men were assigned to a project in Custer State Park where they were "to install comfort but preserve the natural beauty of the park." This ongoing program would build shelter houses and dams at Pinecreek Lake and Doran Lake, parking for "hundreds of cars," picnic sites with stone fireplaces, toilet facilities, footpaths, "and stunning vistas in the heart of the pine forests." The men built bridges of pine logs, including one called the "spiral" bridge, a "pig tail" bridge near Mount Rushmore. Doran Lake would provide the center for this "mecca," and the Custer State Park museum would be built near the game lodge.[45] District Inspector Kenneth F. Jones admitted that they could not "make the park beautiful; that was done before we were born. But we can make it accessible and comfortable to the public and we can do it without marring the beauty that we found there."[46]

Radio began to play a beneficial role in promoting fire control. A forest fire broke out near Deadwood on a Saturday afternoon about twenty-five miles away from the nearest telephone. Assistant Forest Ranger C. C. Averell got in communication with Deadwood officials through his two-way portable radio and with forest rangers in the danger area. He received reports of requests for additional men and supplies to fight the fire and relayed them to the CCC camps at nearby Rochford, Mystic, Nemo, Pactola, and Roubaix. This speeded up the mobilization of men and supplies, and by Sunday about 550 men were there to fight the conflagration. As a result, eighteen sets of radios were installed throughout the forest with several portable sets in "readiness," and the practice quickly spread to other national parks.[47]

By 1935, FDR and Congress were becoming impatient with many states in their delay in reimbursing the CCC for materials used in improving sites, such as Union State Park in eastern South Dakota.

When Fechner wrote to Berry, asking him to prod his legislature to provide their matching funds, the governor's response presented South Dakota's economic and fiscal condition in early 1935 so succinctly and guilelessly that it deserves lengthy quotation:

As of December 31, 1934, the bonded indebtedness of our state was $45,969,000. In addition to $3,900,000 already borrowed from the Reconstruction Finance Corporation, we are now asking for another loan to enable us to meet maturing bond issues.

Due to repeated crop failures caused by drought and grasshopper devastation, low prices, and bank failures the commercial, individual, and state enterprises of South Dakota are now operating on federal relief funds circulating through the regular channels of business. The present case relief load of the State Emergency Relief Administration is 64,000, or approximately 40% of the entire population of our state.

Of our ad valorem tax levy, 18% of the 1931 tax levy is as yet uncollected, as is 27% of the 1932 tax. In view of the existing conditions, the property tax could not be collected, and the 1933 legislature enacted a gross income tax law which provided funds to meet a certain portion of our operating expenses. The collection of nearly one-half of this amount was possible because of federal relief funds.

Although the cost of state government has been reduced one-third during the past two years, our tax collections lack $78,000 of the amount needed to maintain state government for the past biennium. The overdraft in matching federal funds for road building is in the amount of two and one-half million dollars in 1935, and we have been asked to submit an estimate of how much we can contribute in the payment of old ages [sic] pensions should the federal government enact an old age pension law.

Our farmers have no produce to sell, lack of feed has made it necessary to sell one-half of their cattle to the federal government, and there is no visible personal property upon which to impose additional taxes. Insofar as meeting these requests for matching funds with the federal government is concerned, we feel that we are confronted with an unanswerable problem until such time as we have rain and are able to produce crops and new wealth.

We appreciate the benefits our state has derived from the Civilian Conservation Corps camps, and as soon as it is financially possible for us to do so will be willing to assume our share of the responsibility involved in the establishment and maintenance of these camps.[48]

A bill was introduced in Congress in 1937 to make the CCC a permanent organization. While the CCC remained highly popular, by that time President Roosevelt was rapidly losing popularity for various political reasons, and his favorite New Deal program generated some opposition from his enemies. In Congress, South Dakota Representative Francis H. Case spoke for the permanency measure, and many who wanted an extension of the program supported an amendment extending the CCC for two years. Senator Herbert E. Hitchcock, who was completing Peter Norbeck's unexpired term, voted for the extension, as did Representative Hildebrandt.[49]

After Republicans regained control of South Dakota government in the elections of 1936, the position of Catherine Buel, in charge of CCC selection of personnel, was at risk. Appointed by the Democratic administration in 1933, she had performed adequately, although in a partisan way, under Director Eales. At a salary of $135 monthly, she was handling her numerous responsibilities reasonably well in difficult circumstances, but the Republicans were determined to get her position. "An aloof spinster," Buel complained to national CCC officials about the verbal abuse and heckling she was enduring, in addition to coping with a 12 percent salary reduction, but Fechner declined to intervene. The two parties finally agreed to compromise, allowing Buel to keep her position until 1938 with the intent that she could find another position by that time. She was then replaced by Stanton Clark.[50]

From this time until its demise, historian Kenneth Hendrickson asserts, the CCC was in its "heyday" in South Dakota. In particular, camp educational advisors began placing greater stress on vocational education and on-the-job training, and this emphasis proved very popular with the enrollees. Yet 70 percent of the men returned home or to the farm unemployed. In August 1935, the CCC reached its peak of 505,782 enrollees, then gradually dropped to 300,000 in 1938. During its early existence, enrollment information revealed that 84 percent of the men had not completed high school, 44 percent had not completed the elementary grades, and some were illiterate. The study did not include young women. During the worst years of the depression, thousands of boys and girls had taken to "bumming" around the country. FERA transient camps helped many of these youths but more was needed.[51]

The director wrote his final report when the CCC was disbanded in 1942. The CCC had enrolled more than three million men during its existence and had "started a change in the landscape of a nation." The men had planted two billion trees and developed 800 new state parks. They had constructed over 10,000 small reservoirs and 46,000 vehicular bridges, 13,000 miles of hiking trails, 1 million miles of fences, restocked 1 million fish, and eradicated about 400,000 predatory animals. CCC projects altered more than 118,000,000 acres of land, an area larger than California. Statistics from all these categories include work performed in South Dakota.[52] Specifically, by the end of 1941, the CCC had provided employment to 26,500 South Dakotans, and they earned more than $6.2 million for their families. During the CCC's last year, there were only 838 enrollments in the state, but the program left a magnificent legacy in the work it had performed and in the improvements it had made in the region's national and state parks.[53]

5 Berry's Second Term and the Second New Deal

Give a man a dole and you save his body and destroy his spirit; give him a job and pay him an assured wage, and you save both the body and the spirit.

Harry L. Hopkins[1]

POLITICS INVARIABLY INTRUDED into national relief programs, and South Dakota was no exception. H. M. Cass, now the director of Federal Emergency Relief Administration (FERA) in South Dakota, informed Aubrey Williams that the state Democrats "seem to have the jitters" because of a *Literary Digest* poll showing the state to be "on the very ragged edge" of those Americans supporting the New Deal recovery efforts. Governor Tom Berry was concerned and blamed the findings on the politics involved in the South Dakota Agricultural College (SDAC) in Brookings. Cass believed the Republicans on the staff there were playing politics, although not overtly, but neither he nor Berry was happy with the director of extension at the SDAC. Cass noted that he was "handed to us" by Sherman Johnson, regional director of the Agricultural Adjustment Administration (AAA) and a former instructor at the Brookings college. When the New Deal began operations, its bureaucrats naturally turned to state college faculty who were experts in the agricultural areas they were seeking to assist.[2]

More problematic for Berry, however, was the fact that FERA

had issued orders that no one running for political office should retain "a responsible position" in the administration; this rule was Harry L. Hopkins's effort to keep his relief programs above politics. The complication was that John McKee, the popular relief administrator at Sioux Falls, was running for commissioner of Minnehaha County. The governor "tried to straddle the issue by appointing a man named Crowley to perform McKee's duties yet retain McKee in his official position." The local American Legion objected to this arrangement because Crowley, recommended by the Fraternal Order of Workers, was a Canadian citizen.[3] Cass, of course, was directly involved in this issue by appointing Crowley and trying to persuade McKee to resign. Various Democratic politicians disliked Cass, over and above his political preference, partly because of the charge that he was receiving $8,000 annually from the South Dakota Public Health Association, and it was alleged that he received "all the Christmas Seal money that was sent in to the headquarters at Huron." The president of the SDAC further alleged that Cass had "mishandled Red Cross funds." To quell this uproar, Berry finally appointed J. R. Stack to fill the FERA position at Sioux Falls on a temporary basis. McKee reported to the press that "he was forced out," but he resigned before being fired.[4]

That fall T. J. Edmonds, regional relief director from Des Moines, reported that his relationships with South Dakota politicians had deteriorated but now were "in a satisfactory condition." He had ridden on a train from Washington to South Dakota with Berry "in the drawing room" of Fred W. Sargent, president of the North Western Railroad. Berry discussed "some future plans for South Dakota and apparently was his former jovial self," and Edmonds now believed that he and the governor were "again on very good terms." Berry had just fired Cass and replaced him with Michael A. Kennedy. Kennedy was concerned that others might view this shift as coming from FERA pressure, and he hoped that Cass did not feel he had "ever been against him." Berry, however, made his decision because of pressure from the off-year elections coming that fall.[5]

A United Press dispatch headlined a story "Governor Spurs South Dakota Relief as a Campaign Issue." The story noted that South Dakota's reorganization of relief administration "was started at double quick time" when Berry tried to ward off relief as a campaign issue by firing Cass. Republicans were alleging that state relief "had been retarded" by Cass who was "a close friend of FERA administrator Hopkins." This charge appears to be contradictory.[6]

The drought also produced political issues for these elections. In May, Berry announced a plan for the state to purchase 130 carloads of cane, Sudan, and proso millet seed out of relief funds and then donate it to farmers on relief rolls. Recipients had to sign an agreement to repay the state relief commission following the next harvest, plus extra seed to cover the cost of handling. They must plant the seed and not feed it to their livestock or they would lose further relief benefits. Berry expected to distribute this seed to 30,000 South Dakota farmers in time for spring planting. These seeds were both drought and grasshopper resistant, and he predicted the resulting crops would "exceed in value" many times the state cost.[7]

When Hopkins received word of Berry's plan, he asked why the governor had not applied to the Farm Credit Administration (FCA). Berry responded that this program was for those on relief that could not qualify for a FCA loan. He thought they would have to purchase another twenty to twenty-five cars of seed. Hopkins assured him that if he could not find enough funds, FERA would "give you the money to do it."[8]

The South Dakota Young Republican League (YRL) then produced a mimeographed "Weekly Dope Sheet," charging that Democrats were profiting from this generosity. Specifically, they said that Democrats sold four carloads of this gift, which were sent to Plankinton at $19.50 per car. The sheet observed that there was a "possible chance" this money went into the Democratic war chest to pay for "the champaign [sic] propaganda now being shipped out of the Democratic headquarters at Pierre." H. G. Burrell hotly denied this charge with a lengthy letter to Palmer Larson, president of the YRL, which detailed where the donated commodities shipped from Arkansas had ended up in South Dakota.[9]

Prior to the primary election in 1934, Berry traveled to Sioux Falls to attend the annual South Dakota Press Association banquet. Berry informed the gathering that there was little difference between "running" a state and operating a ranch. Instead of using "a trusty and sure-footed pony and a rope," as governor he was riding his "campaign horse," named "Economy," and rather than using a lariat, he was armed with an "axe." He offered the conciliatory opinion that "almost all the members of the legislature are making an earnest effort to do something really worthwhile." One editor noted Berry was "thoroughly competent" as governor, especially in situations where "wise-cracking takes the spotlight" and suggested he was becoming known as "South Dakota's own Will Rogers."[10]

Lieutenant Governor Hans A. Ustrud decided to challenge Berry in 1934, running on the Democratic platform of 1932, because, he claimed, Berry had never used it, except for the purpose of getting into office. This primary race brought the progressive versus conservative feud of the Democrats into the open. Berry used the party machinery he had built up in the previous two years, issuing periodic news releases about the success the gross income tax was enjoying. Ustrud said the administration forces must be convinced showman P. T. Barnum was correct, that "the American people loved to be hum-bugged." Oddly enough, Loriks and Fosheim endorsed Berry in the election, although they had strongly disagreed with him and his proposals. Abandoned by his colleagues, Ustrud "ran a scorched earth campaign" to no avail. Berry inundated him by a vote of 61,484 to 16,037.[11]

The Communist Party of the United States (CPUSA) conducted a "united front" campaign with Knute Walstad for governor, Homer Ayers for lieutenant governor, and Clarence H. Sharp for Congress. The latter later confessed that the effort "was a very militant and not too well conducted campaign." Violent clashes between communists and authorities occurred, for instance, in Roberts and

Marshall Counties, which frightened away many farmers from "radical solutions." This ticket was swamped in the general election.[12]

Berry faced William C. Allen in the general election. A newcomer to politics, Allen was publisher of the Aberdeen *Dakota Farmer*, and he ran on a platform offering a net income tax and a property tax that exempted residences. Berry ran on his record of administering the New Deal relief program. He declined to discuss the gross income tax, or even operations of the state government, observing, "You know me. You know what I have been doing. So if you want change, vote for someone else."[13] Senator Peter Norbeck supported Allen, criticizing Berry for promoting the repeal of Populist and Progressive reforms. Following his defeat in the primary, Ustrud refused to endorse Berry, announcing he would support the Republican candidate in the general election. Berry responded publicly to this announcement by declaring that Charles McDonald, Republican state chair, "used to tell me every time he saw me that the Republicans were certainly glad we took [him] off their hands." It took the GOP "a long time to get rid of Hans" and the Democrats "were welcome to him."

In the midst of this campaign, insufficient revenues for school support became a problem, as South Dakota tax rolls continued to decline. FERA education representative Dr. Howard A. Dawson traveled to Pierre to confer with Kennedy about the crisis. They finally concluded that FERA would have to pay teachers' salaries for three months in those districts without a city of 5,000 or more population and whose "resources had been exhausted." This assistance, Dawson proclaimed, was not to be interpreted as federal support of education but a matter of relief to keep the schools open until the state legislature could act in January. John Hines, deputy state superintendent of public instruction, estimated that 350 districts with 1,500 teachers would be eligible. A *Rapid City Daily Journal* report asserted this was similar to the relief program FERA adopted for 1933, with salaries being paid "not to exceed $60 monthly."[14]

Allen made a political issue of the cost of administering relief programs in the state. This was an issue troubling many citizens, especially Republicans, and estimates of this price were "high." Allen insisted that the middlemen who administered the programs, those standing between federal government funds and needy people, "were getting too large a share" of the money. He believed that relief programs and "all state affairs" should enjoy a "businesslike administration."

Berry responded that these claims were "deliberate falsehoods" and "the product of uninformed minds." When people are told it costs $3.02 to administer each $1 of relief, he declared, the author "is going to be asked to prove that statement." "The books are open to inspection," he noted, and if anyone had examined them, he would not be making "the silly statements that are being made." Berry attributed these "silly statements" to Harvey Jewett of Aberdeen, an ardent Allen supporter.[15]

A week later Berry urged the election of Democrats "sympathetic to New Deal policies." The present team "has given the state of South Dakota the best administration it has ever had," he bragged. He begged the voters not to "send me back with my wings clipped so that I can do nothing but run around circles." He wanted all of his team reelected. T. B. Werner also spoke at this meeting, promising "to continue to support the New Deal," if reelected.[16]

Late in the campaign, Allen charged that state relief administrators "sat idly by" while relief workers in neighboring states "were getting higher pay for their workers." In response, South Dakota officials claimed, "the needy in this state are receiving superior care at their hands." South Dakota relief workers were receiving 35 cents an hour with strict limits on hours, while Minnesota reliefers were getting 50 cents and 30 hours weekly, with overtime available "for special needs." There were "no campaign pictures on the walls" in Minnesota, the Republican continued, "with a minimum of politics entering into the administration." In South Dakota, he declared, it was too much like the man who "gave a dime for missions and $5 to see that the dime got where it was supposed to go."[17]

Just before the election, Berry retorted that if Allen were elected, he would use the Minnesota system of relief "as a smoke screen to try to reduce the amount paid to relief workers." "When the Republicans were in power," he correctly charged, "they gave no money at all to those on relief. They just gave them food and clothing and fuel and not very much of that." The New Deal changed all that in South Dakota. Minnesota paid its relief workers more because of the wage levels of its "three big cities," as New Deal administrators insisted they did outside those cities. But from 1 April to 1 August, Minnesota relief workers outside those cities received an average of $91.03 per family, while South Dakota workers during the same time period received an average of $143.40 per family If he were elected and Allen used this same system, this action would cut the relief money coming into South Dakota by $10 million.[18]

In what the *Argus-Leader* labeled "one of the bitterest battles in years," Allen and Berry continued their fencing over the relief issue. Senator William J. Bulow charged the Republicans with opposing "the farm relief program which brought $37 million into South Dakota this year." Stanley Brekkus of the highway department referred to the Republican charge of farming out relief printing to a plant in which Congressman Werner owned an interest, and asked why they did not also include the fact that Norbeck's company received $20,562 for drilling wells for the relief programs. The charges and counter-charges flew back and forth.[19]

The *Argus-Leader* predicted that this vitriolic campaign would result in a record turnout of voters, and it did, with almost 300,000 votes cast. The newspaper headlined a story that the Democrats would have the "Greatest Power Over State [that] Ever Existed." In the elections that followed, Berry won a second term by defeating Allen 172,228 to 119,447, and the Democrats increased their majorities in the state legislature. In the same election, voters even repealed prohibition that they had adopted in 1914.[20] Republicans took some pleasure in conservative Francis H. Case coming within 3,000 votes of unseating Congressman Werner in the Second District.[21]

When the legislature met in January 1935, Governor Berry advised them to "shun easy cure-alls" and "legislative hocus-pocus." His message urged "economy moves" and outlined "broad principles on liquor control and taxation." Leaning towards "conservatism," he noted that the state was "simply marking time until favorable weather again brings good crops." Both Republicans and Democrats had "favorable" comments to make on his inaugural statement.[22]

The original gross income tax plan carried a two-year limit and required extension. The following day Berry presented the legislature with his version of an extension. The agrarian progressives had other ideas. The Farm Bureau supported a net income tax of 2 to 10 percent on personal incomes of over $9,000 and corporate taxes on incomes over $250,000. Deductions were allowed for a head of family and dependents. Emil Loriks and Oscar Fosheim promoted an ore tax that the Homestake Mine bitterly fought. Both progressive agrarian groups were promoting a common philosophy of taxing the wealthy and an opposition to Berry's gross income tax and sales tax. Both farm groups supported each other's tax plan.

Fosheim and Loriks were circulating a petition and by this time had gathered some 20,000 signatures as a threat to force a vote on the ore tax. The Loriks forces joined with the Republicans to kill Berry's gross income tax fiasco. Berry's supporters amended the ore tax proposal to 4 percent and, to compensate, offered a net income tax of 8 percent maximum and a two-cent sales tax. This net income tax never met financial expectations but the regressive sales tax proved to be a good revenue producer.[23]

The agrarian progressives also promoted civil liberties in this session by joining Republicans to kill Berry's request for a libel law. The governor took exception to the harsh criticism of his management of relief. In 1934 he initiated two libel suits against newspapers and he had "engaged in a shouting match" with Ralph Hillgren, an *Argus-Leader* reporter, at one news conference and barred him from another. The libel bill would apply to editors who rejected a demand for a retraction, but the measure ultimately went down to defeat.[24]

On the last day of 1934, Berry wrote Hopkins, quoting a recent news story that FERA was considering "a change in the relief setup to work relief." The governor noted that South Dakota's highways had benefited more than all the other work jobs combined. He called attention to the public demand for a "surfaced [better than gravel] highway" across his state "giving the traveling public" a route to the state's scenic marvels as well as to Yellowstone and Glacier national parks. Berry referred to the "considerable balance of Public Works Administration (PWA) funds" and suggested that his state might receive 100 percent, rather than the usual 50 percent matching funds, to construct U.S. highways 16 ($2,952,000) and 14 ($2,579,000). This would provide "work for thousands of men, permanently improve our highways and meet the demand of the traveling public."[25]

Pierce Atwater made a preliminary survey of relief work in South Dakota for Hopkins. He concluded that Kennedy was the only person in the state qualified to direct the relief program and recommended that FERA should appoint him as director. Berry was satisfied but wanted something to this effect in writing. Otherwise, both men were willing "to play ball with us on anything we wanted to do." Atwater at first believed that half the people in South Dakota were on stock feed relief, and was astounded to find that almost half the population was on work relief, in addition to those on the stock feed program. The state had 233 caseworkers handling an incredible 70,000 cases. These were rural people who were "miles apart," so they could not be visited more than once every three or four months with this inadequate staff. He concluded that South Dakota presented "a vastly different situation" from other states. He was not satisfied with the explanation from Berry and Kennedy that drought and grasshoppers had caused 50 percent of the state's population to be on relief. "Perhaps that is a good enough reason," but he wanted to carry out a limited case investigation to explore this unusual situation.[26]

In his field report, he informed Hopkins that the governor and the legislature would "do anything that we wanted." The FERA wanted the state to create a Welfare Department "with broad powers," of course, but to obtain this Atwater observed that he had to "write the bill myself, because they don't know what it is all about." In February 1935, during the legislative session, he met with Kennedy "and three lawyers" in Mitchell, and he dictated to their secretary what he wanted in the bill. He further detailed what he wanted Tom Berry to say in the governor's resolution asking the legislature to use $200,000 of the beer tax money to support the department, plus an additional appropriation of $500,000 for welfare purposes. All this was to be in addition to $300,000 annually for mothers' pensions and an inclusion of $1 million for county poor funds.[27]

Atwater determined to make a careful study of work relief in South Dakota beginning with four or five counties. He had a staff of four "qualified case workers with good rural experience" to work on this for four to six weeks. He noted that both Berry and Kennedy, "were very cooperative," following "100 percent of the suggestions I have made," and he was optimistic about the results of the study.[28]

First of all, Atwater deplored the readiness of state office staff in Huron, observing he had never "visited one in worse shape." People in the office were "nice," but not one "appears to have the faintest idea what it [professional social work] is all about." The community's business leaders thought the office was "doing a good job." When pressed on what a competent investigator ought to do, though, they finally agreed that four investigators for 2,800 families "was pretty bad." Atwater concluded that the proper remedy was to find "twenty-five good case workers and bring them to South Dakota as a sort of flying squadron to get at least the elements of decent relief administration" to the counties he was surveying. He believed Berry and Kennedy "would welcome a move of this kind."[29]

Some nine weeks later, Atwater reported to his boss on the new relief administration established for the state. At Kennedy's suggestion, J. C. Byrne was replaced as Director of Relief Work with Phillip L. Ketchum of Omaha in the temporary appointment. They had placed "fifteen trained workers," one in each of the state's districts, to supervise and advise, to offer formal schoolwork in the evenings for untrained staff, and to make recommendations on hiring and firing staff, a move that should have taken place at least eighteen months earlier.[30]

In late April 1935, Berry traveled to Washington and had a lengthy visit with Hopkins over his new relief organization. When he returned home, he was greeted with a news story by Ketchum in which he insisted South Dakotans on relief should be receiving "twice as much money" as they were currently getting on relief. Berry was upset, as he believed his relief program was functioning properly, and he considered this story in the light of "herd instincts" of the public. Atwater got Ketchum and the governor together to discuss "the whole matter . . . carefully" and managed to sooth Berry's ruffled feelings. Atwater assured Hopkins, "This particular matter had been adjusted satisfactorily." The South Dakota relief administration was now ready to meet the challenge of the next work relief program, the Works Progress Administration (WPA), enacted by Congress on 8 April 1935.[31]

The relief situation in early 1935 created a furor in political circles. Critics argued that the numbers of workers on relief and the amount paid them were higher the previous fall, and these numbers declined after the first of the year. They also questioned the accuracy of the amount available for relief. Bulow was quoted as insisting that there was $3,183,000 available and this figure appeared in the *Argus-Leader*. Berry and Kennedy insisted the figure should be $2,108,545, a considerable discrepancy in sums. State senator L. A. Johnson and former state senator Emil Loriks questioned Bulow about the difference. Johnson insisted relief workers were receiving "pitifully small checks, much smaller than they received last fall, and at the same time the number on relief is much smaller." New Deal critics everywhere complained that the opposite happened periodically just before election time. Loriks asked if the difference that was made public might have "gone astray" or was it "only a mistake in bookkeeping?"

Berry called Bulow's claim a bad "misstatement" and insisted the records of the relief office in Pierre showed one million dollars less money available. He and Kennedy denied that "obligations made last fall were being met now at the expense of relief clients," and they "did not need aid worse than they did in November or December." Kennedy further explained, with plausibility, that the previous fall in some counties these relief people had received AAA corn/hog and wheat benefit payments and this should be considered a benefit and naturally relief money would not be furnished them during that time of benefit payments.[32]

Still, the drought and grasshopper plagues continued, swamping Bulow with distress calls from constituents. The special congressional appropriation of $60 million in late 1933 failed to alleviate the farmers' distress. The following March, the Farm Credit Administration announced plans for $60 million in seed loans to be available to needy agrarians. To qualify, the farmers must cooperate with the crop control programs and must be unable to receive credit from local banks or farm credit agencies. The cap on the loans was $500, and the loans would be disbursed at regional offices, with Omaha designated as the center of the project for South Dakota.[33]

The FCA was promoting legislation to make seed loans to farmers without obtaining waivers from their creditors for the right to first lien on their crops. The South Dakota legislature had provided these waivers, but FCA had not, and, "after a series of conferences, exchange of letters, and telephone calls," Bulow persuaded the administrators to divide South Dakota crop loans into two parts. One would be for seed after the state legislature had acted on waivers; the second addressed the need for farmers to give mortgages on crops to cover seed loans of previous years, with the expectation that this would relieve their debt burdens.[34]

Three days later some thousand farmers from drought-stricken states met in Sioux Falls. They sought to achieve three goals: cash relief that would provide "a good standard of living"; relief feed to maintain their livestock; and credit for providing seed, livestock, and machinery for their farms. One of the planners for the three-day conference, Lem Harris of Philadelphia, hoped to unify farm organizations behind their drive and for needy farmers to visit county seats and urge officials there to provide aid.[35]

Farmers and seed dealers were apprehensive over imported Sudan seed being as effective as native seed. The U.S. Department of Agriculture offered assurance that these seeds from Australia, New Zealand, and Argentina "very probably" originated from native American seed exported to those countries. Argentina seed was tested earlier in Kansas, Texas, and Nebraska and found to be "very nearly identical" to native seed. Domestic American Sudan seed production in 1934 "was about half that" of the normal crop and thus the need for imports.[36]

While Governor Berry and the state legislature were engaged in solving the problems in South Dakota, President Roosevelt continued his efforts to bring prosperity back to the United States. The spring and summer of 1935 witnessed the coming of the Second New Deal with three programs that marked a significant change in philosophy and direction by the administration. Revolutionary for laborers, the Wagner Act signaled a different approach to labor relations by creating the National Labor Relations Board (NLRB) to maintain the guarantee that workers had the right to organize and to bargain collectively. The Social Security Act marked a new commitment of the national government to assist the weaker elements of society, the aged, the blind, dependent children, and the unemployed. The Emergency Relief Appropriations Act was the third legislative program.

One might validly accuse New Dealers of radically flip-flopping on the question of the dole during the early years of their reign. First, they eagerly accepted Hoover's FERA for doling out relief while Hopkins experimented with his Civil Works Administration (CWA) in the winter of 1933–1934, promoting creative public projects to put people to work. In the spring of 1934 they reverted to the FERA dole until the summer of 1935, when they accepted a huge, modified public works program. The reasons for these violent fluctuations were twofold: first Franklin D. Roosevelt's conservative advisors in the Treasury and the Bureau of the Budget pressed him to redeem his pledge to balance the budget; second, these work relief projects were "enormously expensive," which surely unbalanced the budget.

While Congress was recessed in late 1934, FDR was vacationing in Warm Springs, Georgia, enjoying the effect of the soothing waters on his polio-stricken limbs at the "Little White House." Included in his study group at Warm Springs were Henry Morgenthau, Jr., Harold L. Ickes of Interior, Rexford Tugwell of Agriculture, and Hopkins. The group was hammering out a plan for "making profitable work for the unemployed until private industry can take up the slack." His "primary consideration" was a new work relief program.[37]

When Congress reconvened in January 1935, Roosevelt asked for, among other programs, $4.88 billion to take 3.5 million people off the dole and put them on work relief. It passed the House rather easily but ran into opposition in the Senate in the person of Huey Long, the "Kingfish" from Louisiana. Some congressional representatives, unhappy over Secretary Ickes's dilatory management of PWA, feared he might be put in charge of the program, but Roosevelt had already decided on Hopkins.

While the relief bill was debated in Congress, as usual, amendments achieving other goals were added to the popular measure. Senator John William Elmer Thomas, an inflationist Democrat from Oklahoma, wanted a currency expansion of $375 million through issuing silver certificates, and Senator Patrick Anthony

("Pat") McCarran, Democrat from Nevada, added a requirement
that all bureaucrats earning five thousand dollars or more must receive senate confirmation for their positions. This action prompted
Hopkins, who had heretofore managed his responsibilities without
playing politics, to decide Congress was using politics to hit him,
and he became more political.[38]

Congress appropriated the requested and unprecedented
sum of $4.8 billion in the spring of 1935 for relief purposes, with
$800,000,000 to phase out FERA and $4 billion for relief purposes.[39] When the Emergency Relief Appropriation Act became
law on 8 April 1935, Roosevelt created out of these funds the WPA
and other projects. In contrast to the PWA, which spent about 85
percent of its funds on materials, WPA spent about 85 percent of
its money on labor. Instead of simply establishing relief jobs, often
meaningless in purpose, to dole out money, WPA sought to create
real public project work and give laborers meaningful work with a
livable wage.

Hopkins would approve no project in competition with other government agencies; the programs must add significantly to society;
and they must be completed within a calendar year. Wages must be
competitive with those prevailing in the community where the work
took place. During its existence, WPA built over 650,000 miles of
highways, constructed or repaired almost 125,000 bridges, 125,000
public buildings, 8,000 parks, and 850 airport landing fields; it expended about $11 billion on 8.5 million persons. In South Dakota,
WPA spent more than $35 million to complete 131 buildings and
refurbish 250 others, in addition to many miles of hard-surfaced
highways to the Black Hills.[40] Much of the nation's current infrastructure is crumbling today because it has had three-quarters of a
century of hard use, dating back to the New Deal.

One important advancement that came to the Midwest through
the WPA was the advent of electricity, which greatly eased the
workload on rural farm families. Its availability came slowly because
private utility companies were reluctant to build infrastructure in

outlying areas. It cost about $2,000 to build a mile of distribution line, and receipts of power companies in rural areas were about one-fifth the return on the same investment in urban areas. As a result, of the 6.3 million farms in 1930, only 571,000 had running water, and about one in ten had electric service. New Dealers were determined to rectify this, FDR in particular. The house he owned in rural Georgia had no electricity, and his experience made him especially empathetic to this rural problem.[41]

When Roosevelt created the WPA in 1935, one aim was to use the laborers hired through the program to electrify the countryside through the establishment of the Rural Electrification Administration (REA) that May. When advisors noted that these relief workers lacked the necessary skills and there were no funds to purchase wire and poles, he then approved the alternative cooperative approach. Units of farmers could organize into a cooperative and apply to REA for loans to construct lines into the hinterland. In May 1936 Congress passed the Norris-Rayburn Act to approve these loans at 3 percent interest. Each co-op had to demonstrate, though, that its program was economically feasible.[42]

In South Dakota, the Clay-Union Electric Corporation was organized in 1936, soon after Congress authorized funding. Clay-Union Electric constructed 136 miles in the area by 1939 and was such a popular success that neighboring Union County Rural Power Company was organized and began construction in 1938.[43] When REA began to pose a real threat, private companies then built "spite" lines into the more lucrative areas to head off REA projects; this construction harassed the co-ops but did no permanent damage to the REA. By 1940 private companies ceased this effort, making the relationship between them and REA more cordial. In 1941, REA had 780,000 subscribers in forty-five states, acquired at a cost of $11 billion, and the percentage of farms with electrical power had increased to thirty-five. This change reduced the great burden of farm work, eliminated the "coal oil" lamps, and permitted plumbing to be installed for running water, which ended the need for the outdoor "privies." Farm homes became cleaner, brighter, and more enjoyable. The farm wife could now use electric utilities to lighten her workload, ending many of the great differences between town and country. These improvements came, of course, primarily during World War II when the agricultural economy had greatly improved.[44]

After WPA started functioning, FERA officials were ordered to begin cutting their relief rolls. From July through November 1935 about 1.5 million families, or 87 percent in rural areas, left FERA rolls to seek employment with the WPA. During this period, WPA officials conducted a survey of counties in seven states to determine the effects the new program had on rural relief. Fortunately, South Dakota was one of those, with Brookings, Corson, Custer, Edmonds, Grant, Hand, and Meade as the sample counties.[45]

In July FERA began cutting its rolls of the 23 percent remaining on relief in South Dakota, with an order to complete the process in December. The survey found that 35 percent of rural South Dakotans were employed by that time; 10 percent were being helped by the RA, 5 percent were on some other kind of relief, and 10 percent had no assistance. It would be difficult to project these percentages from seven counties to the entire state except that South Dakota had a high percentage of rural population and this was a study of rural relief. The best that can be concluded from this is that those percentages closely reflect the state numbers for rural areas.[46]

By December 1935 the median income of rural households in South Dakota was thirty-five dollars, one of the highest of the seven rural states surveyed. Of those seeking work, 61.2 percent were males and 38.8 percent were females. In November 65.5 percent working or seeking work came from the agricultural segment of population. The study showed that South Dakota had the highest rate of separation from WPA, but this undoubtedly resulted from the difficulty of keeping rural projects going during South Dakota winters. Earnings from these programs averaged forty dollars monthly, compared to thirty-two dollars in private industry. In conclusion, the study noted that with the closing of FERA, the old county relief offices were continued as County Welfare Offices, a change in nomenclature only, and the legislature created the State Public Welfare Commission on 1 July 1935 in anticipation of the new work program.[47]

Governor Berry immediately traveled to Washington to lobby for his state. He and Frank D. Kreibs, secretary to the State Highway Commission, along with Senator Bulow, met with officials of the Farm Credit Administration to "untangle confusion about handling seed loans." They spent the afternoon with Thomas H. MacDonald, chief of the U.S. Bureau of Public Roads, lobbying for funding the construction of a hard-surfaced road "from one end of the state to the other." They emerged, "expressing confidence MacDonald understood the state's road problems," but were told that funding depended on "President Roosevelt's plans for utilizing relief funds on roads."[48]

After a week of conferences with federal officials, the governor announced he was returning to Pierre, where he would draft "a comprehensive proposed state-wide work relief program." He wanted to have his proposal ready to submit as soon as FDR was prepared to consider work relief plans. He noted that projects already submitted to the state planning board and the rural rehabilitation division of the state relief administration would provide the nucleus for his works program. He wanted to space the projects in order to "keep people at home" by distributing the projects "across the state." He added that he was considering dividing the state into three districts for planning purposes—East River, West River, and Black Hills.[49]

President Roosevelt kicked off the campaign for the "greatest peacetime spending machine" in history with a fireside chat. He expressed the hope that it would be "the most efficient and cleanest example of public enterprise the world has ever seen." He reported that work would start "soon" on low-cost housing projects in sixteen cities, and work relief projects would be in full swing by autumn. He also warned that when any program was extended over "more than 3,000 counties throughout the nation," there might be "occasional instances of inefficiency, bad management, or misuse of funds" so the public should not let the opposition convince them "that the exceptional failure is characteristic of the entire endeavor."[50]

After Berry returned home, some 100 delegates met in Mitchell and elected a committee of ten, representing each county along Highway 16, to lobby for paving or oiling the road from Sioux Falls to Rapid City. A larger meeting was planned for Pierre later, representing all counties in the state, to plan cooperation with various county relief boards and the State Highway Commission "to push for completion" of paving Highway 16 across the state.

At this point, U.S. congressional representatives were concerned over the appointment of Harold Ickes as chair of a board that would recommend WPA projects to the president because of his "arrogance," for being discourteous to them, and for being "too slow" in spending PWA money. In contrast, Hopkins was considered a "good spender" in his direction of the CWA program in 1933–1934 in dispersing three billion dollars for relief, so his appointment met with widespread relief and approval.[51]

With the pressure of millions on relief in the Great Depression, Roosevelt put protection for the elderly through improving old age pensions on his wish list for the Second New Deal. On 14 August 1935, six months after establishing the WPA, FDR signed the Social Security Act. The second program, Old-Age and Survivors Insurance program (OASI), was to provide assistance for retirees to supplement their retirement plans. Over the years, this title was shortened to Social Security, and seventy-five years after its establishment, the elderly came to view it as an entitlement, with, theoretically, each generation of wage earners providing the sums necessary for the retirement of the current aged.

The Social Security Act replaced systems, such as those in South Dakota, of poor farms and mothers' pensions. Scarcely a half-dozen states had any mechanism in place to handle the OASI program, and the remainder had to establish one to comply with the federal program. The South Dakota legislature began by creating a state Department of Public Welfare to commence operation 1 July 1935. This move would allow the state to take advantage of any new federal program of relief, old age pensions, unemployment insurance, or other welfare activities. Whatever developed, the structure would be in place, and the personnel could change titles to fit the need. South Dakotans were learning the ways of federal bureaucracy.[52]

The program required no state action. Workers paid one percent of their salary, matched by their employer, into a fund that accumulated until they reached age sixty-five, when they would be entitled to a pension, the amount calculated on the basis of how many quarters they worked times the number of dollars earned quarterly. This was the greatest taxing program in the world at that time and would be amended and extended many times in the next several decades.

The remaining three OASI programs did require direct state participation. Employers would pay a payroll tax into a federal fund to establish a federal/state system of unemployment compensation designed to promote substantial uniformity of plans among the states. Each state was to manage its own system and receive federal grants to handle the costs of administration.

The other plans were grants-in-aid to assist states in their provisions for old age pensions and assistance to the blind and to dependent children. The matching grants for elderly pensions would be limited to the amount provided by the state, up to a minimum of fifteen dollars and a maximum of eighty-five dollars monthly. Grants of one-third of costs for dependent children would be limited to eighteen dollars monthly for the first child and twelve dollars for each additional child. Cases were rushed to the Supreme Court to test the constitutionality of the involved taxes, and in 1937, in *Stewart Machine Co. v. Helvering*, the newly emerging liberal majority on the Supreme Court sustained the taxes in a five-to-four ruling. The decisions overturned the majority opinion of *U.S. v. Butler*'s narrow interpretation of the taxing power, with the justices grounding their interpretation in the General Welfare clause. Congress, the court majority insisted, was not coercing states to participate, but was offering an attractive partnership to meet a national need.[53]

The staff of the Social Welfare Department in South Dakota, after poring over the state's laws dealing with its welfare system, concluded that "sweeping changes" would be required to comply with the new federal programs. The commission's staff, with W. J. Cohen speaking, concluded that South Dakota "appeared to have no laws for old age pensions nor care for the blind that would "furnish even a start" for the new programs. Current county funds being used for this purpose were not sufficient to comply and state funds would have to be provided. South Dakota, though, had neither the resources nor the tax base to supply the money.[54]

W. L. Eales used the occasion of the transition from federal relief programs to the new work relief phase to resign from his office. He had not originally pursued his position and had in fact refused it at least once, and was now suffering with an injury from a car accident. This seemed to be a good opportunity to retire, and there was an experienced, capable person as a replacement. Edmonds appointed Governor Berry as director of the new WPA, and the governor, in turn, named Kennedy as his assistant. Kennedy proved to be a most capable administrator in adapting to his new career.[55]

The WPA integrated social work on a statewide basis for the first time in state history. Because South Dakota did not have trained social workers, skilled professionals were imported to assist. After investigation, relief was granted "on a budgetary deficiency basis." Each county was a unit by itself but did not receive grants; a direct disbursing system in the State Emergency Relief Administration handled them. Because of the current economic conditions, counties that received some help from the state cared for unemployable indigents, and the RA and WPA provided work for all those employable.[56]

In preparing for the projects, Kennedy, now serving as administrator for both the WPA and relief, divided the state into five districts and mailed circulars to counties soliciting proposals. Cities, counties, and other public units were requested to submit proposals on anything except those "the local subdivision could carry out normally." The units were to furnish materials if they were able financially, but the federal government would provide them as long as the payment per man per year did not exceed seventeen dollars. Kennedy's suggested programs included canning plants, sewing rooms, and completion of work projects already undertaken. If relief clients refused a WPA job or one offered by a private employer at "the prevailing wage," they would be removed from the relief rolls.[57]

The city of Pierre pressed the advantages it held for being chosen the center for "accounting, disbursing, and procurement" of the new program, but Kennedy rejected the offer because of a lack of adequate facilities or competent personnel for the administration. In addition, the capital city enjoyed the service of only one railroad, and practically all of the work would take place in the eastern third of the state where the majority of the population resided. The administration listed all of the advantages of Sioux Falls, but the officials in that city made "no official offer." Watertown was eventually chosen because it, like Sioux Falls, enjoyed the services of five railroads, and regular airmail service.[58]

When harvest time arrived that summer, relief officials faced a different crisis. By that time, WPA was being launched in earnest and many unemployed were drawing a decent check for the first time in months. As a result, farmers were experiencing a difficult time in attracting sufficient labor to bring in their harvest. This issue of work relief versus the need for harvest labor presented the most vexing problem faced by relief officials. The farmers needed these workers during the critical time when crops were ripe, but the laborers were accustomed to better pay, or at least to shorter hours and less strenuous work.

Governor Berry declared, "No Work, No Eat," notwithstanding the fact that farmers paid low wages, and many who promised cash "after marketing" forgot to pay at all. In mid-summer 1935, state officials ordered suspension of relief employment until harvest needs were met, affecting 19,000 family heads on relief. Relief officials, in turn, promised these workers, forced into the fields by the governor, that they would be reinstated in their relief jobs immediately after harvest. Hopkins, caught in the middle of this controversy, left these decisions to local authorities to determine who were "shirkers" who refused to work for farmers until compelled to and to place them back on relief rolls later.

Reports came in that people were accepting this "in good spirit," but this hardly agrees with contemporary written accounts. Farmers and the general public rushed to judgment that these workers were "loafers," but they failed to realize how difficult it sometimes was to get back on relief rolls once a person left them.[59] The dilemma seemed to require force to get the crops in before bad weather and resulted in the usual emergence of protest groups. This situation was ripe for exploitation by "professional radicals" who came from urban areas "to troubled communities to make capital of a farm controversy."[60]

Kennedy also shut down relief gardens, canning plants, and sewing rooms until after harvest. This shutdown affected "some 890 families in Pennington County." Relief would remain closed, he announced, until "all farmers needing harvest help have been supplied with workers." Other states were following the same national procedures in berry picking, the sugar beet industry, onions, and melons, but, as *The Nation* described it, "in somewhat less drastic form."

The difference in pay was not always the issue. Farmers were required to pay $1.50 daily, approximately the same as relief, but they worked the men ten to twelve hours daily in terrific heat, and the differential in exertion was substantial. One investigator in Sioux Falls found the relief workers had been organized by the Fraternal Order of Workers whose president was unable to provide statistics on how many relief workers there found work in the harvest fields.[61]

Several groups censured Berry and Kennedy for this decision, with the unemployed in Sioux Falls demanding the latter's resignation. Alice Lorraine Daly, editor of Aberdeen's *Dakota Free Press*, denounced Berry's order as "the most unhuman [*sic*] act of any governor, not only in South Dakota's history, but also in the entire annals of the north." Feelings in some areas ran high for some time because of this seemingly arbitrary action. But farmers had to have laborers to bring in their harvest.[62]

By the end of July the harvest had progressed sufficiently for the administration to resume adding unemployed to the relief rolls.[63] In late August 1935, Berry was able to speak glowingly of his state's agricultural prospects for the first time in his administration. At a speech at the Minnehaha County Fair, he stressed the bountiful rainfall received that enabled the state to sell "a large number" of the rural credits farms. He also noted that "the rapid return to normalcy" allowed "scores of persons" to be removed from relief employment and "given permanent jobs."[64] Berry always had the support of taxpayers and public opinion in this, plus the farmers, but earned the wrath of workers.[65]

New Dealers were able to add to Berry's good news a month later when Secretary Ickes announced that a new $200 million PWA program would go to the president for approval, and it promised to be "the best and finest available" that the money could provide. At the same time Roosevelt reported an additional $800 million of funding was "dropped . . . [into] the coffers" of the WPA to put 3.5 million people to work by 1 November. Hopkins had approved $724,748,082 in funding for South Dakota, saying his policy was to "approve twice as many developments as could be financed with available funds so as to give state administrators a wide selection of projects from which to choose."[66]

After WPA workers in five South Dakota cities asked the governor for a raise to fifty cents an hour, with no cut in hours, he passed the request on to Howard O. Hunter, Hopkins's assistant. He believed their plea was reasonable, given the drought and rising prices. The workers stressed that the current thirty-five cents was insufficient for an average family's needs. Field representative R. C. Jacobson wired Berry that he would discuss the situation with Hunter but gave no indication whether or not the appeal would be granted.[67]

WPA-proposed projects were approaching completion by this time to the amount of $10 million, half of which were slated for the Civilian Conservations Corps (CCC) employment. While these were developing, news came that President Roosevelt had declared that those who declined WPA jobs would be denied all types of federal relief. At issue was the demand of New York City workers who struck over the issue of WPA wages ranging from $19 to $94 monthly, "depending on locality and type of work." Unions argued that this scale "threatened to tear down the wage scale in private industry." William Green, president of the AFL, had argued fruitlessly for a wage scale similar to the private sector when the relief program was debated earlier in the year, and now announced, "we told them what would happen—and now it has."[68]

Two weeks later President Roosevelt approved $46,402 for seventeen projects in eight South Dakota counties. These included improving school grounds and athletic facilities in Aberdeen; farm-to-market roads, school repairs, street improvements, and dams in Clark, Faulk, Hughes, McPherson, Minnehaha, Pennington, and Spink Counties. Soon thereafter $1,250,000 in WPA projects was approved for West River counties. Rapid City alone requested more than $200,000 to spend on Dinosaur Park, straightening Rapid Creek, completion of a stadium, and airport improvements. The South Dakota School of Mines requested funding for a new football field.[69]

Shortly thereafter, the governor called a special conference of relief officials in Pierre to plan for winter work. PWA Director W. F. Cochrane announced, "There was no better time than the present" for government agencies to plan their public works projects. Kreibs explained that officials had been criticized unjustly for their "piecemeal" highway construction. It had to continue to be that way, he asserted, because these programs had to be allotted "according to relief needs and caseloads of the communities." State officials declared that when the dole ended, all people employable would be at work by 1 November because FDR had approved $3,331,072 in WPA funding for the state. The sewing rooms in Rapid City would employ forty-five women alone.[70]

The state welfare commission faced the difficult task of determining the unemployable needy. At a meeting in October 1935 of representatives of the welfare commission, highway superintendents, and county commissioners, it was agreed to designate a director in each county, to be paid by the government, to ascertain the unemployables in each county and "provide for their needs." This would establish a uniform system of care for the needy who were unemployable by the WPA and included 4,540 heads of families and 2,077 single people, in addition to the thousand women who fell under the mothers' pension plan. Kennedy assured the group that WPA would have all these people on their rolls by the first of November. Haste was necessary as county poor relief funds were "already exhausted with two months of the year remaining." This problem would not be resolved until the state established a viable Social Security program with pensions for destitute unemployables.[71]

Kennedy wrote Berry in mid-January 1936, noting that they were both currently receiving heavy criticism from those who were on relief and certified for WPA employment but were unable to find jobs. But they were receiving even greater blame from people who were not relief clients between 1 May and 1 November 1935 and thus could not *ipso facto* be placed on WPA employment. State relief officials were being flayed because those workers who sought seasonable employment during harvest and managed to stay off relief rolls were now being punished, while those who continued to accept relief "were being taken care of by the federal government." Kennedy estimated the former category to contain between two to three thousand people who were "in destitute circumstances" and badly needed assistance.

To meet this critical situation, Kennedy proposed employing another 20,000 people from "now [January 1935] until the first of April" at a cost of $1.5 million, when the situation would correct itself with renewed funding for the WPA. He reminded Governor Berry that WPA funds for South Dakota had been increased by $400,000 two weeks previously. He wanted to take this money, plus some from the RA that had thus far spent only $5,000 of their allotted $306,000, and some of the $6 million in highway funds, of which only $1 million had been committed, and put these people to work immediately. He suggested the governor might explain the dilemma to Hopkins and seek additional funding from that source. He further noted that it was impossible to get checks to WPA workers "within the time limits as set in his [Hopkins's] recent bulletin" unless the state decentralized into offices in Rapid City and Watertown, as well as Pierre. The meager mail connections between Watertown and Rapid City, he insisted, made a solution "essential."[72]

That February the weather was too cold to work outdoors so WPA workers continued to draw their wages with the understanding they would make up the work at a later date. Of the 160 workers involved on one job, all but forty-seven agreed to this arrangement. Those who were intractable were informed that if they persisted in their decision, they would be discharged. They remained adamant and were duly fired according to WPA regulations. The men fired, it turned out, were former leaders in the Morrell meat-packing negotiations and had been terminated there for their role in the strike.

One of the men, Cecil Gossard, wrote Hopkins about the imbroglio, stating that the forty-seven had taken possession of the toolshed in their efforts to prevent the other 100 members from complying with their agreement to make up for the lost work. The state director of the Division of Operations traveled to Pierre, found that the WPA foremen could not access their tools, and asked the police to remove the objectors and to protect the others in their efforts to return to work, a request that was granted. The holdouts ceased their activities, and WPA officials agreed to hold a hearing, "and it may be that some of these parties will again be re-instated."[73]

These recalcitrants were strong union men who had joined the Workers Alliance of America (WAA)—a 1935 merger of representatives of the Socialist party, A. J. Muste's Conference on Progressive Labor Action, and the Communist Party. Nationally, the WAA sought to force the WPA to recognize it as the sole representative for its workers. Chairman David Lasser lamented the "more and more frequent resort to the armed forces of the state, the use of tear gas bombs [which] indicates the determination of the masters of our industrial system to crush the labor movement." The WAA endorsed the Lundeen bill, introduced in Congress in 1934, that would provide unemployment insurance to laborers and farmers alike who were unsuccessful in searching for employment. The WAA was generally unsuccessful in recruiting South Dakota workers, except the more vociferous activists in the populous areas of the eastern part of the state, and South Dakota did not rate a position on its board of directors, as did Kansas.[74]

A survey of pending PWA projects in South Dakota that would utilize WPA labor was made in mid-1936. Those using the most labor and of longest duration were an auditorium for Aberdeen (90 men); a courthouse for Mound City (40); school buildings for Pollock and Martin (69); a municipal building for Lead (40); a school for Sioux Falls (70); street improvements for Huron (60); an electric plant, swimming pool, and recreation center in Yankton (247); a disposal plant in Sturgis (100); and a city hall and waterworks system for Rapid City (130). Hiring these men was contingent on WPA funding. Unfortunately, the South Dakota quota had been reduced from 16,000 in March to 10,000 by July.[75]

Badly deteriorating environmental conditions accompanied this reduction. Berry reported to Hopkins that "starting with the tier of counties on the east of the Missouri River, and extending to the west border of the state," a serious drought was worsening, except for the counties "adjoining the Nebraska line." In addition, a grass-hopper infestation was recurring, and even if crops were planted, they would be lost to the locusts. Farmers, realizing they "would be without cash income," were flocking to county commissioners, welfare agencies, and the governor, seeking assistance. The WPA could not employ these agrarians, even if the agency were fully funded. The Resettlement Administration (RA) had been making "substantial grants" of about eighteen dollars monthly to 18,000–20,000 rural families and their funds were "practically exhausted." The counties these farmers lived in were far in arrears of tax collections and had "exceeded" their "constitutional debt limits." He asked Hopkins if there were any way possible to employ 5,000 of these "destitute" people. The governor reminded the bureaucrat, "We have never asked for anything that was not absolutely needed."[76]

In July 1936, Berry related a tale of woe to Hopkins after South Dakota's WPA quota had just been reduced again. He and relief officials had depended on harvest employment to absorb the reduction of 6,000 workers, but the grasshopper plague spoiled this expectation by destroying the crops. The RA was attempting to provide for the helpless farmers, but now the state relief officers faced problems with former grain elevator employees, store clerks, auto mechanics, and employees dependent on agricultural patronage, who were losing their jobs because of the terrible harvest.

The termination of FERA "left the states with an enormous general relief burden." One report noted that a national sample of 10,800 general relief cases showed almost 50 percent wanted to be on WPA rolls but quotas prevented their employment. Another 22 percent were receiving relief to supplement their inadequate WPA wages. All this placed additional burdens on state relief resources. Yet the New Deal administration continued to seek inadequate budgets for WPA spending goals. This can be partially accounted for by the rise of a "conservative coalition" in Congress composed of Republicans and conservative Southern Democrats who were beginning to vote together to oppose deficit spending and public employment strategies.[77]

Governor Berry announced to his citizens that federal relief administrators were insisting that the states pay a "fair share" of relief costs. South Dakota needed more aid, however, because both drought and depression were clinging tenaciously to the land. Hopkins would again come to their aid with a new type of work relief that would provide succor to Dakotans until Mother Nature finally relented with more favorable weather.[78]

WPA employees were 86 percent male and 14 percent female. The nation and the New Dealers in control held "a masculine vision of useful work, and therefore of what public works should be." Construction work, building dams and bridges, was men's work. Also, there was a widely held view during this period that men supported their families and, therefore, women did not need jobs. Many school districts, for example, would not employ married female teachers, as their husbands could support their families. The WPA allowed only one job per family. Hopkins endorsed these concepts, dumping women into the category of "unemployables." Eleanor Roosevelt was most upset over this problem of needy women being unemployed and fought to convince Hopkins to employ them in WPA jobs.[79]

The first women's projects of the WPA were instituted in the fall of 1935, directed by Ellen S. Woodward, who had previously headed the women's division of FERA. Florence S. Kerr was Woodward's regional director for Iowa region IV, and Ethel M. Dowdell was director for South Dakota. Woodward discovered that only sewing rooms and recreation projects were available to women under WPA jurisdiction, in keeping with the traditional male philosophy that all women were capable of sewing but had few other vocational skills. About 3,000 women who were heads of families—widows, divorcees, or those who for whatever reason had no spousal support—sought a living in this women's division. In addition to sewing, these women were involved in canning foodstuffs, working in school dormitories and libraries, and performing household duties. By December 1935, Woodward had 275,000 women at work that represented 57.3 percent of those eligible, but by mid-1936 this number rose to a peak of 460,000. The garments they sewed were distributed to those on relief who had no purchasing power, but to satisfy complaints from the garment industry, Woodward pointed out that these women earning 40.6 cents per hour were potential customers of commercially made clothing.[80]

Dowdell wrote to Woodward about upcoming projects in South Dakota in the summer of 1935. They were arranging to set up community service centers across the state. Communities were drafting proposals for dormitories for rural high school boys and girls and for "hot lunch" programs for "undernourished children." Finally, the community service centers planned to provide rural home-aid service.[81]

A regional conference in Chicago in August produced "statements" repeatedly that projects with "out-put" would not be accepted. Keeping this mandate in mind, the planning in South Dakota "developed many possibilities," and Dowdell informed Woodward that their "ultimate returns" would be "worthwhile in character particularly from the viewpoint of more socially minded communities and better mental attitudes throughout the state." Conditions accelerated the need for projects that would "increase their morale and build up educational and recreational facilities for moral growth." She included a list of sewing machines and comforter frames in the various counties and their origins. Dowdell was learning the bureaucratic jargon necessary to deal with Washington.[82]

Before schools opened in September, Hopkins asked for a report on clothing needs of children from relief families for the next school year. Dowdell responded with a list of 34,395 school garments to be made, including dresses, sets of underwear, overalls, and shirts. She observed that as soon as the projects were approved, the emphasis would be on "intensive construction of winter garments," including "warm underwear, coats, caps, and mittens."[83]

A report on the South Dakota women's division in February 1936 noted that 4,025 women were certified and 3,995 were employed: 2,581 in the work program, 1,067 in "service," and 347 in "professional and statistical" categories. The report proudly noted that every sewing unit and Community Service Center of twenty-five or more members was "neatly uniformed in cover aprons or smocks," as well as "many of lesser membership."[84]

Dowdell reported on an observation trip she made around the state. Despite the fact that 14,375 mattresses and hundreds of straw tick covers were distributed in the previous year, there remained "an appalling lack of mattresses." Could Ellen Woodward produce 500,000 pounds of cotton and 100 yards of ticking for mattresses? If so, Dowdell's people "were admirably equipped to make them," and she was "proud of the products from our centers." She also lamented the dilatory approval of projects they had proposed to the national office. Woodward responded by expressing the hope that Dowdell had submitted a surplus of proposed programs because Hopkins and his office had attempted to secure final approval of approximately twice as many projects "as could be financed out of available funds." She assured Dowdell that new allotments for her "will probably be forthcoming soon."[85] As evidence of the dire situation in South Dakota, Dowdell wrote to Woodward that, contrary to her instructions, her local could not make soap from the slaughtered beef because the local butchers retained everything but the beef itself. She further added that South Dakota cattle were so thin their beef had no tallow from which to make soap.[86] By the time FERA transitioned into WPA, there were 5,189 women on work relief rolls.[87]

An unidentified man holds on to his hat during a dust storm, 1936.
Courtesy of the Franklin D. Roosevelt Presidential Library and Museum, Hyde Park, N.Y.

As both governor and senator, Peter Norbeck advocated for Black Hills tourism. Here he holds Clyde Jones's burro outside the Custer State Park Game Lodge, ca. 1927. *South Dakota State Historical Society, Digital Archives 2008-07-07-032*

TOM BERRY WILL USE THE AXE!

Tom Berry's gubernatorial campaign slogan appeared in newspapers throughout South Dakota. *South Dakota State Historical Society*

President Franklin D. Roosevelt, Governor Tom Berry, and Senator William Bulow during the president's visit to Mount Rushmore, 1936. *Historic Black Hills Studios, Deadwood, S.Dak.*

President Roosevelt delivers his sixth Fireside Chat to the American people, 1934. *Courtesy of the Franklin D. Roosevelt Presidential Library and Museum, Hyde Park, N.Y.*

Dressed in white, from left, Eleanor Roosevelt, James Bourne, and Lorena Hickok visit a village during the first lady's tour of Puerto Rico and the Virgin Islands, 1934. *Courtesy of the Franklin D. Roosevelt Presidential Library and Museum, Hyde Park, N.Y.*

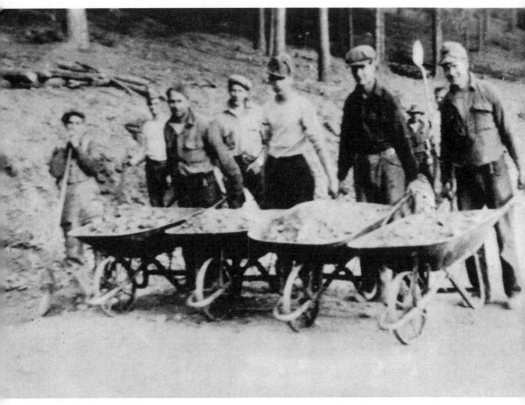

Nine men from Civilian Conservation Corps (CCC) camp no. 792 pose with shovels and wheelbarrows as they build a road near Newell, South Dakota, 1934. *South Dakota State Historical Society, Digital Archives 2010-08-31-025*

A South Dakota family plants a shelterbelt during the 1930s. *South Dakota State Historical Society*

CCC recruits conduct a survey in the Black Hills National Forest, 1933. *Courtesy of the Franklin D. Roosevelt Presidential Library and Museum, Hyde Park, N.Y.*

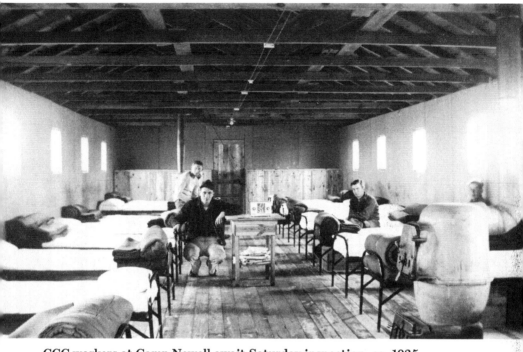

CCC workers at Camp Newell await Saturday inspection, ca. 1935.
South Dakota State Historical Society, Digital Archives 2010-08-31-019

CCC recruits worked on the construction of dams throughout South Dakota, including at this site near Newell, ca. 1935. *South Dakota State Historical Society, Digital Archives 2010-09-02-012*

Completed by the Works Progress Administration (WPA) in 1936, Rapid City's Dinosaur Park featured a tyrannosaurus, a triceratops, and other creatures. *South Dakota State Historical Society, Digital Archives 2008-02-14-021*

Workers constructed sidewalks in Volga, South Dakota, under the auspices of the WPA, ca. 1938. *South Dakota State Historical Society*

Sewing rooms such as this one in Milbank provided work for women through the WPA. *South Dakota State Historical Society*

A group of men employed by the National Youth Administration (NYA) dig into a hill to construct tennis courts for the town of Rosebud, South Dakota. *South Dakota State Historical Society, Digital Archives 2016-03-30-320*

A bulldozer operator works on a landscaping and park improvement project in Hot Springs, South Dakota, for the NYA. *South Dakota State Historical Society, Digital Archives 2016-03-30-311*

An unknown woman throws pottery on a wheel at the Pine Ridge
Indian School, 1940. *Farm Security Administration, Library of Congress*

Girls work in the wood shop at the NYA's Mission Resident Center at the Hare School, a mile from Mission, South Dakota, ca. 1939. *South Dakota State Historical Society, Digital Archives 2015-04-23-318*

A farm family on submarginal land in Pennington County, South Dakota. *South Dakota State Historical Society*

Vernon Evans and his family paused in Montana on their journey
west from South Dakota to Oregon in 1935. *South Dakota State
Historical Society*

6 A New Deal for Minorities and Youth

We are in need and our young men want work. You solve both our problems and we are today very happy.
Unnamed Indian leader to Jay B. Nash[1]

ALTHOUGH CONGRESS GRANTED citizenship to American Indians as early as 1924, their participation in the political process was negligible until the Great Depression. The New Deal for Indians changed all this and "political engagement of tribes" began at this time because Franklin D. Roosevelt and the New Dealers' introduction of the welfare state "radically altered their political thinking."[2]

The history of relations between American Indians and the U.S. government is a long litany of broken treaties and unkept promises.[3] A brief review of this process helps to understand the situation of South Dakota tribes in the 1930s. After the tribes had endured Andrew Jackson's removal policy, Ulysses S. Grant's "peace" policy, and General William T. Sherman's "force" policy, reformers believed America should start helping the country's first people to improve their situation. The Dawes Act of 1887 led to the termination of the reservation system, which further diminished Indian land claims. In 1500 AD, American Indians could claim three billion acres of land in America, but when the Dawes Act was passed, their holdings had dwindled to about 150 million acres. When the General Allotment Act was replaced in 1934, Indian-owned land had further declined to 48 million acres, "much of it desert."[4]

Before reform of the "Indian problem" could take place, the issue "had to go through the muckraking stage," and this occurred during the 1920s with the Pueblo land case. The government required the Pueblos, who had escaped allotment, to prove ownership of their lands. The tribe reacted vociferously and held a special council in the Pueblo of Santo Domingo to draft a petition alleging they were not consulted in this procedure and this action would "destroy our common life and rob us of everything we hold dear, our lands, our customs, and our traditions. Are the American people willing to see this happen?" The people proved to be unwilling in this case, and out of this issue came the formation of the Indian Rights Association. John Collier, director of social science training at San Francisco State Teachers College, became its administrator.[5]

President Herbert Hoover's Secretary of the Interior Hubert Work asked the Institute for Government Research to survey the current social and economic conditions of the tribes. The subsequent Meriam Report of 1928, funded by the Rockefeller Foundation, was an outstanding unbiased summary of Indian conditions. Their mortality rate of 25.9 per 1,000 was twice the white rate. Measles and respiratory diseases, such as pneumonia and tuberculosis, were widespread, as was trachoma. Congress was spending $750,000 yearly on American Indian medical expenses, and only $200,000 of this was available for field treatment, or about fifty cents annually for each sick person. Nearly half of the nation's American Indian population received $100 to $200 income annually, compared to the national average of $1,350. American Indian heirs had further alienated their lands through sales, including the purchase of mineral rights by unscrupulous whites. The report concluded that the policy of allotment and "Americanization" was an abject failure.[6]

The last phase of the reform movement before the New Deal came when Herbert Hoover appointed President Ray Lyman Wilbur of Stanford University, the president's alma mater, as secretary of the interior. Wilbur, in turn, named Charles J. Rhodes, a wealthy

Philadelphia banker and current president of the Indian Rights Association, as commissioner of Indian Affairs. Wilbur made a feeble attempt to attack the issue of loss of land by Indian heirs by promoting the principle that these inherited lands should revert to tribal ownership after a reorganization of the Irrigation Service. The tribes could then form corporate bodies that could issue shares of stock for these lands and the corporations could teach Indians to farm the irrigated areas. Finally, he persuaded Congress to cancel several million dollars of reimbursable debts charged to Indians for projects that were no longer useful to them.[7]

When President Franklin D. Roosevelt took office, he appointed John Collier as commissioner of the Office of Indian Affairs (OIA). A small, bespectacled man, Collier was determined to revolutionize Indian policy, and his agency drafted its own bill carefully and presented it to Congress. While the committees held hearings, Collier toured the country and American Indian reservations to sell his program. American Indian congresses were held throughout the West to give them the opportunity to listen, discuss, and criticize his proposed changes.

At the same time, the issue remained of what to do with the American Indian claims of about a billion dollars for losses under treaties or contracts broken by the national government. Collier prepared legislation to separate this issue from the Wheeler-Howard Act (also known as the Indian Reorganization Act or IRA), but expressed the opinion that Congress would never acknowledge this monetary obligation. He was correct in his strategy of separating this problem because many congressmen believed that the issues addressed by the IRA were more important and it passed Congress. When questioned, Collier insisted the IRA did not alter existing treaties or American Indian claims.[8]

In 1934 Collier also persuaded Congress to enact the Johnson-O'Malley Act that allowed the government to contract with states to provide educational, medical, and social welfare services for its wards. Some of these functions, especially education, had already been treated during the Hoover administration by making grants to the states to provide tuition and meet other costs of young American Indians in public schools. Collier also abolished requirements that American Indians at boarding schools attend Christian worship services and terminated appropriations to suppress the peyote traffic.[9]

"Historians may record it as the battle of Capitol Hill," one newspaper reported on the IRA, because opposition lines soon formed over the Wheeler-Howard bill in Congress. Progressive Senator Burton K. Wheeler of Montana and Nebraska Congressman Edgar Howard sponsored the bill, and the opposition forces quickly assailed it as "communistic and pagan." It granted American Indians the right to organize themselves. Each tribe would vote on the questions of reviving their reservation system and gradual termination of control by the Department of Interior. Revival of American Indian culture would be encouraged. No more than two million dollars would be appropriated annually to buy former reservation lands, and a United States Court of Indian Affairs would be established. South Dakota Congressman Theodore Werner opined that American Indians should be assimilated into American culture but this could not be done by "segregating them" as this measure provided.[10]

Led by Congressman Werner, the opposition forces in the House of Representatives reported a substitute bill. Werner described it as providing for educational scholarships, provision for tribal property, extension of reservation limits, and "self-government without [Interior] department interference." The scholarships, in effect, would be loans the students would repay "over a period of years." The main thrust of the measure, he said, was "to place all tribesmen on an equal footing with whites. We do not want the Indians to live apart," Werner explained, "but want to apply rules that will encourage them to become a part of the national community."[11]

Each tribe was to vote on accepting or rejecting the Indian Reorganization Act. Not surprisingly, many Indians were skeptical of anything the whites were offering. After holding hearings in Rapid City, Collier noted there was a "little group of selfish men . . . self-seeking attorneys, cattlemen, real estate interests, some lumber interests, mining organizations, water power interests, and some reactionary Indian bureau employees" who, since 1887, "have virtually stolen or bought for a song, two-thirds of the Indians' priceless heritage." These people, he charged, were seeking advantage under the new legislation. One delegate suggested renaming Collier "iron man" because of his obstinacy in defending American Indians. The purpose of his measure, Collier insisted, was to secure "what is left" of Indian lands and to help Indians improve their heritage.[12]

In the first council of Plains Indians since 1851, representatives from eighteen tribes in North and South Dakota, Nebraska, Montana, and Wyoming attended the Rapid City conference and made suggestions. The *Argus-Leader* headlined it "Hear about Radical Schemes for New Relations with Whites." Collier, with Wheeler and Howard, took these proposals back to Congress for a response. Werner unsuccessfully tried to block these changes, such as excluding "oil, mineral, metal and gas rights" on privately owned land from communal ownership.[13]

Richard LaRouche of the Lower Brule Indian Reservation described his boyhood recollection of his father who was on the council that debated and accepted the IRA. Those were "rough times" when "everybody carried a pair of [cardboard] soles in his hip pocket" and when the old ones wore out he'd just sit down and replace them. He said, "People were grasping at any kind of deal that they could get." The implication during the debates was that the tribes would gain more if they accepted the IRA than if they rejected it. LaRouche explained, "If we didn't accept it there would be a lot of benefits that we wouldn't get." He described the Crow Creek tribe, "who lived just across the river from us" and rejected the IRA, as the "Old Dealers," in contrast to the Lower Brule tribe, which became "New Dealers" by accepting the program. Yet "through the years," the Crow Creek tribe "received just as much or more, even better than we have."[14]

Roosevelt's Economy Act of 1933 brought further changes to the Yankton Sioux Indians. In the name of economy, Collier was forced to downgrade the Yankton Agency to a sub-agency and place it administratively under the Rosebud Agency. In addition, he removed the Yankton superintendent from office over "allegations of interference in tribal politics."[15]

Yankton tribal committee chair Clement Smith was particularly opposed to the IRA. He wrote a letter to the editor of the *Argus-Leader*, denouncing Collier's plan as being communistic because it would deny American Indians "the right to determine their heirs," since the secretary of interior would be empowered to assign all inherited lands into tribal holdings.

Elections were set for all tribes, and five in South Dakota accepted the IRA: Cheyenne River Sioux, Lower Brule Sioux, Flandreau Santee Sioux, Rosebud Sioux, and Oglala Lakota. The four reservations of Crow Creek, Yankton, Sisseton, and Standing Rock rejected Collier's plan. Members of the rejecting tribes were conservatives who emphasized that treaties defined the federal obligation to them and stressed Sioux rights. Under the IRA, they argued, the tribes potentially could lose power gained under the treaty process, and they believed previous claims should be adjusted before experimenting with anything new.

The Yankton Sioux defeated it by 80 percent vote,[16] and continued to use their non-IRA constitution of 1932.[17] Their plight illustrates the situation of several of those tribes that rejected the IRA, and perhaps some of the tribes that accepted the New Deal as well. William O'Connor, a former tribal chair, observed, "The times were very deplorable." He had supported the IRA and thought three decades later that it had been "a tremendous missed opportunity for the tribe." Clarence Foreman actively opposed the IRA, blaming it and other New Deal programs "for a loss of initiative on the reservation." He also accused the OIA of withholding assistance from those individuals who did not support Collier's program. This division between Indians lasted for decades.[18]

Reservation Indians were especially in desperate need of help as they were in more straitened conditions than white South Dakotans, if that were possible. The South Dakota Emergency Relief Administration (SDERA) financed a study conducted in late 1933 and early 1934 to determine the best way to help these people. The SDERA Survey focused on government ineptitude and malfeasance, particularly in the Indian Service in the areas of health, education, and land management. When the full report was released in August 1935, the "tremendous poverty" the Yanktons were enduring was clear. Fifty percent of them were homeless, with most of them living in tents or with relatives. This overcrowding, of course, without ventilation, led to the rapid spread of disease, such as tuberculosis and trachoma. They were willing to work but decades of drought had taken their toll. The residents were "completely dependent on work relief for income."[19] The surveys revealed "startlingly high rates of illiteracy, disease and mortality, and low incomes." Per capita income for American Indians nationally was only eighty-one dollars a year. The survey demonstrated an acute need to improve health and education on the reservations.

The eight reservations—Standing Rock, Cheyenne River, Lower Brule, Rosebud, and Pine Ridge in western South Dakota and Crow Creek, Flandreau, and Sisseton in the eastern part of the state— created peculiar situations. The sparse populations on western reservations often lived in isolated areas with dirt trails or bad roads, they often did not speak the same dialect, and vital statistics were frequently incomplete. In one district in Standing Rock, for instance, 590 people, who lived mainly along the streams, received $3,216 for leases on their 600-square mile district, or $1,914 per family yearly. Most of the children attended boarding school to save money and transportation costs. One doctor served the entire reservation.[20]

Another district on the reservation also received little income from their land. Their 92,000 acres were owned by 103 families, and brought in $1,893 from leases, crop shares, and Agricultural Adjust-ment Act (AAA) benefits. Only 65 percent of the population in the district owned their homes. "Overcrowded, inadequate dwellings were the rule, and shortages of bedding and clothing were com-monplace," the report noted. Fruit, vegetables, milk, and eggs were almost unknown, causing numerous health problems, especially rickets and scurvy. Efforts to raise vegetable gardens were negated by drought. Government rations were available but distribution of them was cursory. Ten men, who received a ten-pound slab of bacon for their efforts, attended nine bins where they dumped the recipi-ents' allowances into sacks: a two-week ration consisted of two cans of tomatoes, two pounds of sugar, navy beans, rice, bacon, mutton, one pound of coffee, hard bread, and twelve pounds of flour. The distribution for 169 persons required "less than an hour."[21]

Diabetes and gallstones were widespread, and 50 percent of the Sioux on the Rosebud suffered from tuberculosis. The Pine Ridge reservation had 1,500 tubercular people in need of isolation, but the hospital had only ten beds. The doctors available were poorly paid; one beginning doctor received sixty dollars monthly plus transportation. The Sisseton reservation had $10,000 to pay the salaries of three doctors, one nurse, and their transportation ex-penses.[22] Alcoholism was rampant under these conditions. People often traded their government rations for moonshine, or even rub-bing alcohol and antifreeze, to drink. There was also concern over the widely expanding abuse of peyote, the psychedelic fruit of a spineless cactus that the Native American Church uses for cere-monial purposes.

Education levels were appalling. In the Bullhead district of Standing Rock, which was representative of Sioux reservations, of people seventy or older, twenty-nine had no education and one had "some." Among those 45 to 53, three had no education, for-ty-nine had "some," three were high school graduates, and one had attended Carlisle Indian School in Pennsylvania. All but one of the 179 between the ages of thirteen and thirty had some education.[23]

Indian boarding schools were notorious for their harsh discipline and poor food, but many families sent their children to them to lessen the cost of their care. In turn, the children, especially females, often preferred the boarding school to living in the squalid conditions at home. Similarly, teachers complained of bad housing, poor schools and equipment, isolation, and exposure to diseases. Men assigned to work relief jobs often had to travel long distances to work. They frequently camped out at the site or brought their families who had to live in tents. This bleak report left no doubt about the fundamental needs of these people.[24]

The SDERA survey officially described conditions that had been obvious to those who had been in charge of efforts to assist Indians living on reservations. When the Civilian Conservation Corps (CCC) was created, the goal was to put unemployed young people to work on the nation's parks and forests. Harold Ickes, Secretary of the Interior, supported the importance of ensuring that Indians would also have the opportunity for relief work that would improve forestry and conservation on reservations. In a memo to Robert Fechner, Ickes argued that the reservations needed the attention but that Indians would resist whites coming on their land to work. The Indians needed the relief money as well but wished to live with their families. President Roosevelt agreed and created the Indian Emergency Conservation Work (IECW), and approved sites for seventy-two work camps on reservations in fifteen western and southern states. The president adopted this concept because he knew American Indians objected to military-run camps on their reservations. The IECW allowed reservation Indians to direct their own projects, with tribal councils helping to select them. The OIA supervised the projects, administered medical exams and vaccinations, and supplied discipline. This branch is usually referred to as the CCC-Indian Division (CCC-ID) and eventually provided relief work for 14,400 men.[25]

Twenty-seven thousand American Indians participated in the CCC. The U.S. government published a periodical for them entitled

Indians at Work. "I saw some wonderful water conservation work done by them, soil erosion, cultural work in the forests, building of fire trails, etc.," Fechner reported, "and their camps compare favorably in every way with those of the white boys."[26]

The Indian CCC differed in significant ways from the regular program. Collier's goal for American Indians centered on self-rule, restoration of tribal government, revitalization of Indian culture and religion, and improvement of the remaining tribal lands of fifty-two million acres. As a byproduct, he hoped to assist the overwhelming majority who wanted to remain in their own culture. At first, the men showed great reluctance to enlist, as they thought the military would run it, as was happening in the regular CCC. Many of them also opposed the medical examinations and the required vaccinations. But, as the drought and grasshoppers increased, their resistance broke down and soon they came in great numbers.[27]

The CCC minimum of 200 men per camp was not plausible on the sparsely populated reservations, so the CCC-ID ran camps of forty to fifty men. There were three types of camps: the boarding camp for single men, the home camp for those who wanted to live at home, and the family camp where entire households could live in tents on projects of short duration. There were eventually so many enlistees that administrators began using a "staggered employment" concept where two crews worked half-time and alternated shifts. The tribal council appointed a committee to select enrollees, who had to be eighteen or older and free from communicable diseases. They received thirty dollars monthly for a twenty-hour-work week, plus sixty cents daily subsidy for those who lived at home. They would also receive an extra one or two dollars daily if they used their own team of horses.[28]

New Deal public works projects provided some employment through the CCC-ID and WPA. Some 95 percent of the Rosebud residents had received some form of aid by the end of the decade. For many residents, this was the first experience at working for wages. By 1942, per capita income on the Pine Ridge reservation reached $120, or 60 percent earned income and 40 percent un-earned, "figures that were representative for other reservations."[29]

An inspection report on the Pine Ridge agency declared that Indians "appreciate very much the opportunities given them to earn money." Their only economic resources came from the soil, "grazing and farming," and the superintendent believed they could eventually "become self-sufficient, happy and contented if they can once be started in cattle and horse raising." The superinten-dent further expressed the hope that the native language would be preserved, "as it is a beautiful language," as well as the native arts. Finally, he concluded that a tribal history for their schools would be "of great interest," because "the pride of race among the Sioux is very strong."[30]

As with forts and bases in World War I, these camps were ideal for the spread of diseases. An influenza epidemic took the lives of four men at Camp Lodge near Custer. Flu had invaded the camp two months earlier, and Captain C. M. Kuhns was summoned from the Seventh Corps area laboratory to try to suppress it. Although temporarily halted, it flared up again and Captain Kuhns returned. His imposed quarantine of the camp, limiting the epidemic to only 30 percent of the personnel.[31]

The Sisseton reservation presented relief workers with a pecu-liar situation. The reservation was in the most northeastern part of the state, where the soil was quite suitable for wheat and much sought after by whites. During the allotment period, tribal mem-bers had sold much of their land to whites, and the little remaining tribal land was not enough to reconstitute the reservation. Sisse-tons voted against the IRA, and the few remaining tribal members became "ward Indians" (dependent on the national government).

For 1934, the BIA allotted the Sisseton Reservation $24,000 to build "Indian roads," but the difficulty was, from W. L. Eales's viewpoint, that there was "no such thing as an Indian road" in the area, as dominant white farms were interspersed with a few Indian farms. As Eales expressed it, a mile of Indian road would lead to four or five miles of white road, then another mile of Indian road, etc. The Indians remaining on the poorest land in these counties subsisted by renting their hay and pasture lands. The "grasshoppers, blister beetles, dry weather, [and] hot winds" combined to produce the situation of whites being unable to pay their rents, leaving the Indians "in a horrible situation." Eales described the Sissetons as "really the forgotten man," and wrote to Harry L. Hopkins for advice.

The Bureau of Indian Affairs (BIA) with its red tape constituted a serious delay in relief for these people, and Eales requested Federal Emergency Relief Act (FERA) funds until the BIA acted. These people need "fuel, groceries, meats and clothing, and many of them need medicine, medical attendance and hospitalization." He asked Hopkins to contact Collier about the situation or to provide funds to Eales to care for them. The Indians were "perfectly willing to work," and Eales would ask the relief directors in those counties "to immediately arrange to spend some monies with them." Hopkins had sent Lorena Hickok to assess the relief situation in South Dakota and he now sent an investigator to the Sisseton reservation.[32]

John Collier thought the Sioux needed rehabilitation and sought funds to provide it. The Office of Indian Affairs was awarded two million dollars through the Emergency Relief Appropriation Act of 1935 (with which FDR established the Works Progress Administration [WPA]) to create the Indian Relief and Rehabilitation Division (IRRD). The following year, "rehabilitation" became the catchword. Most emergency conservation and public works heretofore had put Indians to work for wages. The rehabilitation program, by contrast, put them back on the land, farming and raising livestock. Grants and loans were made to build or repair homes and outbuildings; develop water access for homes, such as artesian wells; improve land for expanded gardens; and begin furniture-making and other crafts. Other rehabilitation projects might cooperate with other agencies, with IRR providing the funds, WPA the equipment and expertise, and CCC-ID the labor. Some twenty of these colonies were established for resettlement and subsistence homesteading. Preference was given to the landless and those physically able to work.[33] Unfortunately, New Deal retrenchment began shortly after "rehabilitation."[34] In the meantime, the depression, drought, and grasshoppers combined to provide a difficult milieu to experiment with the lives of these poverty-stricken people.[35]

Collier, though, considered housing to be one of the major obstacles on reservations that presented both economic and social problems. Without decent housing, he declared, there was "an inevitable drift to the vicinity of the agency with its work relief rations and [livestock] feed" and subsequent emergence of "tents and shacks." He acknowledged that it would require more than "things." Rehabilitation took "will and one's own intelligence." By 1935 the Sioux owned almost seven million acres of submarginal land and received an average of $440 in family income yearly, most of which came from relief of one kind or another. In addition, after building a shack near the agency headquarters, many families were forced to barter household items for food. These proved irredeemable and the entire situation needed changing. At this point, the WPA provided the equipment and the Indian CCC was the source for labor for helping the Sioux in building new experimental colonies.[36]

Drought and geography "forced the CCC-ID to concentrate on water development and irrigation to control erosion and overgrazing." Few areas on the reservations had sufficient timber to concentrate on lumber as an economic source. The Indian reforestation project was located on fifty-three different reservations nationally, working on wind and soil erosion problems. Members built "catch" dams to provide water for cattle and secondary roads and trails. In addition, the Public Health Service inspected campsites to assure sanitary conditions. J. B. Nash, director of Indian reforestation, reported, "Indians have received the message about conservation work with great enthusiasm."[37]

The Billings headquarters, having jurisdiction over South Dakota projects, insisted on constructing small, irrigated garden developments of two-to-fifteen-acre plots. The Crow Creek, Yankton, and Sisseton Sioux were able to carry out projects of constructing fences, roads, and telephone lines, and small dams for impounding water for irrigation use. The CCC-ID performed the earth-moving operations, and the reservations controlled the garden phase. These yielded sufficient crops for family consumption and a surplus for sale on the reservation. The dams also assured a dependable supply of water for people and livestock, as well as for sanitary purposes. The program provided opportunities for destitute Indians to improve themselves by developing these truck farming gardens and production of livestock for cash needs.[38]

At first, few Indians were capable of operating the machinery required for this construction. By 1936, though, many were able to run the large equipment that eliminated the need for horsepower. On the other hand, use of this machinery often nullified the original purpose of putting men and horses to work.[39] This points up another profound difference between the white and Indian programs. The CCC had as a major goal the training and education of enrollees for future employment and advancement. In the Indian CCC, because of the philosophy and prejudices of many of its supervisors, the enrollees were given insufficient opportunity to learn to operate the machinery or to receive the necessary experience or training for employment or advancement. The emphasis appeared to be more on expanding facilities for destitute people.

On the other hand, the CCC-ID program was dealing with many illiterate people and, as the supervisor at Pine Ridge expressed it, "work is the basis of the CCC and is the all-important thing. I am never going to allow anybody to take time out of our working day for training." This, plus the fact that enrollees who lived at home could not devote their evenings to self-improvement, meant they were limited to on-the-job training. Nonetheless, many of the Sioux received training in Red Cross safety and farm machinery maintenance and repair that they might not otherwise have received. At the end of the decade, officials at the Pine Ridge and Cheyenne

River reservations had equipped a truck with a traveling library. Those who lived in the camps had leisure time for sports and native songs and dances.[40]

The education offerings changed significantly in 1935 when, apparently under pressure from Robert Fechner, Robert M. Patterson was appointed education director of CCC-ID. His primary achievement was to set up a program for first aid and safety with Red Cross instructors. President Roosevelt introduced another significant change in 1937 when he ordered a retrenchment in both CCCs. He froze the number of salaried officials and ordered the agencies to curtail the number of workers to one for every $930 in CCC funds. This led to an increase in emphasis on projects using more labor and less machinery.[41]

Similar to the regular CCC, the Preparedness Program affected the CCC-ID. Those officials inclined to do so opened up courses for training in defense work, and Indians subsequently obtained employment as carpenters, truck drivers, mechanics, and welders, opportunities not available previously to them. As with the white CCC, the CCC-ID remained "one of the most popular and productive Indian programs of the decade." It had employed 8,405 Indians and spent over $4.5 million in the Rosebud, Standing Rock, and Pine Ridge reservations alone. Obviously, it helped some more than others. A study in 1937 of the Lower Brule revealed that the Indians there received 18 percent of their income from agriculture, 50 percent from the CCC, and the remainder from various kinds of relief. This revealed the fact that the CCC "could not really be effective, except as a dole, until the allotment system was destroyed and adequate land resources were given to Indians."[42]

In 1936, Michael A. Kennedy reported the deplorable conditions of the Rosebud tribesmen to Hopkins. There were 1,564 families and 10 percent were "patent fee" and thus eligible for WPA employment. That left 1,400 families not taken care of and 250 of these were self-supporting. The remaining 1,150 families were in dire need of assistance and 250 families were "ration Indians," or unemployable, and were cared for through the "regular ration fund." The 900 employable Indian families had no means of support. The CCC-ID and the Indian Road Fund employed 230 families. The people remaining were in "dire circumstances," he reported. Hopkins's assistant Josephine Brown responded that these people should be receiving FERA aid and thus were eligible for WPA jobs.[43]

The Cheyenne River agency suffered loss of their WPA jobs when the administration cut back funding late in 1936. This affected 206 Indian families. The assistant commissioner wrote Hopkins that he could understand the curtailment of funding but he could not accept having any reservation with "its WPA work entirely wiped out." A Hopkins assistant responded that state WPA officials were advised to make funding adjustments but not to "discontinue the employment of any particular group of persons" and changes should be made accordingly.[44]

Kennedy wrote Colonel F. C. Harrington of the national WPA concerning the planning of winter work for both Indians and whites and raised the interesting jurisdictional point of repairing homes of trust patent for "ward Indians." He had discussed this problem with a reservation superintendent who was "quite sure" he could purchase the necessary materials if WPA would provide the labor. Kennedy asked for an interpretation of this confusing situation because WPA labor was limited to projects "considered public property." Those land titles were held in trust by the national government but would this, in itself, constitute "public property"? There was "no question but what this work is badly needed," he asserted, but their CCC-ID would be inadequate for the project and additional assistance was required. He observed that if the work were done by WPA, he did not believe it would constitute a precedent for similar demands by non-ward Indians.[45]

Collier had promised the tribes increased self-rule and economic development. The IRA produced neither, unfortunately. He blamed this not on the law, but on Congress, for its failure "to go as far as he proposed." The Department of the Interior continued its control of its "wards." Members of tribes that accepted the IRA complained that Interior Department review of their council ordnances merely changed wardship from involuntary to voluntary. Preserving the paternalistic BIA, however, made certain the tribes did not make irrevocably bad decisions. Critics blamed Collier's love of bureaucracy for this betrayal. They were particularly critical of field offices for setting aside only two days weekly for tribal members to come in to conduct their business, and reserving the remainder of the week to conduct bureau business, requiring appointments on those three days. At the same time, they saw whites receiving immediate consideration without appointment.[46]

Individuals also complained of having to wait for their lease money, yet BIA officials were quick to collect rent money. They perceived keenly the double standards held for whites and Indians, which made them believe Collier was betraying them and only exacerbated the long-standing and traditional dislike of Indians for the BIA.[47]

Collier and his reformers fared no better with the promise of economic development. The decline in the agricultural economy was not quickly reversed for either the stagnant white agrarian situation or that of the Indians. South Dakota weather affected Indian and white alike. Even Collier admitted the Sioux condition was "desperate," opining the IRA "may have come too late." The Pine Ridge Sioux, for instance, had been hungry for so long they had eaten their horses and now they had them "neither to eat nor to carry firewood for winter fuel." They blamed Roosevelt and the Democrats for their plight.[48]

While in Washington seeking funding for highways and relief work, Governor Tom Berry also consulted Collier about assistance to South Dakota Sioux. He received assurance that new land use policies on reservations "would not mean such quick changes as to injure white livestockmen" and from the rural rehabilitation division of the BIA that "funds would be provided for a soil erosion control campaign on the Rosebud and for purchases of 800,000 baby chicks."[49]

The FERA created the Submarginal Land Program in 1933 to purchase land unsuitable for farming but that could be added to tribal acres for grazing and water control. The program was later put under the auspices of the Resettlement Administration, with separate funding for the BIA. In 1935, the BIA purchased a small tract of land on the Little White River on the Rosebud reservation. The tribal council decided to use some of the funds from the IRRD to initiate a colony there, called Grass Mountain, for irrigated gardens and the raising of livestock for landless Indians. The CCC-ID built a dozen houses and assigned nine of them to families with the stipulation that any assignee could be removed for negligence or lack of cooperation. The other three structures would serve as a schoolhouse, dining area for students, and living quarters for the superintendent.[50]

The colony used a cooperative plan for the garden crops and considered the livestock as communal property. In 1937, the tribe took out a loan of $2,500 and purchased ten milk cows and some light farm machinery. Each family received two quarts of milk daily and families rotated in tending the cows. Residents sold surplus garden produce on the reservation. In 1937–1938 the colony received sixty-six heifers from the national government and built a barn for their livestock. The experiment was a success within three years.[51]

The Yankton reservation built its colony, named after Chief Rising Hail, of chalk rock mined from the bluffs along the Missouri River. The rock proved to be durable, easy for the cutters to work with, and impervious to weather changes. This colony contained nine cottages arranged in a semicircle, a chapel, a two-story cannery, a schoolhouse, and a barn. A windmill provided the settlers with water. BIA officials worked with an ex-officio committee of delegates from various reservation districts. In 1938, members organized the Rising Hail Cooperative Development Association and submitted a constitution and by-laws for the Secretary of the

Interior's approval, thus enabling it to borrow money from the national government. A loan of $8,000 provided for expenses, including a twenty-dollar monthly allowance for the families who were required to work forty hours weekly. If a member owned livestock, machinery, or other property, it became a part of the association and was reimbursable if he left the organization. By World War II, the association had expanded to 600 acres of good bottom farmland, 900 acres in pasture, a shelterbelt orchard, and an irrigated vegetable garden, all combining to make the colony self-sufficient and with surpluses to sell. At that point the colony possessed 200 cattle, 180 hogs, 30 horses, 900 chickens, and an annual cash income of $13,000—a very successful experiment.[52]

Then disaster struck. Anthrax killed half of the cattle, grasshoppers destroyed the garden, and the barn burned after the inexperienced farmers stored newly cut alfalfa in the hayloft and it caught fire through spontaneous combustion. In addition to these calamities, farming became highly mechanized during and after the war, the colonists could not compete in this environment, and most families migrated to seek other opportunities. In 1949, the cooperative was dissolved and the venture changed from a cooperative one to a family venture.[53]

The Pine Ridge reservation experimented with the Red Shirt Table colony that "represented the most complete attempt . . . to rehabilitate a band of Sioux." By 1930 some 90 percent of the Sioux there were reduced to living on government rations and Red Cross assistance. Finally, eighteen families organized the Red Shirt Table Development Association and adopted a constitution and by-laws. They borrowed $5,000 from the BIA to purchase breeding cattle. In 1941 the BIA extended the loan and secured land on the Cheyenne River where the association built houses, a cannery, dairy barn, schoolhouse, poultry shed, and an irrigation system. Wanting to build a turkey shed, they obtained permission to cut trees at Harney National Forest, but had to borrow trucks from the BIA to haul the logs. After buying 600 turkeys, a tornado killed most of the flock, but the community made enough from the survivors to purchase 1,000 more the next year. After five years the association had paid off most of its debts and had a net worth of $6,500. Again, they also were unable to survive the war and postwar problems and the Sioux began to lose interest in communal living.

In 1941, the National Defense Vocational Training Act provisions were extended to Indians. The government offered classes of six to eight weeks in radio operations and maintenance, carpentry, welding, sheet metal, and auto mechanics. After taking the courses, enrollees could take proficiency exams and, if they passed, they were "almost automatically guaranteed" a job in the Preparedness Program.[54]

Young people were particularly hard hit by the depression because graduation from high school with no special skills—and few rural schools in South Dakota were capable of offering training in highly specialized fields—meant facing the real world where they were competing for the same job with experienced and better-educated workers. Many young people preferred to complete high school or attend college if some means could be found to acquire even a few dollars a month to assist the family in keeping them on an education track. Something was needed, in addition to the CCC, for these young people. The National Youth Administration (NYA), created within the Works Progress Administration in June 1935, helped fill this need.

The NYA sought to provide funding for part-time employment for needy secondary school, college, and graduate students to continue their education; offer valuable work experience to benefit youth and their communities; encourage the establishment of job training, counseling, and placement for youth; and facilitate the development and extension of constructive leisure-time activities. The president named Aubrey W. Williams to direct the program. Like his former boss, Hopkins, Williams endeavored to make certain the NYA employment would not be "make work."[55] He appointed a youth director in each state.

Williams and the national office insisted from the beginning that recipients receive not only funding, but also training and counseling. This concept was difficult to implement, at least in South Dakota, because the local selection committees were unpaid volunteers and had little access to and, apparently, insufficient concern over the problem of student counseling. The state NYA staff was stretched too thin to monitor this important aspect of the program, and school principals who might have done so usually would not take the time to do the job. The conflict continued, with most of the work assignments being clerical or mechanical in nature, and little in the way of research, counseling, or training. After 1937, the situation improved with increased oversight of student work and assignments, but the ultimate goal of the NYA was never fully realized.[56]

As Kenneth Hendrickson notes, "one would expect to find that the relief program was received amid great public rejoicing ... [but] it was not reflected in the press." The *Argus-Leader*, "cool to the New Deal from the beginning ... now became openly hostile." The newspaper voiced the usual conservative complaint that New Deal deficits would "surely ruin the country." In response, Kennedy announced that the program would proceed "slowly and cautiously."

It did just that under South Dakota's first youth director, Philip L. Ketchum, who found numerous work projects that failed to measure up to "the ideological standards" of the national NYA. The program, though, remained popular across the state. In its second year, the local advisory committees began to take effect. The projects then began to demonstrate "greater efficiency and usefulness." Favorable public opinion also began to emerge with this change. The Home Service Center in Sioux Falls also proved quite successful. Headquartered in an abandoned fire hall, the project provided training in sewing, cooking, and recreational skills. Participants visited shut-ins throughout the city and the program remained popular until termination of the NYA in 1943.[57]

After John Erwin replaced Ketchum in 1936, criticism increased from the national office. The program changed significantly when Anna L. Struble replaced Erwin in 1937.[58] Struble, headquartered in Pierre, named her staff of nine administrators located with her in the capital and at Aberdeen, Watertown, Sioux Falls, and Rapid City. This network was designed to adapt the NYA to the needs of local youth. The previous FERA program furnished aid only to undergraduate college students. The NYA, by contrast, operated on "a work project basis where performance of some kind of work is required" in return for wages. College undergraduates received fifteen to twenty-five dollars monthly. First-year graduates could earn an additional ten dollars. High school students were limited to six dollars monthly.[59]

Struble ignored Kennedy's advice to move cautiously from the beginning of her tenure. She was a professional social worker with a strong personality, a lot of energy, and little patience with bureaucratic red tape. Despite Washington concerns over her administrative methods, she "ran a tight ship at home," insisting on the best efforts from her subordinates. She was particularly displeased with the work of NYA finance director Charles A. Reutsh who "generally mishandled his work." He was a close friend of Kennedy's, though, and it took her a year to bring about his dismissal.[60]

To be eligible for NYA relief, a student had to be between the ages of sixteen and twenty-four, be from a relief family, and be in good academic standing. Unfortunately, there was never sufficient funding. Rules required funds to be sufficient to cover 10 percent of the school's enrollment, but the ratio in South Dakota was never more than 6 percent. A total of 5,732 high school and college students received their six and fifteen dollars respectively, and, though meager, this funding permitted these students to remain in school or to acquire some type of advanced training.[61]

In-school students were employed on campus projects, such as building sidewalks, painting, typing, and serving as library and laboratory assistants. The out-of-school phase of the NYA tried to combine work with assistance to the community. In this case, the rules required the recruitment of local sponsors and planning of projects; age limits between ages eighteen and twenty-four; a maximum of forty-six hours monthly; and a pay one-third the rate of similar WPA jobs. The program in Watertown to fight juvenile crime and idleness proved to be one of the more successful programs. Civic clubs organized and rented an Odd Fellows Hall for headquarters. It employed eighty-six part-time people who performed minor repairs and provided a library and public health and recreational units for wayward youth.[62]

Some of the projects entailed outdoor work. The engineer at Redfield supervised fourteen NYA boys in landscaping the artificial lake there, built by WPA labor. The city sponsored the work and provided $500 for materials. The boys also built a 200-foot boardwalk, a six-foot pier, rafts, two diving ladders, a safety line of buoys, a guardrail, and seating for spectators.[63]

From 1935 to 1938, the NYA fostered educational camps for young women. More than forty of these schools were conducted in unoccupied hotels, schools, or clubs that could be rented at "nominal" rates. Each had a director, a project supervisor, a nurse or doctor, teachers of home economics, English, economics, and recreation. The major goal was to teach young women "the responsibilities of living in a democracy," or instruction in handwork, athletic games, and "some classroom instruction."[64]

Struble defended her program's attention to Indian youth. She said, "We give whites and Indians the opportunity to learn the same things, while also stressing handicrafts and the types of things that are supposed to be peculiarly Indian." Indians, she believed, needed "to be taught the work ethic and be judged by the same yardstick as that applied to whites." These concepts sound similar to the attitude that formed the basis for the IRA implemented at the same time. The resident center, located at the Indian Vocational School in Flandreau, provided training and work experience in highway engineering, masonry, welding, agriculture, carpentry, baking, and barbering. Enrollees built a new house for the superintendent, a cattle barn, a hoghouse, and a gymnasium. In this center, white and Indian enrollees worked together, although they were segregated for housing and recreation.[65]

The center at Madison provided women with sewing and home-making skills while they attended the Normal School there. They worked four hours daily, earning thirty dollars monthly, out of which they returned eighteen dollars for cooperative living expenses and six dollars for tuition. Most of them remained in the program for two years and completed the requirements for a one-year teaching certificate. The center "had one of the best job placement records in the country, with graduates employed in various types of work from coast to coast."[66]

The theater branch of the NYA occasionally presented performances to promote their programs and to raise funds for special purposes. The Pine Ridge group, directed by Marie Nylan, offered an entertainment called "Folk Festival" in Rapid City. The program featured a "Grecian urn" dance, a French doll dance, a "sword dance" from England, and an "Irish lilt." The "star applause" went to a costumed group from Pine Ridge who sang "Sky Blue Waters" and Joe Horn Cloud's trumpet solo of "Indian Love Call." The performance raised $239.50 in free will offerings dedicated to building a year-round swimming pool and recreational hall at Roosevelt Park.[67]

As the nation's preparedness program advanced, increasing numbers of these students received training in woodworking, sewing, sheet metal working, welding, radio and automotive repair, and foundry work, skills that were increasingly demanded for national defense work. Many of these NYA projects were converted to defense work training. In addition, the Selective Service, or draft, that became law on 16 September 1940 opened other possibilities for unemployed young men. War production training centers were established in Pierre and Mitchell that administered shop units in various towns across the state.

Prior to 1 September 1935, FERA granted more than $4,000 to

the School of Mines, $7,000 to Augustana, $6,000 to Dakota Wesleyan, $3,000 to Huron College, $11,000 to Northern Normal, and over $12,000 each to State Agricultural College in Brookings and the University of South Dakota in Vermillion for student aid. The NYA gave $15,000 to Mines, $20,000 to Augustana, $19,000 to Dakota Wesleyan, $13,000 to Huron, $35,000 to Northern, $33,000 to State College, and $40,000 to the University of South Dakota. The FERA and NYA granted to South Dakota schools of higher education a grand total of $361,186 from 1935 through 1938.[68]

7 Developing the Black Hills

South Dakota is helping to nourish these beasts whose tentacles reach into every corner of our land. Do you know they are sucking 18–19 million dollars out of one gold mine in South Dakota annually?
Emil Loriks[1]

I N LATE 1933, when President Franklin D. Roosevelt made use of the power the Agricultural Adjustment Act (AAA) gave him to combat the country's financial crisis by stimulating inflation, he and Secretary of the Treasury Henry Morgenthau, Jr., eventually set the price of gold at $35, making the value of the gold dollar 59.06 cents pre-1933 value. While FDR's goal was to inflate prices, especially to encourage farm production, the effort proved to be a colossal windfall for the Homestake Mining Company in Lead, South Dakota. Homestake was the largest gold mine in the world, and it stimulated a healthy economic boom in the Black Hills region throughout the depression years.[2]

General George Armstrong Custer and his troops discovered gold in the Black Hills during their military expedition in 1874. This created a rush similar to the Forty-Niners in California and the Fifty-Niners in Colorado. After the placer mining phase ended, a lode was discovered that would prove to be the richest vein in the western hemisphere. The Homestake eventually was owned by a syndicate headed by George Hearst, father of William R. Hearst, the renowned publisher of a huge chain of newspapers.

Over the next few decades the mine enjoyed great success by being adequately capitalized and soundly managed, having a paternalistic relationship with its employees, and, not incidentally, an enormous body of ore. The government price guarantee of the New Deal cemented its position as number one producer of gold in the western hemisphere.[3]

The government embargo on gold meant that an individual could legally own only $100 in coin or bullion but could ship it abroad freely. With this development, the New York Stock Exchange "took fresh courage and rallied substantially under the leadership of mining issues." Homestake shares jumped 26 points to a new high of 351. When the company reported that gold bullion would begin moving from Lead to the mint in Denver, the Homestake recorded an increase in the price of their dividends from nine dollars to twelve dollars annually. Roosevelt's tinkering with the price of gold meant an immediate windfall of $15 million for Homestake and "much more if gold mining is as stimulated as many experts anticipate."[4]

Gold mining in the Black Hills was greatly stimulated when many nations of the world went on the gold standard during the worldwide depression, creating an extraordinary demand for the metal. Gold was being sold freely abroad in England at no fixed cost much like other commodities, such as wheat. When the price of gold in London reached thirty dollars per ounce, American miners were not allowed to benefit from this rise because of the embargo on gold. Now, with New Deal changes, any new gold could be refined into gold bullion in the U.S. "and sold to the highest bidder any place out of the country," under Treasury supervision. The United States "had no special need" for more gold for monetary purposes, the *Rapid City Daily Journal* noted, and "the rest of the world does need it."[5]

The New Deal price of gold stimulated others to develop new mines or to reopen old, abandoned shafts. The American-Rushmore Mining company of Keystone was soon capitalized at $3 million and held "old and new claims near Keystone, [and] at least thirty-five men" were newly employed since the price change. A. L. Putnam, state securities commissioner, reported that "slowness of financing was holding up operations" of "several of the new companies." Professor Bancroft Gore of the State School of Mines declined to comment on "the new process which he is believed to have invented" for processing ore because he had not yet applied for a patent. Gore was on the board of directors of the American-Rushmore Mining Company and was reported giving "a group of Chicago businessmen" a tour of the Black Hills. Interest in gold mining was booming.[6]

The 1930s were "the golden years for the Homestake and its employees." While the rest of South Dakota struggled, Lead and its surrounding area boomed. Wages were good, there were no cycles of unemployment, citizens and merchants prospered, and employees enjoyed the company's paternalistic program of good medical facilities, recreation, modern safety requirements, and a minimum of labor strife. Homestake also pioneered in providing old age pensions. At that time, more than eighty men had received pensions since the program began in July 1917, in addition to free hospital service equivalent to what they received while employed. The Black Hills were "a veritable oasis of prosperity" surrounded by a desert of unparalleled depression and desolation.[7]

The state legislature, desperately searching for means to raise revenue, found the prosperous Homestake to be an obvious source of untapped revenue. Many states had levied severance taxes on ore taken from their jurisdiction over the centuries, but hardy, pioneer-spirited South Dakotans had always resisted this temptation—until the Great Depression made them desperate for revenues. An ore tax was introduced in the legislature in 1927 during the farm depression, but failed, and again in 1933 it was debated and again failed to pass. Emil Loriks became president of the South Dakota Farmers Union (FU) at this time and declined to run for the state legislature for another term. He was, however, determined to press the ore tax issue, and he and his friend and fellow FU leader Oscar

Fosheim became known as the "Gold Dust Twins." The two laid out a sound strategy for achieving their goal, with their slogan "tax gold, not Russian thistles."[8]

In 1934, Loriks noted that with the increased government price, Homestake had sold $16.5 million in gold in that year, and the price of its stock shares soared from the depression price of $50 to $430. From 1875 to 1932, $308 million of South Dakota gold was mined without being taxed. Now, in one year, the company received a bonus of $8 million in increased profits. It was time, he insisted, that the state profited from this bonanza.

Loriks even suggested that the state of South Dakota should confiscate Homestake. Why should the state permit the mining company to "remove permanently its greatest natural resources without any compensation?" he asked. He saw "the Eastern owners of the mine" as the profiteers, but if the state operated the mine, "the cost of all state government and much local government costs could be paid and taxes thereby reduced." He made no headway with this idea and soon reverted, instead, to a drive to tax the industry to allow the state some benefit from its greatest asset.[9]

He led a petition drive to gather signatures to put the issue on a popular ballot in 1935 if the farmer-dominated legislature failed to enact the tax that session and set up headquarters in the Waverly Hotel in Pierre that winter. He called the ensuing struggle "the battle of the century" to decide "who is going to determine the policies of the government of South Dakota, the people or the privileged few." In addition, he periodically sent out the FU message to farmers via WNAX, the farmers' radio station in Yankton owned by D. B. Gurney.[10]

Loriks headed for the Hills to deliver his message in several speeches, telling the voters there they had as much to gain from an ore tax as anyone. "The ore tax will not handicap new or unprofitable mining ventures," he insisted. He managed to get 20,000 signatures on his petition that required only 15,000. He recalled that, years later, when he gave a promotional speech in the Black Hills,

Homestake miners surrounded him, claiming they could lose their jobs and threatening to hang him. They were "busted" farmers who had found employment at the booming Homestake. "I really felt sorry for them," he responded, "but not a single miner lost his job" because of the tax.[11]

Meanwhile, Homestake was fighting back. The company took out a half-page ad demanding that the miners and their families be heard. The ad read: DO YOU WANT A TAX ON BLACK HILLS ORE? Four days later the editor of the *Rapid City Daily Journal* reported on his poll: 11,322 opposed the tax, while 129 supported it. The company also ran a half-page explanation on how much it had contributed to the area in taxes, employee salaries, etc.[12]

Governor Tom Berry, who had voted against the ore tax while a legislator in 1927, now proclaimed that he favored an ore tax because the miners "should pay their just share of taxes," but thought the present drive for one constituted too hasty an effort. At the last minute, the Berry administration stepped in and proposed a gross income tax of 4 percent rather than the 10 percent ore tax. Even Loriks and Fosheim agreed, because this would mean tax collections of $500,000 immediately, rather than waiting two years until the election in 1936 when the 10 percent tax they favored could collect $1,000,000.[13]

A rally was called in Sioux Falls in February 1934 to discuss the issue. Loriks encouraged his followers to write their legislators and to continue the pressure on them. A bill was "smoked out" of committee when twenty-three representatives signed a petition to the assessment and taxation committee, which then reported it out "without recommendation." The bill passed the lower house, but a similar one in the senate was amended into an unacceptable form, and Loriks announced that petitions would be filed to force the statewide vote. The house refused to accept the senate bill on a second vote, so the two went to conference. Here, the legislature reached the compromise to lower the rate to the governor's proposed gross income tax rate of 4 percent. Loriks accepted this compromise, which gained about $2 million in extra revenues, a not insignificant amount for state coffers at that time.[14]

Despite its protestations, neither Homestake nor the mining industry as a whole suffered tragically, or even marginally, in operations or profits, because of Roosevelt's price fixing. According to a survey done by the South Dakota State School of Mines, by 1936 twenty-nine abandoned mines or placers had been reopened since the price of gold increased, compared to five such mines in 1933. This meant an increase of 312 new employees, in addition to Homestake's 2,000 men. The mines included those with a capacity of five tons or less up to Homestake's 4,000-ton amalgamation and cyanide plant.[15]

Some South Dakotans early saw the possibilities of the Black Hills region producing gold from another source, the tourist industry that, during the Great Depression, was beginning to demonstrate it could become the state's second most important enterprise. With proper advertising and promotion, innumerable tourists wanted to view the awesome panoramic view, or as a Standard Oil description expressed it, "a Marvelous Hundred Square Miles." Visitors had long noted the area's breathtaking beauty but also its inaccessibility.

Custer State Park was one of Peter Norbeck's pet projects. In 1905 he and two friends were the first to drive across the Black Hills in an automobile. He entered politics soon after, moving up the political ladder until he was elected governor in 1916. In 1913, with Norbeck's help, the legislature enacted a bill to make a game preserve of Custer State Park. Thenceforth he tirelessly promoted the area's development. During his second term as governor, he successfully pressed the legislature to create Custer State Park, and he later served on the board. After election to the U.S. Senate, Norbeck continued his passionate interest in nature, conservation, the Black Hills, and Custer State Park. During the 1920s he conceived of the Needles Highway, saw the road to fruition, and helped develop the Iron Mountain Road linking the eastern gate of the Black Hills to the emerging carving at Mount Rushmore.[16]

During this period, the Custer State Park Board became a political issue despite Norbeck's efforts to keep tourism nonpartisan. When Warren Green was elected governor in 1930, he tried to ignore the fissures that had developed in his party during the bitter three-way race for governor in 1926 in which the incumbent Carl Gunderson, a Republican, was defeated by Democrat William Bulow. Green's faction blamed Norbeck and his supporters, who had opposed Gunderson in 1926 and again in 1928.

Governor Green proceeded to replace Bulow's appointees, John Stanley and Berry, with two Republicans on the Custer State Park Board. In addition, he replaced the park superintendent, Charles Robertson, with Republican Frank T. Fetzner, which Norbeck interpreted as an attempt to minimize his own influence on the park's future. When Green's appointees fired several park personnel, Norbeck and his faction concluded Green's supporters were turning the park into political patronage. The park again became a political issue in the New Deal when politicians squabbled over the architectural style of the new game lodge.[17]

Mobility was the key to touring the Black Hills. Early visitors arrived by railroad and later visitors came by automobile, but they all needed transportation to local spots or wanted "to be guided through the Hills." As early as 1926, Rapid City native Paul E. Bellamy established the Black Hills Transportation Company to meet these needs. Soon railroads were advertising these services, selling tourist tickets that included "tours, accommodations, and meals."[18]

Rapid City and the Black Hills community set about creating special attractions for these visitors. They placed great emphasis on Native Americans, appealing to tourists' inclination to glorify Indians. The Sioux Indian Pageant featured Black Elk, who had traveled with Wild West shows in America and Europe that were popular in the late nineteenth century. Black Elk was recognized as a spiritual leader of the Lakota nation, and he helped organize and direct seasonal shows and often performed leading roles in the dances of healing, mourning, and burial. The Lakota also profited by selling artifacts and handicrafts in their shops and to visitors in their camps.[19]

The region had numerous railroad lines by the turn of the twentieth century, which in turn retarded the construction of expensive mountain roads. Tourists could take advantage of numerous forty-odd-mile excursions with costs ranging from $1.05 to $2.70, with the promise they could make any unscheduled stop at any point and the train would pick them up on the return trip. This would allow them time to fish in the mountain streams, hike, enjoy a picnic, or pick wild berries. The Crystal, Wind, and Jewel caves were another three attractions for tourists to explore.[20]

Besides the beauty of the Badlands and Custer State Park and its breathtaking Needles Highway, artist Gutzon Borglum was sculpting the monumental Mount Rushmore, soon to become the nation's "Shrine to Democracy." Local facilities and access highways were all that were lacking to make this a great tourist center, and New Deal programs helped fill that void.

The dearth of funding greatly retarded Borglum's progress until supporters won over President Calvin Coolidge. The president announced that Mount Rushmore should be a national project and, after assuring donors that Coolidge would not appear on the mountain, Congress agreed to pay half the projected cost of $250,000, with the remainder to be raised on a matching basis. The solons also created a commission to oversee the work and to continue to raise funds. The work then proceeded rapidly. Washington's figure was dedicated on 4 July 1930. Carving was halted in 1932, again due to lack of funds, until the Reconstruction Finance Corporation (RFC) granted $50,000 to continue it. In 1936, FDR went to the dedication of the Lincoln face. In 1939, Theodore Roosevelt's figure was completed.

For the dedication of Washington's bust, protocol required South Dakotans should occupy the "chief places of honor" because state historian Doane Robinson "made the original suggestion" for the monument and also because President Washington was "regarded as belonging to the nation rather than to any one state." Virginia would have the honor of unveiling Jefferson, Illinois would do the honors for Lincoln, and New York later for Theodore Roosevelt. Dr. C. C. O'Hara, president of the School of Mines, presented a brief "scientific" address at the dedication of George Washington's bust. The scientist noted the Rushmore monument "will probably last a million years due to its geological formation."[21]

Along with the automobile and the demand for better roads came "the revolutionary idea of sightseeing," the vital ingredient of tourism. In the April 1919 issue of *Pahasapa Quarterly*, Arthur I. Johnson promoted the concept of building scenic highways, such as the Needles Highway, for tourism. He lamented the fact that bad roads in the Hills vicinity accounted for poor attendance at the three caves and limited access to "the more scenic areas of the Hills." He insisted, "It lies within these hills to become as attractive to the American tourists as the mountains of Switzerland." Access was all that was lacking, but state road building in the area was not supported by the remainder of the state because it was considered localized spending for the benefit of the extreme western portion of the state. Someone needed to show East River voters that they also could benefit from tourism to the west. This role was filled by Governor Berry and the New Dealers.[22]

Meanwhile, despite the paucity of publicity, tourism was increasing in the region. During the summer of 1931—the first time an attempt was made to count them—26,449 visitors registered at Mount Rushmore. In 1932 the number quadrupled to 108,000, and the following year, 135,000 came to view Borglum's emerging masterpiece. As better roads were built from Rapid City, and more carving of the monument took place each year, the number of tourists visiting America's Shrine to Democracy increased geometrically.

During these years of development, Deadwood quickly emerged as a major tourist attraction. The town adopted the slogan "the historical city," emphasizing its colorful history as a gold rush town. It had been the home of Calamity Jane and Wild Bill Hickok, who was killed holding a "dead man's hand" in a poker game—two pairs of black aces and eights. The town developed its annual "Days of 76" celebration, emphasizing "Deadwood Dick," the dime-novel character of the Old West who was "a daring Robin Hood."[23]

Signs, such as the Burma Shave ones on highways, became both entertainment for travelers and direction for tourists to entertainment spots. Ted and Dorothy Hustead were young University of South Dakota graduates struggling to establish their drugstore at Wall, on the edge of the Badlands. Dorothy conceived the idea of erecting signs along highways advertising free ice water to travelers to Wall Drug. This concept soon ballooned into making Wall the "unofficial entry to the Black Hills" and after the signs spread around the world, they became "a hallmark of Black Hills tourism."[24]

In January 1931 Congress passed the Park to Park Highway Act that made roads eligible for federal funding beginning at park boundaries. The National Park Service had made improvements at Wind Cave, with the installation of electric lights, a ranger dormitory, and oil surface for its north-south road. Now Senator Norbeck was able to obtain funding for a road from Newcastle, Wyoming, to the Custer road that intersected with one leading to Wind Cave, linking the Hills to the national road system from the west.[25]

In promoting tourism, the Roosevelt administration "instituted a new emphasis on planning and recreation." The National Park Service implemented this planning and "assumed responsibility for recreational development on public lands." The Federal Emergency Relief Administration (FERA) provided matching funds for highway construction. In the House bill, South Dakota's share would bring the state $237.29 per unemployed worker, compared to Iowa's share of $65.20 and New York's $12.66. When debate began in the Senate, it was reported that "certain Midwestern states would take advantage of the situation" that they possessed in the upper house and were expected "to have a good opportunity to increase their allotments." Five days later the Senate bill was passed. The $400

million provided by the national government would be matched by
$200 million from the states.[26]

The following day delegates from eleven counties in South Dakota met with representatives from the State Highway Department
to divide up these "goodies." The state's expenditures of $1,500,000
or 25 percent of the total federal commitment to the state would be
spent on secondary or "feeder" highways over the next two years. It
appeared that distribution of the funds would be on "a basis of relief
needs," which were extensive across the entire state.[27]

The question of spreading relief work by building many miles of
gravel roads or concentrating funds on fewer miles of more expensive hard surface roads was hotly debated for years. The *Rapid City
Daily Journal* carried a large printed telegram on its front page. The
governor's secretary, E. H. Bremer, advised editor E. F. Lusk that
Berry favored "a hard-surfaced road across the entire state" and
the highway commission was "working toward the development of
such a project." Rapid City, of course, would eagerly support this
plan because it would obviously terminate there, and editor Lusk
wholeheartedly gave his endorsement.[28]

Arno B. Cammerer, director of national parks, toured the Black
Hills area in the summer of 1934 and enthusiastically declared,
"Development of the Bad Lands monument will make Rapid City
one of the tourist capitals of the nation." He recognized that what
Mount Rushmore lacked was a parkway drive similar to those in the
Green Mountains or the Great Smokey Parkway and it would come
soon with the Iron Mountain road.[29]

In November 1934, South Dakota officials received word of their
road money for the remainder of the fiscal year. They had $3,100,000
available in federal funds, with 50 percent of it earmarked for the
federal highway system in the state, 25 percent for federal highways within municipalities, and 25 percent for secondary roads.
With half of the four cents per gallon gasoline tax earmarked for
rural credit debt retirement by the 1934 legislature, this left only
enough of these funds for current maintenance and none for vehicle

expansion. Desperately searching for additional revenues in 1935, the legislature began requiring two types of drivers' licenses, regular for a two-year period and one year for chauffeurs, each costing one dollar. The revenues would be divided, with 25 percent for administration and 75 percent for highway construction.[30]

For years highways 14 and 16 had competed with each other as the preferred route to the Black Hills. Then, following the primary elections in 1934, a meeting was called by the associated commercial clubs of the Black Hills where they decided to join forces in the common cause. B. C. Dow of Sioux Falls pointed out the obvious, that both used the same route from the junction at Kadoka and Philip to the Hills. Dow believed that supporters of both routes should unite in their efforts for mutual benefit to get these last ninety miles blacktopped. Federal funds were available to complete that portion in the fall and even authorities in the eastern part of the state believed this was "a good investment of their funds." The decision to press the blacktopping of the remainder of either 14 or 16 could come later.[31]

It was essential to build these two highways as channels to funnel tourists, not only from eastern South Dakota, but from the eastern United States, to the Black Hills and Mount Rushmore. In September 1934, the *Argus-Leader* reported that the highway commission was "apathetic on the topic." If they were spoils politicians they would build "disconnected strips of roads here and there in a crazy-quilt pattern;" if they had "vision and courage," they would construct roads in "a definite scheme." At the end of 1934, Tom Berry disclosed the welcome news that the Highway Department was planning to hard surface both highways 14 and 16 "at the earliest possible date."[32]

Although the subject had "been discussed for years," this was the first official indication of which roads would have priority. Number 14 ran from the South Dakota Agricultural College in Brookings through the capital to Mount Rushmore, and Highway 16 from Sioux Falls through Mitchell, then joined 14 at Wall and ran through Rapid City into Wyoming. "Most" of this mileage would receive oil surfacing but planners would use "pavement" where "heavy traffic justified the cost." Route 14 would connect with hard-surfaced roads leading to the Twin Cities and 16 with good routes from Chicago and the south and east. Connecting routes for other parts of the state would be built as funding became available. The total cost of these two major thoroughfares was estimated at $4.5 million, a sum unthinkable without New Deal assistance.[33]

Through income from the gasoline tax, motor vehicle registrations, drivers' licenses, and motor carrier tax, the South Dakota Highway Department became one of the few in the nation to become almost financially independent of its legislature. As a result, as traffic increased, so too did its annual budget, from $30,000 in 1917 to more than $4 million in 1940. This fund also could be used to match the increasing federal aid, especially during the New Deal. After 1937, the department cooperated with the Bureau of Public Roads to make federal aid highways coincide with the state trunk system.[34]

The Good Roads Association of South Dakota was one of the state's strongest supporters of tourism in making citizens "hard surface highway conscious." In the summer of 1935, its directors decided to devote their efforts to working for the election of a legislature that would push for this program. Noting that the state would have to build "its own roads and will have to borrow money to do it," the association promoted the election of state senators and representatives who would support increasing the gasoline tax. The extra funds would pay the state's share for a proposed RFC loan of $20 million and a matching fund of $4 million of federal aid and highway money.[35]

Their efforts proved successful and the legislature in 1936 raised the gasoline tax to four cents. The highway commission was then able to tap the federal sources, and it reported by September that only eighty-five miles of Highway 16 remained unpaved. This remainder required substantial grading before completion. This, plus the new modern hotel at Sylvan Lake, completed in 1937, the Rapid City newspaper editor reported, made it possible for the Black Hills to become "the Midwest goal for tourists." The Black Hills Chamber of Commerce began planning a series of visits to the region's towns "as a friendly gesture to promote its tourist attractions." After completion of Highway 16, the commission could concentrate on hard surfacing the remainder of Highway 14, South Dakota's historic "Black and Yellow Trail." The interstate project was finally completed in the summer of 1938 and opened amid great fanfare. Chamberlain, for example, hosted "an Indian village, races, and an air show as the principal attractions," along with "blaring bands, [and] shows in full swing."[36]

Presho, the largest town between Chamberlain and Rapid City on Highway 16, would particularly benefit from this expanding tourist industry. The more facilities a town offered, the more tourists it could attract. B. R. Stevens and C. S. Hubbard built tourist camps in Presho in the 1920s, and Anton Safer and Henry Blocker constructed two additional camps in the 1930s. These included a tourist home with individual rooms and a filling station. The juncture of Main Street and Highway 16 lay at the top of the hill on the south side of town and the problem of tourists navigating this stretch in bad weather was not resolved until 1957, when Main Street received a hard surface.[37]

The New Deal made significant changes in concepts and emphasis on the Black Hills tourist industry. Norbeck and the original planners had stressed beauty and adventure as amateurs conceived them, and sought to preserve the natural splendor of the area to attract tourism. Practical New Dealers viewed the Hills as a great opportunity for work relief, but also to enhance practical change, particularly in outdoor recreation. The Public Works Administration (PWA) and Works Progress Administration (WPA) offered opportunities to build facilities with Civilian Conservations Corps (CCC) labor, not only roads, but fire prevention posts, picnic tables, campgrounds, hiking trails, and location signage.

The New Deal period presented an issue that exemplified the changes. After a fire destroyed the hotel at Sylvan Lake in 1935, the decision to replace it produced a heated debate over architectural style. The traditional Native American rock and peeled log style had hitherto prevailed and fitted in well with the rugged and difficult accessibility of the Hills. Robert Lusk of the state planning board, with Norbeck's support, promoted Frank Lloyd Wright as the architect to continue this schema with the new hotel. Wright, though, detested the "Park Rustic" type of architecture dominating the area, such as the recently constructed ranger camp built by the CCC at Jewel Cave. The Custer State Park board, now dominated by Governor Berry's appointments, rebelled. After serious and prolonged discussion and with the support of the National Park Service, the board awarded the contract to the firm of architect Harold Spitznagel of Sioux Falls, and he designed a hotel that incorporated local rock and knotty pine combined with the use of American Indian motifs.[38] The PWA granted $57,240, to be matched by $70,000 in state emergency building funds. The decision on style was awaiting approval of the grant by PWA for the three-story structure with forty rooms and when it came, construction preceded immediately.[39]

Another type of gold gathering was just beginning to surface at the end of the depression. Ring-tailed pheasants were first introduced to South Dakota in 1905 from China. They flourished, despite the harsh winters, and South Dakotans were soon bragging about having more pheasants than people, which became a gross understatement. At the end of World War I they were so numerous that the first hunting season opened for one day in 1919. By 1929, some 2,760 out-of-state hunters purchased licenses, and people from all over the nation began spending money for licenses, motel rooms, food, and guides. Soon the numbers would reach tens of thousands chasing the wily birds each autumn and bringing precious cash to the Land of Sunshine.[40]

8 Republicans Administer
the WPA in South Dakota

Perhaps the most noteworthy development of the entire 1936 South
Dakota presidential campaign was Sen. Peter Norbeck's decision to
endorse Roosevelt.

Philip A. Grant, Jr.[1]

PRIOR TO THE ELECTION campaign of 1936, the highly re-
spected *Literary Digest* conducted a series of nationwide
polls on general citizen attitudes toward New Deal programs. They
showed a steady increase in opposition in 1935. In the spring of
1934, polls indicated that three out of every five voters favored the
New Deal. In a later one, 44 percent were positive and 55 percent
were negative. South Dakotans in December 1935 voted negatively,
with only 35.83 percent positive and 64.17 percent registering negative opinions. This growing opposition in South Dakota definitely
emerged in the next election.[2]

When Tom Berry decided to seek a third term as governor in
1936, rather than to confront a divisive primary with William Bulow for his Senate seat, he faced the growing unpopularity of New
Deal programs, as the polls reflected. Running on his success as relief administrator, Berry noted that in 1932 the state's income from
agricultural production and government benefits totaled $56.7 mil-
lion but had jumped to $103.9 million in 1936, an increase of 83.2
percent. He also took credit for the "Tom Berry pennies" from the

sales tax that relieved property owners. Though uncontested in the Democratic primary, Berry had the serious handicap in the general election of running against the state's anti-third term tradition and the strong reaction in the Black Hills against the ore tax.[3] Berry "may have been aiming" for Norbeck's seat that would come open in 1938, although the Republican was very ill and his future uncertain.[4]

The conservative faction of the Republican party won a victory at their state convention when they replaced progressive, long-time Norbeck supporter S. V. Way, as party chairman, with Harlan J. Bushfield, a conservative from Miller. The latter vigorously attacked the New Deal for "criminal waste." He declared, with obvious relish, "The fight is on."[5]

Republicans were hard-pressed to find candidates to run against the still-popular governor. The publisher of the Aberdeen *Dakota Farmer*, Leslie Jensen, finally emerged on the state level. A former Internal Revenue Service collector and telephone executive from Hot Springs, Jensen had a winsome smile, a good sense of humor, and many acquaintances across the state. On the national level, President Franklin D. Roosevelt and Vice President John Nance Garner were nominated for second terms, marking the first time in American history that both candidates on the same ticket were nominated in the space of twenty-four hours. The *Argus-Leader* described this as "the already accelerating presidential campaign." Tom Berry was given the honor of seconding FDR's nomination, delivering "a brief impromptu speech" in which he called the president "the greatest man alive." The governor stressed the benefits of federal relief spending, noting that "if it had not been for relief, the people couldn't stay out there [in drought-stricken South Dakota]." Republican governor Alf Landon of Kansas became Roosevelt's opponent. Landon enjoyed the distinction of being the only Republican governor elected west of the Mississippi in 1932 and the only GOP governor elected anywhere in 1934.[6]

The Republicans were growing optimistic for a couple of reasons.

First, they were aware of the increasing public pessimism over Roosevelt's very limited success in "revitalizing" the sick economy, and many farmers were returning to their traditional Republican roots. In addition, Alf Landon appeared to be a more attractive candidate than Herbert Hoover had been, and they held out hope that the Union party candidate William Lemke of North Dakota might siphon off the votes of angry Democrats and Independents in South Dakota.[7]

Prior to his reelection campaign, Franklin Roosevelt decided to tour the drought-stricken areas of the Midwest in late August. He participated in weather conferences in Pierre and Rapid City, where he reminded listeners of his unwavering commitments to agriculture and conservation. In Aberdeen, he expressed concern over both the drought and South Dakota's expressed relief needs for the coming winter. He also stressed the need for urban dwellers to realize that "there would not be any cities if there were not any farms," exactly the correct posture for an easterner to take with South Dakotans. He promised to "take back to Washington . . . the picture of a whole lot of people with courage, with their chins up, who are telling us they are going to see things through. And I am going to help." After unveiling the face of Jefferson, he hailed Mount Rushmore as a shrine to democracy, "not only in our own beloved country, but, we hope, throughout the world."[8]

This campaign season brought out incidents of "red-baiting" in South Dakota. Karl E. Mundt of Madison, seeking to unseat Fred H. Hildebrandt, discovered the congressman had employed a Communist named Linn Gale in his Washington office in 1919. Hildebrandt responded that he had employed Gale for a month, and he felt "highly complimented that my opponent has apparently found nothing to criticize in my record as a member of congress and, therefore, is left to resort to childish and picayunish tactics of this kind." Mundt would successfully use this Communist issue over the next many years of his political career.[9]

In late October the Republican state chairman asked Berry if he supported Hildebrandt's candidacy, citing the congressman's recent observations that "we must move much further to the left" and that the Supreme Court's power should be "limited." The people of South Dakota want to know, Bushfield insisted, if Democrats supported a man who was "working hand in hand with a communist down in Washington."[10]

Two days later the major candidates held late rallies in what the state's leading newspaper described as "political oratory" rising to "new heights" as candidates "continued to hurl broadsides at each other." Jensen reminded listeners he had promised, if elected, to "fire Frank Kriebs [*sic*] as secretary of the state highway commission" and to "kick the white collared parasites out of the state relief setup." He also assailed Berry for using funds "earmarked for relief to set up a pension program which could hardly last until after election," adding that this pension plan constituted "the cruelest hoax ever perpetuated on the people of the state."[11]

Early in 1936, Berry charged, with plausibility, that "anonymous literature" containing "deliberate misstatements" was being distributed to the press." Bushfield immediately challenged him "to furnish a bill of particulars," observing that, as far as he knew, there had been "nothing either anonymous or untrue" distributed by the Republican committees, "nor will there be as long as I am chairman."[12]

Yet, in mid-October the *Yankton Press and Dakotan* carried an advertisement signed by H. W. Apted and W. H. Baggs, Republican county chairman and state central committeeman respectively, concerning the state relief programs. South Dakota, the pair insisted, was last among the forty-eight states in relief allotment per client. "No family, no matter how large," the notice claimed, received over $44.50 monthly in comparison to $55 in Iowa and a $50 average nationally. The notice charged that the governor, senator, and representatives have "deserted us in this time of disaster and need." Voters were asked to "repudiate our faithless leaders."

Michael Kennedy enclosed the ad in a "confidential letter" to Harry Hopkins. He called attention to the "whispering campaign in the state to try and influence Progressive Republicans to vote for Roosevelt and Jensen." The Democrats were showing how the Works Progress Administration (WPA) arrived at its wage rates in South Dakota, but no one could legally release "earnings of clients in other states" for comparison. He asked Hopkins to send Berry a list of WPA earnings in neighboring states. Hopkins's assistant, Aubrey Williams, responded that such stories were "without foundation" and any such comparisons were "not valid." South Dakota workers on WPA jobs were paid on the same basis as communities of comparable size in other states in Wage Region I. Community size, not state, was the criteria used. That the WPA officials in South Dakota were correct was of no assistance in countering the slanted presentations of the political opposition. Republicans were trying to have their cake and eat it too by enjoying federal relief money at the same time they criticized the Berry administration's handling of the program.[13]

Late in the campaign Bushfield charged Congressman Hildebrandt with "exacting a tribute" from postmasters in his district. In one case, he asserted, the solon had actually removed a postmaster and his assistant who refused "to kick through with contributions." John Delpherdang of Tripp was Bushfield's star witness. He testified that he and his assistant had made payments to the Democratic party for six months, then quit, and were subsequently removed from their posts. Hildebrandt responded, not surprisingly, that he had "never exacted a solitary dime" from any of his appointments and never permitted any of them to "even discuss contributions with me."[14]

In the election, Roosevelt defeated Landon in South Dakota by a margin of 35,000 votes but his percentage dropped from 63.3 in 1932 to 54 percent in 1936, while his national percentage rose from 57 to 60. Jensen, one of three Republican governors elected nationally, won the gubernatorial race by 9,000, indicating that the popular Berry could not buck the anti-third term sentiment. Senator Bulow won a second term and Hildebrandt retained his House seat, although Karl Mundt made a good showing against the latter. The Republicans lost fourteen House seats nationally in this Democratic landslide, but Francis H. Case picked up a seat for them in the Second District by defeating Theodore B. Werner. Republicans carried the state house by a substantial margin and won a majority of one in the senate. Both parties won some elections but, looking to 1938, the trend was towards the Republicans.[15]

Before he left office, Berry had an important duty to perform. U.S. Senator Peter Norbeck succumbed to cancer in late December, and the governor had to select a successor. His obvious choice was to resign and let his lieutenant governor, Robert Peterson, name him to the Senate, a position he desired very much. Peterson, however, had just been arrested for bank embezzlement. According to the *New York Times*, Berry declined to resign because of Peterson's legal situation but also because Jensen and his lieutenant governor-elect Donald McMurchie had filed oaths of office on the basis that they could assume office immediately upon Berry's resignation. Many politicians across the country had assumed that Berry would resign and Jensen would then appoint him to the office, but the bitter campaign they had just endured made Berry distrust Jensen to fulfill such an arrangement.[16] He avoided the risk of being named to the Senate by a governor under indictment or the chance that Jensen would appoint a Republican rather than himself by selecting Herbert Hitchcock, a Mitchell attorney and currently head of the Democratic state committee, to serve out the time between Norbeck's death and the next election in 1938.[17]

Herbert Hitchcock had moved to Mitchell in 1894 and practiced law there for forty years. He served terms in the state senate in 1909, 1911, and 1929, but never sought political office otherwise, contenting himself with building his party's influence. He became state Democratic party chair in the landslide of 1932. Aged sixty-nine, Hitchcock was a widower with no children who described himself as "a moderate progressive" in his politics. His appointment gave the Democrats an overwhelming 76–16 margin in the U.S. Senate.[18]

In the meantime, federal marshals arrested Lieutenant Governor Peterson at his home in Centerville, charging him with embezzling funds from his bank in that town. He was also connected with banks at Vermillion, Viborg, and Wakonda, and he resigned from the bank at Vermillion after his arrest. When he was arrested, the Federal Deposit Insurance Corporation (FDIC) in Washington announced that a shortage of $172,000 had been discovered there, but the arrest warrant specified an item of $3,400 on 7 October 1936.

Despite the charges, he presided over the opening session, but postponed resigning after Norbeck's death. At his trial, Peterson changed his plea of not guilty to guilty on two counts of embezzlement and falsifying bank records. He was sentenced to serve three years in prison on each count, with the sentences running concurrently.[19]

The brief Democratic reign thus ended in South Dakota. While Democrats nationally perceived Dakotans to be ungrateful, it was state Democrats who were truly disappointed. Berry and his supporters had proven to be resourceful servants who successfully milked the federal relief cow for all it was worth, and they were frustrated by the return of voters to their habitual trend of supporting Republicans.[20] This trend continued for the next several decades in South Dakota, which elected conservative governors to control state policies but chose Democrats for the U.S. Congress to "bring home the pork." South Dakotans were becoming accustomed to federal largess and wanted it to continue.[21]

There were a few changes made in the WPA and the state welfare office following the Republican victory. Kennedy wrote Hopkins a confidential letter explaining the awkward situation. He had been serving the dual role of welfare commissioner, appointed by the governor, and state WPA administrator, appointed by the national WPA, with his offices housed in Pierre in the Chicago and North Western depot and in some committee rooms in the state capitol building. With the change in state administrations, the building superintendent had notified him that the committee rooms must be vacated by 10 December. The WPA treasury office, however, was located in Watertown. Kennedy anticipated that the Republicans would replace him as welfare commissioner, and he wanted to plan ahead for his role as only the WPA director. In addition, the welfare office had "so many responsibilities with old age assistance and other phases of the Social Security program "that it was advisable to separate the positions," and he had planned to resign the welfare job "very shortly." He was proven correct when Governor Jensen immediately appointed P. L. Crowlie to replace him.[22]

In response, Kennedy proposed moving the WPA offices to Mitchell. Another possibility was Watertown, where the finance offices were located, but that town did not offer sufficient office space or housing facilities. He called attention to the proposed move of the Resettlement Administration to Huron and observed that town could not host both agencies. Aberdeen was not "as well geographically located" as Mitchell, and Sioux Falls had no office space that was "suitable or that could be secured at any reasonable rate." This left Mitchell as his choice.

Kennedy's letter sounded as though he was not too disappointed to leave Pierre. The town, and Hughes County where it was located, were "very strongly opposed to any re-location" of the WPA offices. The Berry people believed, though, that the "business people of this community did not appreciate the business they received from the various federal employees nor the benefits the town and community has received in the line of [federal] improvements." He based this opinion on the fact that in the last election, they failed to give either of the Democratic candidates for Congress, or Governor Berry "a majority." Aubrey Williams responded affirmatively to Kennedy's requests. F. R. Stanley, WPA field representative, called and then wrote Williams of the plans for moving and the decision to combine districts one and two in Watertown and Aberdeen into one district.[23]

Huron did not abandon this issue of locations without a struggle. The city wired Harry Hopkins of its advantages over Mitchell, noting it was on a regular airmail route that gave overnight service to Washington. City leaders noted that 81 percent of the state population lived within a hundred-mile radius and it was closest to the state's major relief load. Huron was only ninety miles from the treasury office in Watertown (city officials were unaware that that office, too, might be moved), compared to the 130 miles from Mitchell to Watertown. In desperation, Huron offered to improve a building of 15,000 square feet and charge no rent for one year. City officials also insisted their housing facilities were "adequate" for employees, all to no avail. The move to Mitchell was made.[24]

The WPA put the finishing touches on the new gubernatorial home in Pierre in time for Governor Jensen and his family to move in. Built south of the capitol, the house was described as "plain on the interior, as it is outside." The ground floor contained a study, a reception hall, and "a long dining room for large dinners." The mansion contained a fireplace made of petrified wood, with others in the basement recreation room, the living room, and the master bedroom. There were four bathrooms, two with shower baths, and the Republican-controlled legislature was currently planning on appropriating $13,500 to furnish the structure adequately for the new Republican chief executive.[25]

Berry reported an administrative problem to "My Dear Harry" after the election. Merle Brown, WPA compensation commissioner, had been arrested. The governor knew him "quite well; he had never been quite right. He has stiff checks all over the country and was wrong politically." Berry recommended firing him because "such fellows as he hurt the administration," and replacing him with W. J. Dawson of Pierre. The latter had served as Berry's state insurance commissioner during his two terms. "Someday," Berry added, "I'm going to write you a friendly letter when I don't want anything." Aubrey Williams discovered that Brown was not on the Washington staff, but worked for Kennedy on the state level, so the WPA director could resolve the issue locally.[26]

As the lame duck governor, Berry had one last issue left to resolve—how to pay for the state portion of the old age pensions now required by the Social Security Act. He had studied the problem thoroughly and concluded that seven million dollars would be required annually for old age pensions alone. Knowing the money was simply not available, Berry refused to call the legislature into special session to consider such a plan. Emil Loriks and Oscar Fosheim disputed this figure, claiming it was exaggerated at least twofold, and condemned Berry for his inaction. They believed that he could "safely trust" the solons, "possibly the best group of lawmakers ever elected" in the state.

Reluctantly, Berry finally called a special session that enacted the necessary welfare measures, adding another two million dollars annually to the cost of state government. During the last quarter of 1936, the Federal Social Security Agency made $290,000 available to give a monthly pension of $21.50 to 8,750 people over age sixty-five. All did not proceed smoothly, however, with this initial effort. The ages of many of these recipients were not verified, and the incomes of many of them made them ineligible. Some were members of public institutions. This overpayment was deducted from future payments.[27]

When the legislature convened in January 1937 in "frigid weather," both Berry and Jensen addressed the two bodies, and the crowd rose to their feet and cheered them. The Republicans held a scant majority of one in the senate but a wider margin of 66 to 37 in the lower house. The Democratic progressives soon discovered the new governor held ideas compatible to their own. In his inaugural address, Jensen praised their net income tax as "the most equitable form of taxation devised." He criticized the regressive sales tax and proposed exempting food purchases under forty cents, but agreed the tax had to remain temporarily to raise needed revenue. He proposed a homestead exemption on the property tax, which was revived in order to repay rural credits bonds, and an extension of the mortgage-moratorium law. He also urged the cessation of budget slashing on higher education. He supported Fosheim's recommended increase in the ore tax from four to ten percent and the New Deal's replacement of the Agricultural Adjustment Act (AAA) with the Soil Conservation and Domestic Allotment Act. Finally, he agreed with the state legislature to match $4 million in Social Security funding, primarily for old age pensions.[28] "As I see the picture," he announced in his inaugural address, "the old Elephant and the old Mule are hitched in double harness. The people are at the roadside with their eyes upon the eveners." One of their biggest challenges was responding to the Social Security Act of 1935, which they did belatedly and shamefully.[29]

The governor had the politically painful task of informing the legislature that there was only enough money in the old age fund to finance pensions until April. Beer and liquor taxes were insufficient to continue the assistance, and they must find additional sources of revenue. State Treasurer W. H. Hinselman disputed the governor's figures, insisting there was enough revenue to last until 1 July. Whoever was correct, additional funding was required to carry the program beyond the fiscal year. Three million dollars seemed to be the most reasonable sum anyone was suggesting, an amount equal to the recent biennial appropriation.[30]

Old age pension plans proved to be a particularly sticky point for the state legislature as they were deemed "indispensable" because of the available federal dollars. Appearing before the solons to deliver a special message, Governor Jensen described the current state plan as "a house of cards," noting that it was questionable if the state currently possessed authority to use its funds for this purpose. Secondly, the state lacked sufficient funding, he insisted, to carry the program beyond April. In addition, New Deal bureaucrats were threatening to shut off funding if the state did not correct a disparity in benefits among counties. The governor urged quick passage of his proposal, which called for a three-member board to administer these pensions. The nit-picking legislature reluctantly enacted his proposal.[31]

First, Governor Jensen recommended the legislature be given

more control over public funding and reduce money spent at the discretion of various boards that received fees and other types of agency income. Then, as usual, "sin" taxes were the first to be increased. "By straight party vote," the Republicans transferred control of the liquor laws to the agriculture department and raised taxes on both liquor and beer to replenish the old age pensions fund. Despite Fosheim and Johnson's measure to increase the ore tax from 4 to 10 percent, the bill ultimately signed by the governor was a smaller increase to 6 percent, which would produce an additional $360,000 in revenue.

In another message, the governor asked for the return to the state of one of the two cents on the gasoline tax diverted to paying off rural credits in order to give it to the highway department. This would give that department three of the four cents for accelerated highway construction to complete highways 14 and 16. The legislature extended the debtor relief program, approved participation in the New Deal's Soil Conservation and Domestic Allotment Act, and approved a child welfare division in the new Social Security division. The solons increased the state's austere budget by 10 percent and appropriated $4 million for matching funds for pensions for the elderly. They also increased the sales tax to 3 percent and killed a proposal to exempt food. Finally, this conservative legislature defeated a request to prevent racial discrimination and rejected the Child Labor amendment.[32] Not to their credit, they also rejected an obvious request to rename Custer State Park after Norbeck.[33]

This legislature set a record for political bickering, increased taxes, and higher appropriations. Political differences over a few dollars in expenditures held up final adjournment for several hours. The appropriations as finally approved stood at $5,608,817 for the biennium, or $508,917 annually above the previous session. Despite Democratic opposition, Republicans deferred the decision on old age pensions until 1 July 1937. Until that time Republicans agreed that payments would be made under the old Democratic plan that the Republicans believed was legally questionable.[34]

The Social Security Act offered the states generous dollar-matching plans if they would establish programs to assist their dependent members of society, which included those who were blind, unemployed, dependent children, or elderly. This was asking a good deal of a poverty-stricken state like South Dakota, whose taxpayers found it hard to resist the dollar-matching enticements, but equally difficult to produce matching money. As Governor Jensen explained to the president, his legislature was "giving their serious attention" to these matters and "we intend to accomplish these results to the fullest extent of our ability," but finding the necessary dollars was very onerous.[35]

With regard to dependent children, however, the solons acted in a shameful manner. Poor families were left with only the inadequate mothers' pensions, while advocacy groups unsuccessfully pressed for a program of one-third federal, one-third state, and one-third local support. The program they enacted carried a proviso that it would not go into operation until the federal government provided 50 percent support, while the Social Security Act clearly spelled out only one-third from federal funding. Was the legislature trying the impossible task of blackmailing the federal government?[36]

Jensen dutifully traveled to Washington, hand outstretched, to the New Dealers whom his state had just repudiated. He sought not merely old age program assistance but also expansion of the Civilian Conservation Corps (CCC) camp quotas, "liberalization of WPA regulations," and Farm Credit Administration (FCA) and Resettlement Administration (RA) assistance for "unlimited funds for spring planting." The latter seemed crucial at the time, but the drought would not be broken that year, and the seed proved fruitless. Jensen also conferred with newly elected congressman Francis Case, who supported his quests. Case asked for sufficient federal personnel to speed processing of applications in the field and leniency with farmers "who have so-called poor credit history" based on impossible payments from drought years. Technical application of regulations "also had occasionally defeated the purpose of emergency loans" for some farmers. Jensen returned home three weeks later with a victory on seed-loan regulations but otherwise empty-handed. There would be no federal emergency funding for old age assistance. The state would have to find money itself to match federal grants to about 11,000 current elderly with "approximately 70 percent" payments.[37]

Bushfield blamed the Democrats in the state legislature for all the state's tax and economic woes because the laws they passed would be in effect until the new ones enacted by the current legislature would go into effect on 1 July. He particularly castigated them for failing to provide adequately for the elderly by not voting emergency funds to allow the program to continue during this three-month interim. This forced Governor Jensen to explain the situation to "the heads of the relief agencies in Washington" and to ask for emergency funding "to bridge the gap" of April, May, and June. A bill to place old age assistance "on a permanent basis" failed of a two-thirds vote, Bushfield claimed, because of lack of Democratic support. Funding for the program after 1 July was approved because Republicans supported it and it required only a majority vote at that point in time.[38]

The 1937 legislature faced an additional chore when President Roosevelt chose that time to submit the child-labor amendment again for ratification. First proposed as part of the Progressive reforms in 1922, the amendment was ratified by twenty-eight states before becoming bogged down and languishing for more than a decade. Interest in it revived when the use of child labor increased significantly in the Great Depression. FDR proposed reviving the ratification process, and he asked the governors of nineteen states whose legislatures were then meeting to approve it "quickly." Governor Jensen informed the president that he was in agreement with the child labor concept but feared subsequent control of the vital labor of farm children if it became part of the Constitution. In addition, such consideration "might jeopardize other needed measures" his legislature should enact. As it had in the past, the South

Dakota legislature again rejected the amendment on 11 February for the fifth time. In 1941 a liberal Supreme Court sustained a new child labor law, and the child labor amendment is still pending today but unneeded because of more liberal Supreme Court decisions.[39]

At the same time, President Roosevelt initiated his Judiciary Reorganization bill to combat the adverse opinions of the Supreme Court that struck down his First New Deal programs. He dropped his bombshell on the nation on 5 February 1937, proposing a law permitting him to nominate up to fifty new federal judges.[40] His proposal touched off the greatest domestic battle of the New Deal thus far, as opponents immediately labeled it his "court-packing plan." Administration supporters argued that the framers of the Constitution never intended for the Supreme Court to exercise the power of judicial review, which was true. After a century and a half, however, the public had come to accept the procedure and wanted no political tinkering with their sacred cow. The proposal bogged down in the congressional judiciary committees. Chief Justice Hughes, with the support of Justices Van Devanter and Brandeis, produced a document amply demonstrating the "nine old men" were encountering no difficulty in keeping up with their docket. More judges would only increase delays.[41]

A "switch in time saves nine" changed the bill's prospects. Soon after FDR presented his proposal, the Court handed down a decision involving a Washington state minimum wage law. In *Morehead v. New York ex rel. Tipaldo*, Justice Owen Roberts joined the court's conservatives to strike down a state minimum wage law. One year later he switched sides and joined the chief justice and the three liberals to sustain an identical Washington state law.[42]

The Washington minimum wage decision presaged a change in court opinions and a return to its interpretations of regulation in the pre-New Deal era. This "Constitutional Revolution" was a rejection of the old "Liberty of Contract" concept precluding regulations. The Social Security provisions were upheld, especially its tax, on the basis of the general welfare clause in the Constitution.

A short time later the Court sustained the second AAA by extending congressional power over farming, even to the point where the agricultural produce never left the farm! By that time, of course, there had been retirements and changes in personnel on the Supreme Court, and it now became known as the "Roosevelt Court."[43]

Soon after the court fight, Roosevelt took steps that led to the "Roosevelt Recession." He sincerely believed in balancing the budget, but the private sector never managed to invest sufficiently in the economy to reduce unemployment significantly. In February 1937, he decided the time had come for fiscal restraint as the economy was recovering, however slightly, and unemployment had dropped significantly. Secretary of the Treasury Morgenthau persuaded him to cut back on relief "to take away the crutches to test whether the patient was able to walk by himself." The president was convinced he had whipped the depression and said so publicly, ordering the WPA to begin stretching its funds. A serious recession resulted that erased all the economic gains made since 1933.

When the Roosevelt Recession hit, FDR and his advisors immediately realized their mistake. The only answer was to reverse course and begin priming the pump again. But it was too late and it would take some time to regain what had been lost. Under pressure from Harry Hopkins, FDR increased spending by asking Congress in April to restore their cuts in relief funding. In addition, the Federal Housing Authority revived its lending policy to small homeowners, and the Farm Security Administration (FSA) began a new lending program to help marginal farmers to buy land on their own. In the summer of 1938 the Public Works Administration (PWA) "handed to cities and states . . . the first buckets of federal money . . . for priming industry's pumps under the huge spending-lending bill. . . . His pen strokes were the signal for the PWA and all federal spending agencies to swing into action."[44]

Senator Bulow deplored this infusion of relief funds, observing, "we can't afford to spend $4 billion every year in excess of our income." On the other hand, he noted, the nation had ten million idle men, and "some method must be made to care for them or a revolution is at hand." He finally concluded, "the new deal was probably the best solution to the economic problem at the time the administration took over the reins of government." Bulow warned of "rabble rousers" and specified Huey Long of Louisiana with his "share the wealth" plan, Francis E. Townsend and his old age pension program, and Father Charles E. Coughlin as being particularly dangerous. Perhaps "it was best the new deal stepped in," he concluded, because otherwise these demagogues "would have led the country to destruction." Further "pump-priming," at this point, though, he emphasized, was not the solution to the present crisis.[45]

In June 1938, Congress allotted almost $200 million to finance 300 PWA projects approved by the president. As the *Argus-Leader* expressed it, the PWA "handed to cities and states today the first bushels of federal money" under the new incentives. The first group of 2,000 more projects at a cost of $600 million were taken from "nearly 2,000 applications held over from the old PWA program of the last five years," which had been approved but held up "because of lack of funds."[46]

In October 1938, the administration announced the "largest peacetime budget" in history. The "bulk" of this money was directed toward WPA spending, PWA projects, and naval construction as part of the "preparedness" program. The PWA estimated that one job on one of its projects "creates two others in the private industries which supply the materials." Sioux Falls soon reported that the city spent $1,289,975 on new construction and improvement since 1938, including the new airport where the city and PWA combined to spend $202,073.[47]

One of the PWA's depression-era building projects created post offices throughout the country. In South Dakota, post offices were constructed at a cost of $75,000 to $80,000 in Beresford, Britton, Canton, Clark, Custer, Flandreau, Gettysburg, Howard, Miller, Parker, Sisseton, Spearfish, Tyndall, Wessington Springs, and a post office and courthouse annex in Pierre.[48] Another was highway construction. Many of the hundreds of miles of these roads were built to cross the state to connect the more populous eastern part to the west and the eastern part of the United States to the Black Hills in the promotion of the tourist industry.

Roosevelt planned to implement his increased government relief expenditures by asking Congress for $1.5 billion for 1 July 1937 to 1 July 1938. This, WPA officials were certain, would still mean a reduction, not an increase, in relief rolls. Their rolls had already been cut from 2,871,637 in 1936 to 2,114,790 in 1937, and "sharp reductions" might have to be made in 1939 as Congress was becoming restive over the continued relief spending. To cut the expected deficit of $2,652,654,000, the president ordered agencies to reduce future expenditures on 14 April, and he planned to send Congress revised budget estimates for fiscal years 1937 and 1938.

Congressional Democrats, led by Senator James Byrnes of South Carolina, a close advisor to the president, were proposing drastic cuts in relief spending. Because of continued drought, however, South Dakota needed increased relief spending, not reductions. Governor Jensen and his Social Security director, J. W. Kaye, sought a meeting with Hopkins when he came to the state. The governor called attention to the fact that "at least 41 counties" required more relief than they were receiving.[49]

Following his dedication of a new armory in Aberdeen, Hopkins announced that "several thousand needy South Dakota farmers" would receive work on WPA dam sites. He indicated that four thousand men would be employed "and the number might be increased as the need arises." "These families can rest assured," Hopkins said, "that we are going clear through with them and see they are given all the assistance possible."[50] But this assurance ignored the power of the legislative branch, and, in an economy drive in early 1938, Congress slashed almost four million dollars from the Tennessee Valley Authority budget and $123,669,000 from the CCC. This eliminated 412 CCC camps and reduced enrollees from 315,000 to 250,000. CCC director Robert Fechner planned to include camps in Roubaix, Deadwood, and two in Custer among those to be closed, which would further hurt South Dakota.[51]

The South Dakota Supreme Court definitely hamstrung one effort in the state to provide relief for unemployment. Minnehaha County commissioners agreed to pay 8.3 percent of the costs of materials for a certain project. The circuit judge determined that the state statutes providing for the support and relief of the poor were sufficiently broad to authorize this type of support. When the Minnehaha County auditor was ordered to approve the payment, however, he appealed, with the argument that he was not authorized to make such a payment. The state supreme court agreed with him, noting that "the duty to relieve and support the poor is expressed in general terms," but "the mode and nature of the relief extended [in this instance] is not left entirely to the judgment and discretion" of the county commissioners. There was nothing in the statute that "points to the intention that the county engage in activities . . . to the promotion of other welfare programs."[52]

This decision prompted Governor Jensen to solicit the opinion of legislators on the advisability of calling a special session of the legislature for the purpose of authorizing the use of county funds to sponsor WPA activities and amending the current Aid to Dependent Children (ADC) to meet the federal demand for a two-thirds matching contribution. He noted the county commissioners association had requested that the special session be called for these purposes, and he refused to accept responsibility for any suffering caused by the failure to declare an emergency.[53]

To offset the need for a special session, Jensen approached the attorney general for his opinion, but he could uncover "no loopholes" whereby counties could directly assist WPA projects. However, this did not conflict with the authorization to construct highways and dams, he added, because spending in these categories saved the "employees from becoming or continuing to be county charges." He failed to note that county spending to promote a WPA project also would help save the workers from becoming "charges."[54]

Jensen announced that he would travel to Washington to confer about federal programs in his state. He planned to talk to the Social Security board to complete the details of the state's ADC program. He also was desirous of obtaining funds to complete the state's WPA projects. At this point, the state had saved enough from its inadequate funding of the children's program to provide ADC. The current law in South Dakota, he noted, had to be amended so that the state would provide two-thirds of the stipend, rather than one-half as the legislature erroneously established it. Jensen would undoubtedly have to confer with these officials before he could call a special legislative session. By this time the political season was upon South Dakotans.[55]

The year 1937 revealed a WPA worker's financial situation that posed an interesting legal question. Fred Most of Aberdeen received credit in 1936 with grocer Peter Schneider but evaded payment of his bill. When he received his WPA job he promised to pay such bills with his relief checks, as required by administration rules. E. J. B. Longrie, state deputy WPA administrator, wrote Most that he had to work out an arrangement to pay his debt in full or make some type of an arrangement with Schneider for installments or he would have his WPA employment certification cancelled. Ervine Lavine, business agent for Unit 416 of the Workers Alliance of America (WAA), protested this action, asking Harry Hopkins if WPA regulations authorized it to become a collection agency. If this were true, WAA "strongly protested" the ruling. In this part of the country, Lavine informed Hopkins, the current WPA wage scale made it almost impossible for a worker "with a family of any size to keep out of debt." He acknowledged that "there are always a few individuals who continue to chisel on any agency of help," but this policy represented a dangerous "precedent." The policy was continued.[56]

Jensen's Republican administration decided to make some alterations in the Democratic welfare policies. Kennedy discussed these changes via telephone with Jensen and immediately wrote

Harry Hopkins to warn him before the new governor traveled to Washington to ask Hopkins to increase the WPA quota in South Dakota. Hopkins told Jensen that he had informed Field Representative Howard Hunter that the quota assigned South Dakota was "large enough to provide employment for the certified urban workers." Kennedy also warned Hopkins that Jensen would ask his permission to employ women who were eligible for mothers' pensions. He acknowledged there were precedents for this because, during "a portion" of 1936, WPA had "weakened" and given work to such women. It was a temporary solution to the financial situation in many counties that had reduced funds for mothers' pensions on the grounds that they were financed by "a direct property tax" which many property owners were unable to pay. On the other hand, some mothers were destitute and needed help immediately. In Kennedy's opinion, it was "highly inadvisable" to take these women out of their homes and place them in a WPA job and leave "minor children neglected." His only solution for this dilemma was for the counties to meet their obligation to these poor women. Jensen would probably request permission to employ "former farm operators and farm laborers residing in towns and cities." Kennedy supported this line of action and had already recommended it to Hunter. His purpose in alerting Hopkins was, if the latter granted these requests, he thought this should be expedited "previous to the governor's visit" because "from the administration viewpoint," the "publicity would be better adjusted prior to his visit."[57]

The issue of mothers' pensions was further clouded by Harry Hopkins's telegram to state WPA officials on 7 March 1937 about employees terminated because of the dependent children benefit provisions under the new Social Security Act of 1935. Kennedy wrote for a clarification of this new policy because the national board had not yet approved South Dakota's legislative implementation plan for the new program. As a result, his WPA administration had not yet terminated any worker under the new approach. The primary difference between South Dakota's old program for mothers' pensions and the new Social Security system was that the old plan was not being fully implemented because of the impoverishment of the counties through delinquent taxes. The Mothers' Pensions program also required county judges to determine eligibility as well as recommend to the county commissioners the amount of the monthly pension. David K. Niles responded for the WPA that employment benefits would continue to be available to mothers until the state began participating in Social Security and then, of course, neither this employment nor the Mothers' Pension would be necessary.[58]

March also saw changes in the financial branch of the WPA in South Dakota. After discussing the problems of coordinating the treasury accounts and disbursing activities, Kennedy wrote the assistant WPA administrator that he wished to make changes in the state system. He wanted to close the treasury branch offices in Pierre and Rapid City that month. If the alteration in district lines as approved by Aubrey Williams the previous December became effective, then Kennedy could provide a liaison officer for the treasury office in Watertown. The national WPA recommended mailing checks directly to workers, but he objected. His experience was that this policy delayed delivery of paychecks. Corrington Gill of the national office approved of Kennedy's requests, including not directly mailing checks "at this time."[59]

Congressman Fred Hildebrandt directed a long-standing personal complaint to Harry Hopkins. He complained of being "embarrassed" on several occasions when he returned to his hometown of Watertown by the disrespectful conduct of J. A. Grande, chief WPA accountant there, toward him. The congressman was unhappy that his efforts to recommend people for positions in Grande's office were repeatedly rebuffed. Hildebrandt learned that job applicants were asked by assistants in Grande's office if "they had been politically active, made political speeches, or assisted in organizing political groups." He considered these procedures to be "rather far-fetched and unethical." Hildebrandt asked Hopkins to remove men in that office "who have made themselves obnoxious," but Hopkins's office responded that the treasury department, not the WPA, was responsible for selecting the personnel, and he would have to pursue the issue with that office.[60] Disappointed that Hopkins could not "bring about harmonious cooperation," Hildebrandt continued to complain. Aubrey Williams graciously responded that the NYA was under his direction and he invited the congressman "to come down and talk to me about it."[61]

At the end of 1937, the South Dakota League of Municipalities sponsored a survey that produced interesting results. Earl Strathman, research director at the University of South Dakota, conducted the study, and Lyle Ford reported his findings on fifty towns and cities in south-central South Dakota. Many towns, especially the smaller ones, he reported, had "large warrant indebtedness caused by . . . the large amount of delinquent taxes." Because of this, the cities had been "forced to register warrants to meet current expenses." They also were delinquent on repayments of bonds and interest obligations. There had been "a rapid increase in the taking of property" through county tax sales that endangered their credit. This increased the tax burden on those who managed to keep their taxes paid. He believed the situation would "continue to grow worse . . . until times change" and "the problem of delinquent taxes disappear." In the counties most heavily hit, "many families" were leaving their farms and moving to town. There had also been "a decided increase in the amount [number] of people leaving the state." On the other hand, this area of the state had not been "most severely attacked by the drought."[62]

The streets and public property commissioner of Yankton reported to his mayor that unemployment would increase there in "the next three or four months" because businesses had ceased hiring and construction "was at a standstill." He estimated that one hundred men and women between eighteen and twenty-two, seventy-five widows with children, and 350 married men were seeking employment. Garbage collectors reported two and three families living in one residence. The latter included many who had lost their farms due to crop failures. He believed the current WPA requirement for cities to contribute to projects should be lessened because of the inability to subsidize programs, and he recommended establishing part-time work projects to keep people "pacified until such time as they can find regular employment."[63]

The director for Social Security for Yankton County reported 184 recipients of Old-Age and Survivors Insurance (OASI) were receiving $14.87 monthly and another twenty applicants were pending verification of birthplace and date. The county had 250 persons on WPA projects and 100 others certified who were currently employed privately. He estimated an additional application of fifty in the "next thirty days." There were forty youths assigned to the NYA. The CCC should accept twenty-five men for January but thus far only seven had applied. Finally, the county supplied 480 families containing 1,286 members with "surplus foods and clothing as needed."[64]

Huron city manager Dow I. Sears wrote Governor Jensen, currently in Washington seeking WPA funding, of the financial condition in Huron. He and the city commission supported the governor's quest for lowering the sponsors' contribution to projects. Beadle County had recently endured "another complete crop failure," and "in the past two months" business had increased unemployment. He wished the governor success in securing "some relief."[65]

The WPA proved to be a godsend to every community it touched. Even tiny Presho benefited from the program in ways other than increased tourism. WPA built a large garage to house the county road maintenance equipment and, more importantly, a swimming pool the town would never have built at this time without federal assistance. Swimming was a favorite summer recreation and this municipal federal project, completed in 1938, "gave hundreds of children . . . a healthy recreational outlet" and the opportunity to learn on their own how to swim.[66]

It was not until early 1937 that South Dakotans began thinking seriously of securing a federal music program under WPA auspices. Gail T. Kubik, director of the Philharmonic Symphony at Dakota Wesleyan University, telegraphed the national office that South Dakota could qualify "between forty and sixty" musicians for the project who were currently working in adult education. He believed "a small symphony orchestra entirely possible." State authorities had pledged "full cooperation" with the idea, and Kubik asked about the process for obtaining WPA approval. Howard Hanson of the Eastman School of Music in Rochester, New York, wrote in support of Kubik's proposal. Kubik was an Eastman graduate, "an excellent violinist," and "a decidedly gifted composer," as well as having "considerable conducting talent," he noted. The national office, after investigation, reported an insufficient number of persons "to warrant the establishment of such a unit."[67]

A year later, Kennedy made another attempt, submitting a list of sixty-seven persons "classified as musicians." He cautioned that a majority were "widely scattered and distances in our state are very great." He assured the national office, however, that he was personally supportive of the concept, but they responded with the "insufficient funding" argument.[68]

Writers also had serious problems earning a livelihood during the depression, and unemployed ones needed help. The Federal Writers Project displayed more sympathy for the predicament of unemployed writers than the proposal for musicians had received. Organizations across the state proved eager to become sponsors. In late 1935, Ethel Dowdell, who had been a high school history and English teacher, told newspaperman Lisle Reese about the Federal Writers Project. On 21 October, he received a telegram offering him the position of part-time director of the state unit at $1.50 per diem, not to exceed twelve days monthly. He reported to Mike Kennedy, who greeted him "warmly," recalling his story the previous winter of "airlifting food supplies to West River ranchers marooned in a blizzard."[69]

The first major project was to develop a state guide. It would consist of "a few essays and a section on major cities" and half would cover "mile by mile tours of all key highways," along the lines of the famous Baedeker tours of Europe. No limits were placed on the number of persons assigned to the project, and Reese decided on "a few writers in each of the larger cities" and a field staff to cover small towns and highways. His Sioux friends were eager to write Indian legends, and the staff began publishing *MSS*, a monthly periodical of poetry, prose, and artwork. "Work on the state guidebook moved slowly and unsteadily," but because the WPA funds were to be spent on the writers rather than publication costs, Reese and his staff were forced to appeal to the state legislature for this funding.[70]

The session in 1937 approved $2,000 for a revolving fund to print 2,000 copies of the *Guide* to sell for two dollars each. Legislators described it as "frivolous," and the governor let it become law without his signature. A 1939 report noted that 4,000 copies of the *Guide* had been distributed and "a second edition is likely." The guide was followed by a *Vacation Guide to Custer State Park*. Kennedy reported to Ellen Woodward that 12,254 hours were spent on the *Guide* with an expenditure of $8,696.60 for the six-month period ending 31 December 1937. One of the great achievements of this project was to initiate a place-names study of the state published in 1944. The University of South Dakota later acquired this project and continued and expanded on it.[71]

The year 1938 proved to be the zenith of WPA work in South Dakota. America was still recovering from the "Roosevelt Recession" and the orders for war material from Europe were just beginning to arrive. These distressed conditions led to the growth of the need for WPA work and an increase in the letters of grievance. When Ralph Wilhelm of the WAA complained of low pay on WPA projects, the national office reminded him that pay scales were determined by the state WPA office in Mitchell and should be addressed to them. Wilhelm proceeded to write Nels Anderson, national WPA director of labor relations, that Michael Kennedy and James R. Kerper,

South Dakota director of employment, were "passing the buck." Kerper's response to complaints such as this was to point out that the men "were satisfied or they would not have accepted their checks." When they held their state WAA convention in March, Wilhelm warned, farmers and laborers were "going to combine their forces." He enclosed the recent letter he had received from Kerper, who noted that carpenters, electricians, and plumbers were "paid 80 cents, [90] cents, and one dollar" respectively. The disagreement was over classification, therefore, with men claiming to be journeymen carpenters receiving only fifty cents. Kepler wrote in the margin that these men received forty cents, not fifty, and complained of this to their foremen.[72]

That summer the state WPA again temporarily suspended its workers because they were needed for the harvest. This move helped farmers who were seeking workers and also permitted the state WPA to stretch its meager funds. The WAA denounced this reasonable procedure, noting that no one could be denied WPA employment where wages and working conditions were similar to WPA work, but farm wages were much lower. This did not include "the mere belief or opinion of some WPA official that private employment might be available." A handwritten note at the bottom of the page said that David Niles would "get further information" on the issue.[73]

Niles also received a complaint from the WAA about workers being forced to travel long distances without pay for their project in Aberdeen. Niles asked for Kennedy's response to this objection, and he replied that Brown County commissioners wanted the dam built thirty miles north of the town, but by Aberdeen men. Kennedy had objected to the long commute time and rejected their proposal. The commissioners sent a delegation to Washington to protest his decision but received no redress. The state later overrode him and approved the project that employed "from 100 to 200 men for a year." Kennedy reported that there had been very little complaint locally, and he believed that "at least ninety-five percent of the persons are satisfied with the present arrangement."[74]

Much of the WPA work in western South Dakota included building dams. C. W. Anderson, WPA regional engineer, inspected these seventeen dams in a 900-mile trip and assessed the construction as excellent. In addition, he insisted that the qualifications of the engineer of the Avon sewer system indicated that he was capable of being "used to much better advantage on some larger project." On the other hand, the Rosebud Indian Agency buildings of chalk rock quarried near the Missouri River "could be better organized." The state capitol building was settling at an alarming rate because of shale movement inclining toward the Missouri River, and the WPA workers stabilized the rotunda with cement. The remainder of the huge building continued to shift around the rotunda, causing cracks and other damage. The walls were plastered over and painted a muckle dun. Decades later, when this paint was removed, it was discovered that the WPA workers had covered up beautiful murals of classical artwork.

In the same region, the Pierre airport was being improved and expanded. Sully Lake, built in 1925, was expanded and improved by the Civil Works Administration (CWA), the Federal Emergency Relief Administration (FERA), and the Works Progress Administration (WPA), but still lacked a proper spillway. Anderson recommended the Cheyenne Creek Reservoir become a WPA project because Potter County was willing to assist in its construction. Finally, he found the Kadoka school building and the Quinn high school and gymnasium to be "tremendous assets" to their communities. This survey reveals extensive WPA contributions to West River country in terms of significant employment and also major lasting contributions to the lifestyle of its inhabitants.[75]

Congressman Francis Case wrote Harry Hopkins about the problems of the central counties of West River and of "the considerable distress through burned crops and grasshoppers." The commissioners of Ziebach County had appealed for his help, and Case noted that Meade, Perkins, and Corson Counties were also suffering, and he was requesting WPA assistance. David Niles responded that farmers could receive assistance from the RA, but when they did, they became ineligible for WPA employment.[76]

In mid-October, Governor Jensen received happy news from Aubrey Williams that South Dakota had a remaining balance of $11,497 for relief purposes. After looking for the best place to apply these funds, Jensen discovered that the state appropriation for transporting and warehousing surplus commodities was insufficient, and that money would be exhausted by December. It "would be of invaluable assistance to South Dakota's needy," Jensen wrote, "to be able to transfer $11,000 of these funds for this purpose, especially to a dozen West River counties" that had reached "the legal limit of their indebtedness" and could not fund distribution of these commodities. Kennedy endorsed Jensen's idea, except he wanted to defer this change until the transfer "of the much disputed relief records" of the FERA program accompanied the exchange.[77]

Kennedy continued to insist that the new Social Security administration in Pierre take responsibility for all "books, records and accounts of the State Emergency Relief Administration as well as the assets and liabilities." This would require an employee familiar with the records and proper reporting in order for that person "to intelligently answer" disputed claims questions, transfers from FERA accounts to the RA, and other financial transactions. With his office in Mitchell and the Social Security office in Pierre, someone on his staff could not "efficiently do this work." Jensen, in turn, reported the reluctance of the Social Security administration to accept responsibility for the files because "they know nothing concerning the condition of these records; they may or may not be complete." They were, however, willing to "simply take them over and give them storage space in the basement of the State Capitol Building."[78]

The *Argus-Leader* tried to make a great mystery of these records. The newspaper carried a story about former governor Berry and "numerous Democratic leaders [who] met in a closed door

session at the St. Charles hotel until 1:30 one morning" soon after the election of 1936. Two truckloads of relief records were then
loaded and left for Chicago. "The assumption in Pierre" was that
the Democratic leaders sent the records out of state for safekeeping
to preclude a Republican investigation of them. Another story held
that "three truckloads of relief records which disappeared from a
Pierre Schoolhouse" were "shipped by freight" to Harry Hopkins.
The stories caused "considerable consternation in state Republican ranks" because of the widespread apprehension that they were
removed to prevent an investigation of the relief activities of the
Berry administration. The Republican-controlled senate chose to
investigate the episode in the belief that the outgoing administration was trying to conceal something. Oreen Reudi, director of
social services for the state public welfare commission under the
Berry regime, testified that Governor Berry ordered the removal
of the twenty-five tons of records. The records eventually were returned to Mitchell but this did not end the story.[79]

P. L. Crowlie, state welfare commissioner, testified that he knew
of no one except Louise Kubler, FERA disbursing officer, who had
anything to do with these records. Kubler accompanied the records
to Sioux City, then back to Mitchell. She first testified that she
moved the records herself because she was under a $5,000 bond
and "wanted to be relieved of any responsibility in connection of
the records." Kubler further testified that the records belonged to
her boss, Harry Hopkins, and she believed they should be sent to
him with federal funds at her disposal to pay for the transportation.
She remained in a Sioux City motel with the records for three days
and denied having consulted the governor about their disposal.
When asked why she moved the records, Kubler responded that
she had heard "several times" that "the records were loaded with
dynamite and should be gotten out of Pierre before the Republicans got in." She also consulted with Mike Kennedy, and he told
her, "I don't care. I am through with them."[80]

At a later hearing, the story began to change. Ruedi testified that she had talked to Kubler after the latter returned from Sioux City, and he told her that Tom Berry had "ordered the records removed from the state." She further charged that Berry had "gone back on her" because he wired Senator Hitchcock about the matter, telling him that Kubler was responsible for moving the records and "left her holding the bag." She again described staying in a Sioux City motel for three days, with $20,000 in shipping funds, while others debated the issue of what to do with the records.

Reudi charged that E. H. Bremer, Berry's secretary, asked her after the election to have county welfare directors process pension applications quickly in order to deplete the pension fund so there would be no money remaining for Republicans to distribute. From late November to early December, she said, the number of pensions rose from 5,720 to 10,160. She had recently been fired for criticism of the program and because she was "impudent." Perhaps this accounts for her antagonistic attitude; or possibly she was being honest. No evidence surfaced either way. In any case, Kennedy, who knew as well as anyone what the records contained, ordered them sent to Mitchell and the $20,000 deposited in a Pierre bank.[81] It is curious that the records remained in Pierre for some time and the Republicans made no effort to exploit them, other than this minor senate investigating committee that found nothing amiss.[82]

These FERA records remained an albatross around the neck of Kennedy neck and later administrators. In March 1939, Senator John Chandler ("Chan") Gurney wrote the WPA that the fourteen tons of records stored in a bonded warehouse in Mitchell needed to be moved to the basement of the capitol building to end the drain on the remaining $11,000 fund. Gurney offered to forward the sixteen sheets, letters, and resolutions on disposing of this issue.

A few weeks later, Kennedy wrote Howard Hunter a confidential letter on the question. For economic reasons, he wanted to move the treasury office from Watertown to his WPA office in Mitchell. He was not "particularly concerned" about helping Mitchell but thought the centralization would be a good move and space was available. He had considered moving his office to Watertown and relocating it, as well as the treasury office, to the federal building, but the latter was "badly in need of repair" and the maintenance expenses would be too great. Actually, the improving economy would provide an answer, as the program slowly shut down thereafter.[83]

9 The Third New Deal
and the Preparation for War

But in '38, why, here was that one little spear [of grass]; you could
find it if you looked real sharp. But it all came back, every bit of it. It
all came back in '38 and nine.
                    Arthur F. McKinstry[1]

HISTORIANS CONVENIENTLY DIVIDE the New Deal into
the first phase of the Hundred Days session and the second phase with the new programs taking the nation in a different
direction with work relief, the Wagner Act (which authorized the
National Labor Relations Board), Social Security in 1935, and for
farmers, the Soil Conservation and Domestic Allotment Act of
1936. The chief beneficiaries of the First New Deal were businessmen and large farmers; small farmers and laborers benefitted from
the Second Deal. Some historians write of a Third New Deal running from 1937 to 1940, which included cutbacks to relief, the subsequent Roosevelt Recession, and the slow, painful recovery from
it, with the specter of war looming. This was a period in which "the
active New Deal was effectively over."[2]

While the Soil Conservation Act improved farming techniques
and soils, it did not address the basic problem Henry A. Wallace
wanted to resolve. Storing up surpluses during good years as a reserve for meeting the needs of the drought years became the basis of his second Agricultural Adjustment Administration (AAA).

Funding for the new AAA would come from the general treasury, eliminating the processing tax of the first AAA. If a surplus threatened, the secretary of agriculture was empowered to establish marketing quotas. After two-thirds of the farmers involved approved these quotas, which made the program voluntary, they would receive acreage allotments. They would receive "parity" payments based on the 1909–1914 period for restricting their production to their allowed acreage. By restricting production to acreage, rather than bushels, of course, surpluses continued through the rest of the century as farmers accelerated their use of insecticides, pesticides, and fertilizers to increase production.[3]

The second AAA, enacted 16 February 1938, also established the Federal Crop Insurance Corporation, capitalized at $100 million, where farmers could insure their crops. It covered losses due to unavoidable causes, ranging from 50 percent to 75 percent of the average yield. The program initially covered wheat, providing badly needed income for Wheat Belt people to pay taxes and to maintain a decent standard of living for their families. This proved so successful that it was later extended to other crops. Again, as with earlier farm legislation, these programs catered largely to large farmers and their organization, the American Farm Bureau Federation (AFBF).[4]

Farmers eventually organized to recover the tax money that had been paid under the first AAA processing tax. In August 1937, Representative William Lemke of North Dakota introduced legislation to allow farmers to retrieve the tax. Deloss B. Gurney decided to use his powerful radio station and influence to support this movement. Although he had opposed the AAA, he viewed this as an opportunity to assist South Dakota farmers. It would not only be a good public relations maneuver, and Gurney was a real showman, but it would also promote his seed and nursery business because farmers would spend some of the money with him. Long-time listeners regarded him as a personal friend. One wrote him, "I have heard you so many times on the radio that I feel I know you real well."[5]

Farmers could join his recovery program by gathering their receipts from the period when the plan was in effect. Gurney included both those who had enrolled in the plan and those who had not, insisting there was no distinction between the two groups with regard to prices they had received for their hogs. The respondents were to list the number of hogs sold, the purchaser, the hogs' total weight, and the total tax. They had to pay Gurney a filing fee and agree to pay him a 6 percent fee if the tax were refunded. With this lapse of time, producing the receipts was occasionally difficult. They were lost or burned, and purchasers were not completely responsive in producing duplicates. Often farmers received a reply from the solicitor general of the Department of Agriculture, quoted in *Wallaces' Farmer*, that trying to recover processing taxes was illegal. Non-signers had great difficulty in proving the claim, but participants also faced the same problem when their county agents quoted the solicitor's opinion and refused to cooperate.[6]

Delegates to the South Dakota Republican Convention in 1938 demanded a return of the tax in their platform. Gurney's son, John Chandler ("Chan") Gurney, had been campaigning that year for the U.S. Senate seat on the issue of failure of the New Deal. When he won and headed off to Washington, the elder Gurney became concerned that his activity might constitute a conflict of interest for his son, so he began diminishing his role in promoting the tax recovery scheme. He turned over his accounts to the National Farmers Process Tax Recovery Association and arranged to forward all future correspondence to that group. Chan Gurney continued his father's efforts in the Senate, but the hog tax refund never overcame the hurdle of the absence of congressional approval because the major farm organizations declined to support it. Producers of cotton and tobacco, however, had powerful Southern support and succeeded in obtaining their refund. The hog processing tax eventually fell victim to the nation's Preparedness Program and concern over World War II developments and was never recovered.[7]

Chan Gurney's emerging success in politics proved to be a

problem for governor Leslie Jensen. He had an important decision to make as the 1938 elections approached. Though favored to win reelection to the governor's seat, he decided instead to try for the Senate seat once held by Peter Norbeck until his death and filled temporarily by Berry's appointee, Herbert Hitchcock. In his announcement for candidacy he declared that he was "in as good a position as any to carry the clear picture of South Dakota to Washington." Chan Gurney defeated him and three other challengers in the Republican primary, while Harlan Bushfield was elected to the open gubernatorial position. Bushfield was a lawyer from Miller, father of three children, and had served three years as the party chair.[8] Former congressman Charles A. Christopherson of Sioux Falls became the new party chair.

In an address to primary delegates, Bushfield expressed great concern about taxation, noting, "much has been said about reduction in taxes but nothing is ever done about it." He wanted his party to write its plank on economy to "mean something" by promising to cut taxes and then do it. "Until we have more money to spend," the state must reduce the work it did and he was ready to campaign on this issue.[9]

The Democratic defeat of 1936 had "shattered the Berry machine," leaving the path open for the progressive wing to dominate in 1938. Oscar Fosheim won the party's primary race for governor and Emil Loriks became the candidate for Congress in the Second District, after defeating five other candidates. Fred Hildebrandt decided to take advantage of the multiplicity of political candidates for the major offices that year to challenge Berry in the primary for Senator Norbeck's seat. Hildebrandt observed, "The reactionary elements are gathering their forces for a drive to discredit the Roosevelt forces and democrats cannot afford to expend any energy quarreling among themselves." At their state meeting, the Democrats adopted a platform pledging "a drastic reduction" in state government costs. They also condemned Bushfield for "loading the administration of old age assistance with an army of political appointees," insisting that 20 percent of state costs for this program were used for administration. Democrats pledged to reduce the sales tax to 2 percent at the next legislative session and eventually "to eliminate it entirely." They believed "demobilizing the army of state employees to actual business requirements" was a solution to overspending. They also wanted to sell rural credit lands in family-sized tracts "with small down payments."[10]

The Senate race was complicated by the fact that the few months remaining of the late Senator Norbeck's term were now open in the election, as well as the full six-year term. By law, Chan Gurney could not run for both the short-term and long-term positions. Tom Berry won the primary and faced off against Chan Gurney for the six-year Senate seat, while, after losing to Gurney in the primary, Governor Jensen decided to run for the few months remaining in the Senate term held by Herbert Hitchcock. He lost again, defeated this time by Republican Gladys Pyle of Huron, who became the first female senator from South Dakota. Pyle, whose parents were early suffragists, was baptized into politics at an early age and experienced many "firsts." She was South Dakota's first female secretary of state, and her election to the U.S. Senate, while brief, gave her a remarkable distinction nevertheless. She took office immediately, but did not actually attend a session since the Senate was in recess during her short tenure.

Karl E. Mundt began a thirty-six-year career in the national government by defeating Loriks for the East River seat in Congress.[11] Francis H. Case had little difficulty in defeating Theodore B. Werner, the man whom he replaced in 1936, for the western seat in the House of Representatives. This left William J. Bulow the sole Democrat to represent South Dakota in Washington.

Good weather greeted the voters, producing a near-record turnout on Election Day. The "approval or disapproval" of the New Deal, concluded the *Argus-Leader*, appeared to be "the main issue for South Dakota voters." This campaign also witnessed the first charges of Communism hurled by Karl Mundt against his opponent,

Emil Loriks, in the race for the eastern seat of the House of Representatives, an issue that would turn ugly in future campaigns.[12]

The GOP candidates, riding a solid majority in Minnehaha County, swept the state. No admirer of the New Deal, Bushfield defeated Fosheim for the governor's seat by a substantial margin, completing the Republican sweep of state offices begun in 1936. The election was interpreted as a solid rejection of the New Deal in South Dakota, although an impartial observer would wonder why, after all the New Dealers had done to save them from starvation, they would repudiate their benefactors.

Republicans attained an overwhelming majority in the state legislature, garnering 30 of the 35 senate seats and 62 of the 75 house positions (after the passage of a constitutional amendment in 1936 to decrease the size of the legislature). Friction was exposed within the Republican Party when Jensen announced his nominees for state office on his last day, which led Bushfield to make his own appointees that afternoon following his inauguration.[13]

By 1938 the drought was breaking, and the Republicans and some leading Democrats were becoming more willing to curtail relief spending. As the nation began producing war materials and a preparedness program of its own, Congress became increasingly inclined to cut relief funding and reduced President Roosevelt's deficiency appropriations request from $879 million for Works Progress Administration (WPA) funding to $725 million in 1938. He asked for an additional $150 million to avoid "drastic reduction" of WPA employment and a stingy Congress slashed this to $100 million. These reductions especially hurt the agricultural state of South Dakota where serious depression continued for both urban laborers and rural farmers.

Colonel Francis C. Harrington, who replaced Harry L. Hopkins as head of the WPA when the latter was promoted to Secretary of Commerce, expressed opposition to a provision in the Senate bill to prevent political activities of WPA workers. Harrington had no problem restricting supervisory personnel in this pursuit, but insisted it should not apply to relief workers. Solons also provided for a formula for determining relief funds that would strip WPA administrators of all discretionary powers to allocate them. The administration forces lost by one vote in the Senate in an attempt to restore the cut.[14]

As WPA was winding down in 1939, Michael A. Kennedy wrote Harrington a confidential letter alerting him to the impending visit of George Fredericks, mayor of Mitchell, and "ex-Senator [Herbert] Hitchcock." Hitchcock, he wrote, "was a good friend of the WPA, both nationally and in the state," and the mission of the two was to get the treasury office moved to Mitchell. Kennedy supported the men's effort because his WPA office was already located in Mitchell, and we "have very satisfactory quarters which are rent free." If the move were made, the state WPA administration could realize a monthly savings of at least $500 in administrative expenses, a not inconsiderable amount given the cutbacks in funding that WPA was enduring. Savings actually could be more than this, he said, because the treasury office in Watertown was "paying $415 monthly" for rent, plus electricity, "and that expenditure could be reduced by at least $250 monthly.[15]

By September 1939, the WPA cutbacks were really hurting the state. Francis Case wrote to Fred Rauch, the national director of WPA employment, that "representatives of several counties" had visited Governor Bushfield with their concerns. Case believed some counties in western South Dakota should be placed on an emergency basis because of the drought. "Conditions in Custer, Pennington, and Fall River were the toughest I have ever seen," he reported. "They had no threshing." War orders "in some industrial districts" had not helped South Dakota because "we have no war industries." Case hoped that increased private employment in those areas would "enable you to adjust quotas to meet our situation."[16]

Kennedy soon received authorization to employ an additional 3,000 people, plus an increase "in our regular operating quota for December." This increase would have "some bearing on retail business in the state," which needed stimulation because the mild winter so far had caused "a number of merchants" to complain about not selling "overcoats, overshoes, and other items of winter apparel." He reported "approximately the same number of persons leaving our program to accept private employment as there are returning to us from private employment." This meant that the increase in the WPA quota was vital. "About the only serious criticism" being received from those whose employment had been terminated was the low standard the state legislature set for unemployment compensation of three dollars weekly under the Social Security Act.[17]

Roosevelt instructed WPA officials to remain within this sum as far as they could. One plan to do this involved rotating the personnel. They planned to replace those who had longest seniority with individuals on the waiting list. If not in the current bill, concerned legislators agreed this formula might be implemented in the next appropriation. Those opposed to weeding out employees favored eliminating the least necessary projects. The growing war preparedness program and increasing private employment in war industries would eliminate the necessity of making this difficult choice. Most importantly, the terrible drought and dust storm patterns had been broken, and South Dakota farmers could again begin to produce. Agricultural production would resume its rightful place in South Dakota's economy in time for the war effort.[18]

From 1938 to 1942, federal relief was curtailed, agricultural production slowly improved, and, step by step, the United States became involved in war production for World War II. The conflict produced real agrarian prosperity for the first time in two decades. At the time this prosperity arrived, citizens were still moving to Oregon and California. Twelve of the West River counties lost 20 percent of their population between 1930 and 1940. The exception was Pennington County, with Rapid City as its center. This outmigration continued in 1942 when good-paying jobs emerged in war production on the West Coast and elsewhere.[19]

In South Dakota, Bushfield, a serious conservative, was re-elected to a second term in 1940, defeating Lewis W. Bicknell, and was elected in 1942 to the U.S. Senate. He died in office; his wife Vera was appointed to complete the last few months of his term.

The depression had struck European countries also, in varying degrees. In Germany, Adolf Hitler came to power in January 1933, and his Nazi party built superhighways and remilitarized, giving his people both guns and butter, to end their depression. Benito Mussolini and his Fascists captured the Italian government a decade earlier and also began militaristic ventures during the depression. So, too, did the militants in Japan. These three authoritarian countries took advantage of the depressed economic conditions of their neighbors to initiate waves of aggression under the guise of ideological promotion. In 1931, Japan invaded Manchuria and six years later attacked Nanking in China. In 1935, Mussolini launched an attack on Ethiopia and the following year Hitler remilitarized the Rhineland.

Victims fell to these aggressors one by one, and most nations allied with one side or the other until by 1939 the world was divided between the Axis of Germany, Italy, and Japanese aggressors with their conquests, and the Allies, with America in the middle, trying to maintain its neutrality. This American effort became much more difficult after Hitler invaded Poland in September 1939, thus igniting the war worldwide. The U.S. continued its preparedness program and this, plus greatly increased sales to the belligerents, eventually brought industrial America out of the depression. This was not true in agrarian South Dakota until the weather cycles changed, the rain began to fall, and improved agricultural production began to find markets after 1939. South Dakotans enjoyed the increasing foreign markets but kept a wary eye on the burgeoning hostilities, maintaining a staunch isolationism and insisting that Roosevelt keep the nation aloof from foreign conflicts.[20]

In the fall of 1939, the *Mitchell Daily Republic* quoted Governor

Bushfield as saying he was "cheered about the economic situation" in South Dakota, which he said was "rapidly improving." Practically all types of business "showed an increase," he said, and the economic picture "is becoming brighter each day."[21]

The New Deal had been assisting cities in construction of airports for some time. The Federal Emergency Relief Administration (FERA), Civil Works Administration (CWA), and Public Works Administration (PWA) had provided financial help for construction of runways if the city owned or leased its airport and, in the case of FERA and CWA, used relief rolls for labor. Partly because of its pioneering nature and partly because of the great distance between cities, South Dakota was in the vanguard of developing the aviation industry. In 1935, the state legislature created the South Dakota Aeronautical Commission (SDAC). The SDAC began work during the greatest economic crisis in American history, at the same time as the New Deal was ready to lend a helping hand in aviation development through its public works programs and national security needs. Aviation in South Dakota and elsewhere had actually received its greatest initial stimulus through mail contracts. The preparedness program further stimulated the business, and by 1936 the state boasted twenty-seven airports, eighty-three registered pilots, and eighty-four registered airplanes.[22]

In 1937, the SDAC recommended that the aviation fuel tax be earmarked for aviation purposes rather than rural credit bond interest. The state treasurer would determine the amount of fuel sold, collect the tax, and transfer that amount to the State Aeronautics Fund for use in operating the SDAC or maintaining airports. President Roosevelt signed the Civil Aeronautics Act in 1938, establishing the independent Civil Aeronautics Board (CAB). The law terminated the old contract-airmail system and replaced it with a negotiated certificate system whereby holders could carry both passengers and airmail. The CAB's three-member Air Safety Board regulated air traffic control, pilot and aircraft certification, and enforcement of safety regulations. This proved to be a boon to many smaller municipal airports. Of the 662 airport sites approved, 461 were in cities with populations under 5,000.[23]

Later in the decade, the largest cities at each end of the state sought to build airports through PWA funding and WPA labor. In February 1938, the Sioux Falls mayor announced that work would begin on a hanger and runways on the flats north of the city. This development, in turn, should assure the attraction of an air route that had previously refused to come to Sioux Falls because of lack of lighted facilities, bringing a resumption of airmail service. A WPA flood-control project for the low-lying area would assure PWA approval and completion of the airport.[24]

In keeping with the trend of WPA officials to approve requests for their paid labor for airport construction, Rapid City officials pursued a project to obtain $25,000 for this purpose. A vote of 60 percent approval was required for their $30,000 bond issue. This would assure Rapid City of becoming an airmail stop and improve its chances for future federal grants for urban improvements. In selling the bond issue, city officials stressed that "airports soon will be as necessary as railroad depots or other transportation facilities."[25]

South Dakota managed to keep WPA and PWA funds flowing longer than many areas because of the relative paucity of airports in the state. At the same time, these landing areas became part of the nation's preparedness efforts. Senator Gurney believed that some of the $75 million approved for WPA construction of small airports should go to his hometown of Yankton. Kennedy pursued funding for an airport in Watertown, and Sioux Falls sought money to complete its municipal airport. The WPA provided $11,830 to supplement Rapid City's expenditure of $17,030 for grading and surfacing of runways at its airport. Some cities were disappointed, however, when the secretaries of War, the Navy, and Commerce announced ten weeks later that $40 million would be expended on this type of work, but the Civil Aeronautics Administration failed to include any South Dakota airport in its survey. In late 1940, the U.S. Congress appropriated $40 million for 250 airports designated as "necessary to the national defense." A few South Dakota airports received some of these funds.[26]

Other than ongoing efforts of bureaucrats to draw funding to South Dakota cities, Kennedy reported to Howard Hunter that the European war would have no effect on the employment picture in the state as there were no manufacturing or other important industries besides agriculture in the state.[27] He released figures in February 1940 that showed his agency's expenditures had passed the $50 million mark in 1939. Combining the total of federal funds with those of local sponsors, WPA had spent almost $56 million in South Dakota since 1935, with $44 million of that coming from Washington. More than 70 percent of this went for labor costs, and the remainder was spent on materials and equipment. Highway construction and "improvement projects" accounted for almost half the funds, or over $25 million. Minnehaha County ranked first in expenditures, with Pennington second and Brown coming in third.[28]

The *Rapid City Daily Journal* headlined a story in 1940, "S.D. Gets Millions in U.S. Grants," relating how the state received $1,834,200 in the previous fiscal year to finance "various social security programs." This was a reduction from $2,531,800 for the year before. On the other hand, state employers and their employees paid $676,900 in Social Security taxes. The amounts paid to the state included $1,498,700 for OASI; $23,100 for aid to the blind; $133,2000 for unemployment compensation; $76,400 for public health work; $56,300 for maternal and childcare services; $29,200 for crippled children; and $17,200 for child-welfare services. All these marked a massive change in societal priorities from the previous decade.[29]

By this time, President Roosevelt was changing his emphasis on budget requests. In 1940, he urged a 26 percent reduction in agricultural appropriations, especially in farm subsidies, because of recent advances in agricultural prices. In addition, he proposed a reduction for the WPA, the Civilian Conservation Corps (CCC), and the National Youth Administration (NYA) unless "business fails to improve" according to his expectations. Roosevelt now wanted to put his money into defense spending. He asked Congress to vote the highest defense budget "in two decades." His increase in naval expenditures would go into building warships, an expansion of twenty-four new ones to meet the growing threat on the Atlantic. The naval warfare there between Germany and Great Britain was accelerating and the position of neutral America on the Atlantic was becoming increasingly tenuous.[30]

The U.S.S. *South Dakota* was part of this new fleet. At the ship's dedication, Secretary of the Navy Frank Knox declared that the U.S. "must establish the greatest sea power the world has ever seen and with it an air force that will make us invincible." Vera Bushfield, South Dakota's first lady, smashed the traditional bottle of champagne on its prow. The *South Dakota* cost $52,794,000 and became the navy's eighteenth ship of the line. The ship first saw action near the Vera Cruz Islands in October 1942, then off Guadalcanal, where it suffered damage, and in the Arctic, where it joined an effort to destroy Germany's battleship *Tirpitz*. Finally, the ship suffered severe damage in the Pacific battles of Guam, Okinawa, and the Philippines, and was decommissioned in 1947.[31]

Increased spending for defense, of course, meant increased taxes to pay for it. The current federal income tax stood at 4 percent of net income above $2,000 for married persons (a substantial income when men were working for a dollar a day), and the corporate rate was 24 percent for net incomes above $25,000. Senators Robert Taft and Walter George of the Finance Committee agreed that individual taxes would have to be doubled and the corporate rate increased to 30 percent. The $2,000 exemption for couples meant that 1.7 percent of South Dakotans paid Uncle Sam some income tax in 1938.[32]

Beadle County commissioners stressed they were subjected to a 30 percent reduction in their WPA rolls as a result of a cut in the special drought allotment that went into effect in November 1939. This crisis led to a meeting in Huron to launch a statewide effort by the South Dakota Association of County Commissioners to persuade Governor Bushfield to fight for the restoration of state WPA funding. In addition, the Beadle County commissioners sent a resolution to Harrington and to members of the South Dakota congressional delegation, stressing the need for increasing, not decreasing, relief spending in the state. Jesse Smith of Yankton, secretary to the state county commissioners' association, proceeded to arrange a conference in Pierre to pressure Governor Bushfield to send a delegation to Washington to plead for "increased WPA rolls."[33]

When the South Dakota County Commissioners Association met in Pierre in April 1940, they determined "to halt reduction of the state's WPA personnel" on the grounds that drought-stricken counties were unable to absorb "the unemployed being lopped off public works rolls." After meeting with Bushfield, the county commissioners complained that the reductions stemmed from the declaration that "several counties were declared drought emergency areas last fall and drained the allocation." There was dissent to this action. William W. Kuehn of Hamlin County "decried" the effort to seek more funding because "now is a good time to call a halt on wild spending." He believed the cry of "drought" and "emergency" was "bad publicity for the state." John Forsting of Brown County placed the blame on the state legislature, saying the last session "did well but it didn't do anything to help the counties." Senators Bulow and Gurney increased the pressure on Washington bureaucrats. Bulow promised to pressure the appropriations committee to insert a provision in the next deficiency bill for an item for relief "in the Great Plains states," and Gurney sent Harrington telegrams from five counties insisting they had no funds to offset the "load created by WPA layoffs."[34]

President Roosevelt soon despaired of receiving new funding for the crisis and asked Congress for permission to spend the entire appropriation in eight months, hoping by then the drought would be broken and South Dakota farmers would again have produced ample crops. Congress finally agreed to appropriate supplemental funds but, reflective of the growing international crisis and the internal fear of threats from "isms," excluded "relief to aliens, communists, and Nazi bund members."[35] Congressmen also agreed the appropriation could be spent in eight months, rather than twelve, and renewed the current restrictions "against wasting relief money." It further retained provisions for a minimum 140-hour-work month, rotation of WPA enrollees every eighteen months, and reemployment after thirty days "on the basis of need."[36]

With the threat of war looming, the need for trained industrial workers became increasingly obvious, and New Dealers sought to help supply this need through several venues. WPA enrollees proved to be one obvious source. Secretary of Education John W. Studebaker announced some 50,000 men throughout the country would be taken off their projects and sent to "vocational trade and engineering schools for industries related to national defense." The workers would be chosen on the basis of "previous occupational experience as skilled workers" and would receive their "present pay" while taking the courses.[37]

The NYA emerged as another promising source. The agency announced its intention to construct shops in Mitchell, Huron, and Rapid City as control centers to train young men in "machine, sheet metal, and woodworking industries." Local and county governments would contribute land on which to erect the "fabricated steel" buildings. The NYA planned to offer training in three shifts of thirty-five to fifty boys monthly. The NYA would close all their other administrative offices in the state, and there would be subsidiary training offices in Sioux Falls, Vermillion, Huron, and at the Mount Marty Mission. This program accelerated the out-of-state movement of young men as they completed their courses and searched for industrial employment in other states.[38]

The NYA director from the state of Washington "widely praised" these South Dakota workers. His shop foremen and instructors were "highly complimentary in their comments on your boys." Of the first 1,000 to complete the courses, 88 volunteered for military service, 14 were selected for "compulsory training," and 24 enrolled in CCC camps. The remainder found employment on the West Coast, Chicago, the Duluth shipyards, the Rock Island arsenal, and other defense installations. As with WPA enrollees, NYA also tried to make their men available for the seasonal harvest work in South Dakota.[39]

NYA administrator Aubrey Williams completed an 8,000-mile tour of defense training facilities for war work for these young men and women. He reported that 60,000 young workers, or half of those entering defense industries "last month," came from NYA shops. Williams noted that NYA administrators began buying five million dollars' worth of machinery for use in worker training "one-and-a-half years before the present emergency," indicating good foresight on their part. He further suggested that "larger future allocations of money" were planned for this phase of preparedness, including a "substantial" increase for South Dakota. He hoped to train 350,000 more workers nationally in 1941.[40]

Aircraft engines were a "bottleneck" in the administration's plans for producing 25,000 airplanes "in the next two years," and one solution was a new program of awarding contracts to companies moving inland. As a result of this official pressure, for instance, the aircraft industry was soon centered in Wichita, Kansas. The army planned to relocate its defense industries to areas "200–250 miles or more away from the coasts or international boundaries." Unfortunately, there was no one in South Dakota pushing the concept of attracting these new industries, as Jesse Clyde Nichols of Kansas City was doing for his state. Nichols was well aware that his region received no war contracts in World War I, and he was determined this oversight would not be repeated. None of this industrial dispersal, however, came to South Dakota.[41]

Mineral deposits in West River country could have played a role in the preparedness program if some industrialist had promoted them. The development "of vast magnesium beds" along the Missouri River could have been exploited, the Corps of Engineers asserted, if cheap hydroelectric power from the river were provided. Dr. A. Karsten of the School of Mines suggested that "a foreign power spent seven million dollars" exploring tin deposits in the Black Hills, and he hinted darkly that this "failure was a very good investment for this power that controls the world's tin supply." The Hills also were rich in deposits of tungsten, beryllium, and aluminum, which could be tapped. In addition, an $80,000 manganese plant was built at Chamberlain three months before the U.S. entered the war.[42]

Bentonite, a nonmetallic substance, was in demand for war production. Foundries both in America and in countries aligned with the Allies abroad used it in the production of armaments. Bentonite was one of the raw materials that helped bring about "a sharp increase" in Black Hills income. Car loadings in Chicago rose to 572 in the first seven months of 1940 compared to 461 for the same period a year earlier. Feldspar shipments from the Black Hills showed a similar increase of 41 to 51 carloads during that period. In addition, wool shipments enjoyed a 15 to 20 percent jump over the previous year. Although cattle shipments had been low, "recent price improvements are bringing herds to the loading pens." The highest prices "in three years coincide with one of the best grass years in the past decade."[43]

The drought cycle began to break in 1938, and by 1941, it was over. In April 1941, the *Rapid City Daily Journal* reported a four-inch rain in the Black Hills, and by June the headline read "South Dakota Counts Wettest Spring in Years." That August brought a report that "Grain Bins in West River Burst with Decade's Best Crops." South Dakotans were again producing bountiful harvests and no longer had to rely on New Deal relief programs for survival.[44]

Meanwhile, President Roosevelt was pushing a policy that could lead to war with the Axis powers. The naval war in the Atlantic, with German submarines sinking British shipping, was taking a heavy toll. Roosevelt was determined to assist Britain as the last Allied holdout, short of entering the war, and when Prime Minister

Winston Churchill informed him of his country's dire need for ships, he was full of empathy. The country at large supported the president in his determination that England should not fall to the Axis powers, but congressional representatives were more isolationist than their constituents. Senators Gurney and Bulow were especially critical of what they considered Roosevelt's dangerous policy in the Atlantic. As a result, the president decided to bypass the Senate in September 1940 when he and Churchill agreed to the Destroyer Deal, whereby the United States traded Great Britain fifty old but serviceable destroyers in exchange for eight naval bases in the Atlantic. President Roosevelt used this executive agreement device to avoid the constitutional requirement that the isolationist Senate give its "advice and consent" to a treaty making this exchange. Churchill told Parliament this agreement in no way affected American status as nonbelligerent; Adolf Hitler believed otherwise.[45]

At the same time, President Roosevelt was seeking congressional support to raise the necessary manpower for his preparedness program. On 16 September 1940, Congress passed the first peacetime military draft in American history when the Burke-Wadsworth bill gained its approval. It required all men between ages twenty-one and thirty-five to register for a training period, followed by a reserve requirement. Some sixteen million men registered and the first draft numbers were drawn on 29 October. Both Francis Case and Karl Mundt voted against it in the House of Representatives, as did Senator Bulow. Senator Gurney was the sole South Dakota representative to support the Selective Training and Service Act. County draft boards had to be established, and many business leaders were reported to have rejected this civic service because of "other obligations" that they failed to specify.[46]

The Burke-Wadsworth law was due to expire in one year, and the battle would be fought again in 1941. Congressman Case argued the ten-year reserve component of the act, plus the National Guard Act of 1940, made "unnecessary any legislation to extend the active service of the selectees for another year." Despite this isolationist representative's disclaimer, Congress approved an eighteen-month extension of the draft on 18 August 1941. The opposition was strong, and again Chan Gurney supported the proposal but the vote in the House ended in a tie. At this point Speaker Sam Rayburn saw that Congressman Andrew Somers wanted to change his vote and recognized him. Rayburn then proclaimed the vote of 203–202 as a victory and, despite Republican congressmen protesting that the voting was not complete, he adjourned the session forthwith.[47]

Prior to this action, Churchill informed Roosevelt the Allies needed economic assistance of all kinds to survive the Nazi onslaught but were unable to repay. After his election victory in November 1940, Roosevelt asked Congress to enact his Lend-Lease proposal. Using the analogy that one needed temporary use of his neighbor's garden hose to douse his uncontrollable fire, he asked permission to sell, transfer, exchange, or lease war materials to any nation whose defense he deemed vital to America. Despite Senator Robert Taft's quip that this was like lending your chewing gum— you didn't want it back—Lend-Lease passed on 11 March 1941. This move took the United States into the war. After receiving authority to lend or lease the supplies, it would be folly to watch the Axis submarines sink the materials in the Atlantic, so the United States began convoying its merchant ships on the high seas. Hostile action in the Atlantic immediately accelerated.[48]

Meanwhile, on the other side of the world, the Empire of Japan continued its aggressions in the Far East, with the United States tightening diplomatic restrictions in response. While still trying to conquer China, Japan sought to swallow Burma to prevent the U.S. from supplying China through that route. In October 1941, Japan sent Ambassador Saburo Kurusu to Washington to negotiate an agreement to allow it a free hand in China. When Roosevelt refused to budge on this issue, a large Japanese fleet left the Kurile Islands headed for Hawaii, where the bulk of the American fleet was stationed. At 7:55 am local time on 7 December, these forces attacked the American fleet at Pearl Harbor without a declaration of war. When news of this arrived in Washington, the Sunday morning newspapers had already been printed, featuring stories of the Kurusu negotiations. A special edition of the Sioux Falls *Argus-Leader* later that day headlined "Japs at War With U.S." and "Japs Kill, Wound 3,000." The next day Congress voted unanimously for war, with the exception of Jeanette Rankin of Montana, who also had voted against war in April 1917. On 11 December, Germany declared war against the United States in support of her ally. America was now immersed in World War II, and depressed economic conditions vanished. The challenge now was inadequate labor for industrial production and the prosecution of the war.[49] With the increased demand for foodstuff occasioned by the onset of World War II and the return to normal rainfalls, prosperity returned at last.[50]

Conclusion

A T FIRST, MANY CITIZENS were too proud to ask for charity or later relief work on the Works Progress Administration (WPA). That they could do so and then "bite the hand that fed" them by voting against New Dealers is baffling. There are at least two possible explanations. One is the denial of some citizens that they had accepted relief work, a psychological abnegation of the idea that they could ever be so weak and still call themselves South Dakotans. The other is the self-deluding claim that "we repaid every loan," failing to accept the fact that a loan was any type of assistance. Even today there are, of course, South Dakotans who denounce Washington waste and abuse of freedom, while using federal highways to drive to protest meetings, who denounce Franklin Roosevelt for his collectivism or Barack Obama for socialism, while drinking water from a WPA water system or driving to a national park for recreation while listening to a radio broadcast. The same people denounced socialized medicine while taking every advantage of the skills of a doctor educated in a public school system or later in using Medicare or Medicaid.[1]

That same split personality allowed citizens to boast of their individualistic self-sufficiency and yet "stand tall at the public trough" when in need. Could a grocery merchant in Kadoka who hated Roosevelt have survived without WPA work funds that were spent on food? Could a Democratic haberdasher in Vermillion have endured without patrons spending their WPA wages on clothes?

Could a city have maintained its public health system without its PWA sewer project or WPA water system? Could Americans do without that greatest socialistic venture of the New Deal, the Old-Age and Survivors Insurance (OASI), or the Social Security program? The national average of people on relief at its highest point neared 15 percent, and at the same time in South Dakota it approached 40 percent. Yet South Dakotans rejected programs that saved them in 1936 and repudiated Franklin D. Roosevelt himself in 1940.

Likewise, these same people declined to tax the vast amounts of gold taken from beneath the surface of their land. It was not until drought and depression forced them to seek novel ways of obtaining increased funding for their state government that they dared confront the Hearst lion in his den. Even then the ore tax was a minimal gross income levy, although in subsequent years it was modified into an ore tax.

South Dakota voters have shown a "recurring pattern of electing Republican governors (to keep taxes low) and Democratic senators (to collect federal dollars) as evidence of South Dakota's pragmatism." Berry was successful at combining both features. He was politically incapable of uniting his party and introducing a true two-party system in the state, but he kept taxes low and did an outstanding job in obtaining relief funds. Although conservative in philosophy, and in some instances playing a reactionary role, this is one case where Berry placed the needs of his constituency above his political philosophy. It is amazing how this home-spun cowboy could successfully woo and win the urbane, urban aristocrat Roosevelt and impress him to the extent of being asked to second his nomination in 1936. There are numerous complex personal relationships of completely diverse personalities who have meshed in their objectives in history that defy explanation and this is one of them.

His successors, Leslie Jensen and Harlan Bushfield, are not so difficult to explain in their relationship with the federal government.

Jensen had seen how Berry cultivated the Washington bureaucrats and gained great popularity across the state for "bringing home the bacon" and tried to emulate his predecessor's feats. Warren Green and Bushfield were arch-conservatives, and Bushfield was a dedicated Republican, unable to adapt to the new federalism. The governor disliked Roosevelt and the New Deal and welcomed the reemergence of Republican power in Pierre and the declining New Deal as a reversion to the past that he cherished.[2]

Roosevelt provided a New Deal for Indians that proved ephemeral but was lasting in many respects. Relief work was often temporary, but its funding was enduring in the projects it developed. Many Indians agreed with the goal of Termination and worked hard to make it succeed. The CCC, like the CCC-ID, made major and lasting contributions to the state, not just in the projects that still remain, but in developing young men who were entering the labor marketplace for the first time, facing the insurmountable odds of one in four experienced men walking the streets, searching for employment. The WPA and Public Works Administration (PWA) also left their lasting mark on the state. Federal support of highway construction added greatly to the development of tourism that profoundly affected state development and eventually became its most important industry.

New Deal farm programs helped many Dakota agrarians survive the ordeal, but New Dealers could not deter Mother Nature. Drought and grasshoppers proved far more influential than bureaucrats in an agriculture-dominated state. This is why the high rate of unemployment endured so long. There was little base to reemploy men once the orders for industrial goods came from Europe. When the rains came late in the decade, South Dakota farmers could exploit the increased demand for foodstuffs coming from war-ravaged foreign countries.

The New Deal had a great impact on South Dakota youth and the state's future. In keeping with the contemporary societal mores, males received greater economic opportunities than females. Young men received great experiences through the CCC, while earning badly needed money to send home to their families. Just as important, young students were enabled to finish their high school or college education, along with learning some vocational skills. In this category, females also benefited, although in keeping with the trends of the times, there was a lower percentage of them attending college than males. The educational camps for young women offered through the National Youth Administration (NYA) were one program specifically designed to help them.

While South Dakota really began its outmigration in earnest during the Great Depression, this continued for its youth into the new millennium. As prosperity returned there were still insufficient industrial jobs for young people, and the best and brightest received a good education, then migrated to Omaha or Minneapolis for greater economic opportunities. During the Populist period, South Dakotans unsuccessfully resisted colonialism from the East. During the Great Depression, New Dealers attempted to colonize the state again with their programs, were successful for several years, then the young people, in their own way, successfully defeated the eastern colonial efforts.

New Deal agencies affected the growth of bureaucracy in South Dakota government. The Agricultural Adjustment Act (AAA), the PWA, and the WPA required the use of local agencies to develop ideas, to assure compliance with federal rules, and to mold public opinion. But they also developed additional layers of bureaucrats who tended to be self-perpetuating. These programs left a very different culture in South Dakota from what they initially encountered. As Paul O'Rourke explains it, one has to be "impressed with how little the basic values of its people changed" in the decade. Americans in other areas eventually accepted the new order, adapted to it, and grew. South Dakotans "never reconciled their beliefs with reality." Their need and greed for federal largess could not be harmonized with their antipathy toward the growth of federal powers and resulting high taxes and deficit spending.[3]

Though harder hit by the drought than neighboring states, South Dakota was not unique in these experiences in the 1930s. Other midwestern states were also altered by these programs. Kansas, for instance, endured the New Deal in much the same manner. Unlike South Dakota, the Sunflower State developed a remarkable relief director, John Stutz, whom Harry Hopkins described as "the best relief administrator" he had in the nation. But Kansas received millions of dollars more for its relief programs than it legally deserved, through Governor Alf Landon's misrepresentations to Harry Hopkins about the legality of the state's ability to raise funds for relief.[4]

Historian David Danbom made a study of Fargo, North Dakota, during the depression. He found that, unlike South Dakota, Fargo continued to grow during these years by 12 percent, serving as a magnet to the region's youth. While fewer people were on WPA rolls in 1940, unemployment nevertheless remained at 16 percent for men and 10 percent for women. Neighbors regarded these unemployed people as "slackers" and "chiselers" who had become "aliens in their native land." The federal government, though, had enhanced the quality of life in Fargo, he added, by improving the public infrastructure and ameliorating the status of their economic life. Unlike South Dakotans, Fargoans "commonly viewed" the federal government "as another customer to be courted." And like their neighbors to the south, they were "seared by the experience of hardship and the specter of dependency, developing habits they carried through the rest of their lives."[5]

D. Jerome Tweton made a similar survey of Otter Tail County in Minnesota. He concluded that the New Deal improved and sustained life for the area, including the county road network, the Rural Electrification Administration (REA), and the alleviation of suffering and hardship, but that it also "fostered a sense of democracy and community." The same could be concluded about the South Dakota experience. Similarly, Otter Tail County and South Dakotans "suffered no penalty for [their] allegiance to the Republican party," and the New Deal did not alter the state's conservatism. Yet reform has continued and expanded over the decades.[6]

Undoubtedly, the greatest legacy the New Deal left to South Dakotans was to drag their ancient system of charity into the twentieth century. New Deal policies forced federal agencies to supplant state ones or, in many cases, compelled the executive and legislature to create new ones to meet new needs. In the 1930s New Dealers taught South Dakotans to provide trained professionals to oversee a system whereby the state provided financial assistance, with the help of Washington on a dollar-matching basis, as Aid to Families with Dependent Children (AFDC). This required establishing an entirely new organization of professional bureaucrats to manage the emerging concept of aid. Referred to henceforth as welfare, the program underwent another transformation, leading to assistance through the Food Stamp program to make certain the needs of the poor were met. This inexorable evolution basically revolutionized South Dakota society, at least in forcing it to meet its financial obligations to the needy. The advent of the Social Security Act led to the establishment of the Department of Social Welfare, Aid to Dependent Children (ADC), old age pensions, unemployment compensation, the modernization of social work, and the "cradle to grave" care of the modern world. Many South Dakotans might never be able to accept the contemporary, interdependent world in which they live, but life under "the old ways" would never return. Like it or not, their forbearers were forced to accept the new world created by those outsiders, the New Dealers from Washington, D.C., who helped them preserve their culture while adapting to the "new ways." Life on the Great Plains "would never again be the same."[7]

Afterthoughts: Memories of the Great Depression on the Great Plains

We farm people went to town (population 500) on Saturday night to see the sights and watch the free outdoor movie, preceded by a short, such as *The Perils of Pauline*. If the class B or C movies were atrocious, we didn't know any different.

Gasoline trucks dragged a chain on the ground because the dust storms filled the air with so much static electricity that the truck could explode if the "juice" was not drained off.

Mother raised a large garden and canned 500–600 jars of fruits and vegetables in the summer.

We children worked hard in the hot sun shocking wheat and chopping weeds. We might have worn a hat but no one thought of sunscreen.

We ate a hearty breakfast, dinner at noon, and supper in the evening, often composed of homemade bread and butter with a large can of Campbell's Pork and Beans. Dad, the breadwinner, always got the "pork."

A cow might splash a bit of manure in the pail when we milked the cows, but the calves didn't complain about the taste, and neither did we.

We drove an old car without a radiator to town a half mile away and let it cool off before driving home, and we were glad for the ride.

We took our lunch of homemade bread and lard to school in a brown paper bag and thought we were lucky if we found a chunk of crispy fat in the lard. If Mom's dessert was a "store-bought" cookie, we felt lucky.

Our school district grouped elementary grades together in the same classroom. In first grade, one of the students was mentally disabled and wanted to roam with freedom. He began running away from school, so Mrs. Jones tied him in his desk, which was disturbing because of his wails and struggles with the constraint. There was no special education room to meet his needs.

At school, the girls played jacks and the boys had a marbles championship and played their favorite game at recess. "Dumps" involved the larger boys carrying the smaller ones piggyback while the riders tried to pull each other off down to the ground. Our clothes were quickly worn out, but the games never stopped.

Santa Claus came to town on the fire truck two weeks before Christmas. The city fathers drove him down Main Street, where he gave each of us a brown bag containing an orange, a few unshelled peanuts, and some hard candy. If there were better gifts somewhere, we couldn't imagine.

We shocked the neighbor's wheat at ten cents an hour to buy fireworks. We made noise, blew up tin cans, and held a "fizzler" too long in our fingers, but the Fourth of July was always a celebration.

Aunts, uncles, and cousins came for a delicious Sunday dinner for Mother's fried chicken and homemade ice cream, or we went to their house. It was simple fare, but there was always room for everyone and nobody went away hungry.

Mother bought a hundred chicks every spring, which meant a rooster for Sunday dinner and fifty hens for laying eggs. When the hens stopped laying and molted, this meant fifty delicious meals of chicken and noodles, and we never minded the routine.

Torgesons' grocery store had to stop selling on credit because it became difficult and often impossible to collect bills, but we only bought what we could pay for. On Saturday night, that's where Mother took her eggs, cream, and butter to "trade" for clothes, shoes, and condiments.

One of my aunts was midwife to deliver my oldest sister born at home. I was born at home, too, but I had Dr. Randles on hand.

Our pail of drinking water, with its common cup, froze at night in the kitchen. We had to remember to remove the cup before bedtime. One of Mother's early morning chores was to empty the common chamber pot.

✦

Dad's income from the farm paid the rent, taxes, and livestock and implement replacement. Later, when he obtained an F-12 Farmall, he also had to buy gasoline and oil. If this was a hardship, our parents never complained.

✦

We all took baths on Saturday night in the metal washtub. My sisters went first so they would smell nice for their friends. When my turn came as the last, the soapy water was pretty dirty, but I never knew the difference.

Notes

Preface

1. Catherine McNicol Stock, *Main Street in Crisis* (Chapel Hill: University of North Carolina Press, 1992): 17; percentages on relief are from W. F. Kumlein, *A Graphic Summary of the Relief Situation in South Dakota (1930–1935)*, Bulletin #310, Agricultural Experiment Station, Brookings, S.D., May 1937, 23. Drought statistics from Paul A. Landis, "Rural Relief in South Dakota," Department of Sociology, Brookings, in cooperation with FERA Division of Research and Statistics, Bulletin # 289, June 1934, 4.

1 Before the New Deal

1. Richard Lowitt and Maurine Beasley, eds., *One Third of a Nation* (Urbana: University of Illinois Press, 1981), 85.

2. Theodore Salutos, *The American Farmer and the New Deal* (Ames: Iowa State University Press, 1982): 3–9.

3. Ibid., 9–12.

4. *See* John Kenneth Galbraith, *The Great Crash* (Boston: Houghton Mifflin, 1954) for this financial crisis.

5. Benjamin Stolberg and Warren Jay Vinton, "The New Deal vs. Recovery," *American Mercury* 33 (Dec. 1934): 386.

6. David B. Danbom, *Born in the Country* (Baltimore: Johns Hopkins University Press, 1995): 199.

7. T. H. Watkins, *The Hungry Years* (New York: Henry Holt, 1999), 44; Melvyn Dubofsky, "Not So Turbulent Years: Another Look at the American 1930s," in Melvyn Dubofsky, ed., *The New Deal* (New York: Garland,

1992), 125; Conrad Black, *Franklin Delano Roosevelt: Champion of Freedom* (New York: Public Affairs, 2003), 316; Timothy Egan, *The Worst Hard Time* (Boston: Houghton Mifflin, 2006), 130–31.

8. Stock, *Main Street in Crisis*, 2–23.

9. Paula M. Nelson, *The Prairie Winnows Out Its Own* (Iowa City: University of Iowa Press, 1996), 117–23.

10. Lorena Hickok to Harry L. Hopkins, Aberdeen, 7 Nov. 1933, in Lowitt and Beasley, eds., *One Third of a Nation*, 181.

11. Salutos, *American Farmer*, 3–9.

12. Dorothy Schwieder, "South Dakota Farm Women and the Great Depression," *Journal of the West* 24 (Oct. 1985): 6–18; Barbara Handy-Marchello, *Women of the Northern Plains: Gender and Settlement on the Homestead Frontier, 1870–1930* (St. Paul: Minnesota Historical Society Press, 2005).

13. The description of the work of farm women here and following comes from Schwieder, "South Dakota Farm Women," 10–17.

14. Ibid., 13.

15. Ibid., 17.

16. "Tax Delinquency Status of Farm Land in South Dakota," State Planning Board, Brookings, 1 July 1937, South Dakota State University Archives.

17. Michael Johnson Grant, *Down and Out on the Family Farm* (Lincoln: University of Nebraska Press, 2002), 11.

18. R. Alton Lee, *Principle Over Party* (Pierre: South Dakota State Historical Society Press, 2011), 175.

19. R. Douglas Hurt, *The Big Empty* (Tucson: University of Arizona Press, 2001), 74.

20. Gilbert C. Fite, *Peter Norbeck: Prairie Statesman* (Pierre: South Dakota State Historical Society Press, 2005 reprint), is the definitive story of this towering figure in South Dakota history.

21. Gilbert C. Fite, "Peter Norbeck and the Defeat of the Nonpartisan League in South Dakota, *Mississippi Valley Historical Review* 33 (Sept. 1946): 220–22; Herbert S. Schell, *History of South Dakota* (Lincoln: University of Nebraska Press, 1968), 286.

22. Gilbert C. Fite's *George N. Peek and the Fight for Farm Parity* (Norman: University of Oklahoma Press, 1954) is the classic account of this failed program.

23. "William John Bulow," in Lynwood E. Oyos, *Over a Century of*

Leadership (Sioux Falls: Center for Western Studies, 1987), 117; Alan L. Clem, *Prairie State Politics* (Washington, D.C.: Public Affairs Press, 1967), 36.

24. Donald D. Parker, "Warren Everett Green," in Oyos, *Century of Leadership*, 122.

25. Fite, "Peter Norbeck," 224–27.

26. Nelson, *Prairie Winnows*, 9–12; W. F. Kumlein, *A Graphic Summary of the Relief Situation in South Dakota, 1930–1935* (Brookings, SD: Agricultural Experiment Station Bulletin #10, May 1937): 7; C. Hartley Grattan, "Who is on Relief?" *Scribners Magazine* 97 (June 1935): 25.

27. Schell, *History of South Dakota*, 283.

28. R. Alton Lee, "Drought and Depression on the Great Plains," *Heritage of the Great Plains* 39 (spring/summer 2006): 6; A. R. Mangus, *Changing Aspects of Rural Relief*, WPA research monograph 14 (New York: Da Capo Press, reprint, 1971): xvii.

29. *Daily Journal*, 14 Nov. 1932; *Argus-Leader*, 8 Aug. 1932.

30. *Daily Journal*, 21, 22, 26 Nov. 1932.

31. Arthur M. Schlesinger, Jr., *The Coming of the New Deal* (Boston: Houghton Mifflin, 1959), 238–41.

32. John L. Shover, ed., "Depression Letters From American Farmers," *Agricultural History* 36 (July 1962): 163–641; *Argus-Leader*, 22 July 1932.

33. John E. Miller, "Restrained, Respectable Radicals: The South Dakota Farm Holiday," *Agricultural History* 59 (July 1985): 429–47. Miller's thorough analysis and description of the activities of the Farm Holiday in the state during the years between 1932 and 1934 is an excellent resource on this topic. Included here is a brief review of the significant events leading up to the implementation of the New Deal. For an excellent study of the FHA in a broader region, *see* John L. Shover, *Cornbelt Rebellion: The Farmers' Holiday Association* (Urbana: University of Illinois Press, 1965).

34. Miller, "Restrained, Respectable Radicals," 433–34.

35. Ibid., 437.

36. Ibid., 430.

37. William C. Pratt, "Rural Radicalism on the Northern Great Plains, 1912–1950," *Montana: The Magazine of Western History* 42 (winter 1992): 48; Matthews, "Agrarian Radicals," 412.

38. For this episode, *see* Matthews, "Agrarian Radicals," 408–21.

39. Ibid., 420. For a survey of these sales, *see* John Shover, "The Penny-Auction Rebellion: Midwestern Farmers Fight Foreclosure," *American West* 2 (fall 1965).

40. Pratt, "Rural Radicalism," 49–50.

41. Ibid., 51. *See also* William C. Pratt, "Rethinking the Farm Revolt of the 1930s," *Great Plains Quarterly* 8 (summer 1988): 134.

42. *Daily Journal*, 16 Nov. 1932.

43. Christopher Howard, "Sowing the Seeds of 'Welfare': The Transformation of Mothers' Pensions, 1900–1940," *Journal of Public Policy* 4 (1992): 193.

44. William W. Bremer, "Along the American Way: The New Deal's Work Relief Programs for the Unemployed," *Journal of American History* 62 (Dec. 1975): 639.

45. Howard, "Sowing the Seeds," 193; table on p. 202.

46. Cohen, *Nothing to Fear*, 248–49.

47. For a first-hand account of the drought in Laura Ingalls Wilder's county, *see* Lyle R. Johnson, "Decade of Drought," *South Dakota History* 43 (fall 2013).

48. Quotes in Egan, *Worst Hard Time*, 103–4.

49. Frank Freidel, "Election of 1932," in Arthur Schlesinger, Jr., and Fred L. Israel, eds., *History of American Presidential Elections* (New York: Chelsea House, 1978): 2311–12, 2318. The "deflation" quote is from Joan Hoff Wilson, *Herbert Hoover: Forgotten Progressive* (Prospect Heights, Ill.: Waveland Press, 1992 reissue): 146.

50. James McGregor Burns, *Roosevelt: The Lion and the Fox* (New York: Harcourt, Brace and World, 1956): chap. 6.

51. Schell, *History of South Dakota*, 281; Suzanne Barta Julin, *A Marvelous Hundred Square Miles* (Pierre: South Dakota State Historical Society Press, 2009), 109.

52. Matthew Cecil, "Democratic Party Politics and the South Dakota Income Tax, 1933–1942," *South Dakota History* 26 (summer/fall 1986): 140.

53. *Argus-Leader*, 29 Oct. 1932.

54. Joseph V. Ryan, "Tom Berry, 1933–1937," in Oyos, *Century of Leadership*, 127–28.

55. Ibid., 128.

56. Ibid., 139–40.

57. Paul H. Carlson and Steve Porter, "South Dakota Congressmen and

the Hundred Days of the New Deal," *South Dakota History* 8 (fall 1978): 328–32.

58. Ibid., 327–38; Norbeck quote from Lewis L. Gould, *The Most Exclusive Club* (New York: Basic Books, 2005): 113.

2 The New Deal Comes to South Dakota and the Nation

1. Lowitt and Beasley, eds., *One Third of a Nation*, 83.

2. Black, *Roosevelt*, 269. The bank failures are from Schell, *History of South Dakota*, 284.

3. William E. Leuchtenburg, *Franklin D. Roosevelt and the New Deal* (New York: Harper Torchbacks, 1963), 45.

4. Black, *Roosevelt*, 171–72.

5. Salutos, *American Farmer,* 39–42.

6. Miller, "Radicals," 445–46. For Reno's views, *see* Shover, *Cornbelt Rebellion*, 100–101.

7. John L. Shover, "Populism in the Nineteen-Thirties: The Battle for the AAA," *Agricultural History* 39 (Jan. 1965): 18–19.

8. Gilbert C. Fite, "Farmer Opinion and the Agricultural Adjustment Act, 1933," *Mississippi Valley Historical Review* 48 (Mar. 1962): 659–61.

9. John C. Culver and John Hyde, *American Dreamer: A Life of Henry A. Wallace* (New York: W. W. Norton, 2000), 57, 199, 229.

10. William R. Johnson, "National Farm Organizations and the Reshaping of Agricultural Policy in 1932," *Agricultural History* 37 (Jan. 1963): 35–37. For Simpson's views, *see* Gilbert C. Fite, "John A. Simpson: The Southwest's Militant Farm Leader," *Mississippi Valley Historical Review* 35 (Mar. 1949).

11. Grant, *Down and Out,* 65–75.

12. Fite, "Farmer Opinion," 662–65.

13. Shover, "Populism," 23–24.

14. Cohen, *Nothing to Fear,* 144–45.

15. Shover, "Populism," 20–22.

16. Lynwood E. Oyos, *The Family Farmers' Advocate* (Sioux Falls: Center for Western Studies, 1999), 54.

17. Fite, "Farmer Opinion," 670–73.

18. Johnson, "Farm Organizations," 41–42.

19. Alvin Rosenman, "Old Age Assistance," *American Academy of*

Political Sciences 202 (Mar. 1939): 53; Gregory M. Hooks, "A New Deal for Farmers and Social Scientists: The Politics of Rural Sociology in the Depression Era," *Rural Sociology* 48 (1983), is quite thorough on the topic.

20. Rosenman, "Old Age," 57.

21. William E. Leuchtenburg, *Franklin D. Roosevelt and the New Deal* (New York: Harper & Row, 1963), 120–21.

22. James T. Patterson, *America's Struggle against Poverty, 1900–1985* (Harvard University Press, 1986), 44–46.

23. *See* Bremer, "Along the American Way," for how New Dealers altered this conceit of the unemployed. They failed, however, to modify significantly this denigrating image in South Dakota.

24. Adam Cohen, *Nothing to Fear: FDR's Inner Circle and the Hundred Days That Created Modern America* (New York: Penguin Press, 2009), 47.

25. Fite, *Peter Norbeck*, 161–65, 193.

26. Carlson and Porter, "South Dakota Congressmen," 328–32.

27. John E. Miller, "Restrained, Respectable Radicals: The South Dakota Farm Holiday," *Agricultural History* 59 (July 1985): 31–32; Parker, "Warren Everett Green," in Oyos, *Century of Leadership*, 124.

28. Biographical Files, SDSHS, Pierre; Elizabeth E. Williams, *Emil Loriks: Builder of a New Economic Order* (Sioux Falls: Center for Western Studies, 1981), 32.

29. Paul A. O'Rourke, "South Dakota Politics During the New Deal Years," *South Dakota History* 1 (summer 1971): 237–39.

30. Cecil, "Income Tax," 144–45; "cheered" from *Argus-Leader*, 3 Jan. 1933.

31. Ibid., 146–50.

32. Ibid., 148.

33. Ibid.

34. Ibid., 156.

35. Ibid., 151–54.

36. O'Rourke, "New Deal Years," 239; *Argus-Leader*, 13 Jan. 1933.

37. Oyos, *Family Farmers' Advocate*, 22.

38. O'Rourke, "New Deal Years," 241–43.

39. John E. Miller, "Setting the Agenda: Political Parties and Historical Change," in Jon K. Lauck, John E. Miller, & Donald C. Simmons, Jr., eds., *The Plains Political Tradition* (Pierre: South Dakota State Historical Society Press, 2011): 87.

40. *Daily Journal*, 25 Apr., 9 June 1933.

41. R. O. Carte to Paul Webbink, 13 Oct. 1933, RG 69, box 272, National Archives (NA). *See* Eduard Lindeman, "Social Workers in the Depression," *The Nation* 138 (7 Mar. 1938): 275–76, for a survey of the role of this profession during the early New Deal years.

42. Nelson, *Prairie Winnows*, 134–37.

43. John Finbar Jones and John Middlemist Herrick, *Citizens in Service* (East Lansing: Michigan State University Press, 1976), 35.

44. Van L. Perkins, "The AAA and the Politics of Agriculture: Agricultural Policy Formulation in the Fall of 1933," *Agricultural History* 39 (Oct. 1965): 220–22.

45. Ibid., 225–26.

46. Ibid., pp. 227–28. Berry's quote is from Miller, "Restrained, Respectable Radicals," 442; Biographical Files, SDSHS, Pierre.

3 Work for the Unemployed, Food for the Hungry

1. Michael Golay, *America 1933* (New York: Free Press, 2013), 168.

2. John L. Shover, "The Communist Party and the Midwest Farm Crisis of 1933," *Journal of American History* 51 (Sept. 1964): 266.

3. Cohen, *Nothing to Fear*, 61.

4. *Argus-Leader*, 15 July 1932, 14 Oct. 1934.

5. Watkins, *The Hungry Years*, 356–57; C. Roger Lambert, "The Illusion of Participatory Democracy: The AAA Organizes the Corn-Hog Producers," *Annals of Iowa* 42 (fall 1974).

6. C. Roger Lambert, "Slaughter of the Innocents: The Public Protests the AAA Killing of Little Pigs," *Midwest Quarterly* 14 (Apr. 1973): 247–48.

7. C. Roger Lambert, "Want and Plenty: The Federal Surplus Relief Corporation and the AAA," *Agricultural History* 46 (July 1972): 390–95.

8. C. Roger Lambert and Kevin F. Mykill, "Federal Food for the Hungry, 1930–1940," in R. Alton Lee, ed., *Agricultural Legacies* (Vermillion: University of South Dakota Press, 1986): 94.

9. Ibid.

10. For an expanded presentation of the Food Stamp and School Lunch programs, *see* ibid., 96–100.

11. Jean Choate, "'Dear Mr. Gurney': D. B. Gurney's Campaign to Recover the Hog Processing Tax for Farmers," *South Dakota History* 22 (winter 1992): 157–58.

12. Ryan, "Tom Berry," in Oyos, *Century of Leadership*, 128–29.

13. *Daily Journal*, 8 Sept. 1933.

14. Deborah Epstein Popper and Frank J. Popper, "Dust to Dust: A Daring Proposal for Dealing with an Inevitable Disaster," *Planning* 12 (Dec. 1987).

15. *Argus-Leader*, 8, 13, 14 Sept. 1933.

16. *Daily Journal*, 30 Oct. 1934.

17. Ryan, "Tom Berry," in Oyos, *Century of Leadership*, 129.

18. *See* Gregory M. Hooks, "A New Deal for Farmers and Social Scientists: The Politics of Rural Sociology in the Depression Era," *Rural Sociology* 48 (1983): 393.

19. Lorena Hickok to Harry L. Hopkins, 7 Nov. 1933, in Lowitt and Beasley, eds., *One Third of a Nation*, 80.

20. Ibid., 82.

21. Ibid., 85.

22. C. Roger Lambert, "The Drought Cattle Purchase, 1934–1935," *Agricultural History* 45 (Apr. 1971): 85. For the Berry story, *see Daily Journal*, 30 Oct. 1934.

23. *Argus-Leader*, 2, 12, 22 June 1934.

24. Lambert, "Drought Cattle," 86.

25. *Daily Journal*, 6 June 1934.

26. Irwin M. May, Jr., "Cotton and Cattle: The FSRC and Emergency Work Relief," *Agricultural History* 46 (July 1972): 408–9.

27. *Daily Journal*, 30 Oct. 1934.

28. *Argus-Leader*, 17, 20 Nov. 1933.

29. Robert E. Sherwood, *Roosevelt and Hopkins* (New York: Harper & Brothers, 1950), 53; *Daily Journal*, 16 Nov. 1933.

30. *Daily Journal*, 17 Nov. 1933. *See also* Nancy E. Rose, *Put to Work* (New York: Monthly Review Press, 1994), 53.

31. Reinholtz, Parrager, and Brown to Frances Perkins, 27 July 1933, RG 69, box 275, NA.

32. Ibid.

33. Ibid.

34. *Argus-Leader*, 28 Oct. 1933.

35. *Daily Journal*, 5, 6 Apr. 1935.

36. E. E. Sudan to Franklin D. Roosevelt, 15 Dec. 1933, RG 69, box 46, NA.

37. *Daily Journal*, 19 Feb. 1934.

38. Ibid., 30 Dec. 1933, 26 Apr. 1934.

39. R. O. Carte to Paul Webbink, 29 Sept. 1933, RG 69, box 273, NA.

40. W. L. Eales to Harry L. Hopkins, 31 Jan. 1934, RG 69, box 46, NA; W. L. Eales to Corrington Gill, 10 Feb. 1934, RG 69, box 272, NA.

41. W. L. Eales to "Mr. Williams,"13 Feb. 1934, RG 69, box 46, NA.

42. Boyden Sparkes, "The New Deal for Transients," *Saturday Evening Post* 208 (19 Oct. 1935): 90, 92–95; Rose, *Put to Work*, 23, 39.

43. FERA Transient Division, Pierre, n.d., RG 69, box 274, NA.

44. T. J. Edmonds to Aubrey Williams, 28 July 1934, RG 69, box 273, NA.

45. *Daily Journal*, 6 Aug. 1934.

46. Ibid., 5 Jan. 1935.

47. Martha H. Swain, "The Forgotten Woman: Ellen S. Woodward and Women's Relief in the New Deal," *Prologue* 15 (winter 1983): 202–4.

48. T. J. Edmonds to Harry L. Hopkins, 13–14 Feb. 1934, RG 69, box 275, NA.

49. *Daily Journal*, 8 Sept. 1933.

50. Ibid., 10 Oct. 1933.

51. Ibid., 13 Oct. 1933.

52. Ibid., 21 Mar. 1933.

53. Tom Berry to Harry L. Hopkins, 2 Mar. 1934, RG 69, box 46; Aubrey Williams to Tom Berry, telegram, 10 Mar. 1934, RG 69, box 272, NA.

54. Hopkins to Eales, 16 Feb. 1934, RG 69, box 46, NA; *see also Daily Journal*, 12 Mar. 1934.

55. W. L. Eales to Harry L. Hopkins, 2 Mar. 1934, RG 69, box 46, NA.

56. *Daily Journal*, 31 Mar. 1934.

57. Beadle County Farmer Labor Committee, 17 Mar. 1934; E. T. Gitchell to William Bulow, 19 Mar. 1934, both in RG 69, box 47, NA; Theodore Reise to Harry L. Hopkins, 24 Mar. 1934, RG 69, box 275, NA.

58. *Daily Journal*, 27 Nov., 18 Dec. 1935.

59. Tom Berry to T. J. Edmonds, 19 Apr. 1934, RG 69, box 272, NA.

60. Lorena Hickok to Eleanor Roosevelt, 11–12 Nov. 1933, in Lowitt and Beasley, eds., *One Third of a Nation*, 91; Tom Berry to Harry L. Hopkins, 25 Apr. 1934, RG 69, box 46, NA.

61. RG 69, box 272, NA. Tables indicate that from June 1933 through March 1934, FERA spent $4,473,504.58 for South Dakota relief.

62. Hickok to Eleanor Roosevelt, 11, 12 Nov. 1933, in Lowitt and Beasley, eds., *One Third of a Nation*, 90. *See* Joseph E. Perisco, *Franklin and Lucy: Mrs. Rutherfurd and the Other Extraordinary Women in Roosevelt's Life*

(New York: Random House, 2008), chap. 24, for the close relationship between Eleanor Roosevelt and Lorena Hickok.

63. Lowitt and Beasley, eds., *One Third of a Nation*, 91–92; *see also* Michael Golay, *America 1933* (New York: Free Press, 2013), chap. 6 for Hickok's visit to South Dakota.

64. Allan J. Soffar, "The Forest Shelterbelt Project, 1934–1944," *Journal of the West* 14 (July 1975): 95.

65. Ibid., 96–97.

66. Ibid., 97–98.

67. Ibid., 99–100.

68. Ibid., 101–5.

69. Quoted in Debra O'Connor. "Union in His Blood," *Sioux Falls Argus-Leader*, 20 Oct. 1981.

70. Lynwood E. Oyos, "Labor's House Divided: The Morrell Strike of 1935–1937," *South Dakota History* 18 (spring/summer 1988): 69.

71. Ibid., 70–75.

72. *Daily Journal*, 11 Mar. 1935; Wolff and Cash, eds., "South Dakotans Remember," 252.

73. *Daily Journal*, 20 July 1935.

74. Ibid., 22 July, 4 Aug. 1935.

75. Ibid., 7, 8 Aug. 1935.

76. Oyos, "Labor's House Divided," 76–78.

77. *Argus-Leader*, 11, 13, 14 Apr. 1936, 10 Mar. 1937.

78. Salutos, *American Farmer*, 164–73.

79. Ibid., 156–60.

80. *Argus-Leader*, 17 July 1936.

81. Salutos, *American Farmer*, 178.

4 Building Public Projects

1. Arthur M. Schlesinger, Jr., *The Coming of the New Deal* (Boston: Houghton Mifflin, 1959), 99.

2. Rural representatives blocked a state NRA in South Dakota. See James T. Patterson, *The New Deal and the States: Federalism in Transition* (Princeton University Press, 1969), 116.

3. George E. Socolsky, "The Political Burden of Relief," *Atlantic Monthly* 158 (Sept. 1936): 334, 340.

4. Bernard Bellush, *The Failure of the NRA* (New York: W. W. Norton,

1975), 48. Patterson, *The New Deal*, 103–4, notes that PWA provided a boon for states unwilling or unable to appropriate substantially for public works, "especially on the local level."

5. *Argus-Leader*, 15 Oct. 1933, 10 Feb., 17, 26 Aug. 1934.

6. Ibid., 26 June 1933.

7. Ibid., 5, 18 Aug. 1933.

8. Ibid., 26 Aug. 1933.

9. Ibid., 22 Sept., 2, 15 Oct. 1933.

10. Ibid., 26 Oct. 1934.

11. Ibid., 17 May 1935.

12. Ibid., 30 Oct. 1934, 11, 26 Feb., 17 May 1935.

13. Michelle L. Dennis, National Register of Historic Places Multiple Property Documentation Form for Federal Relief Construction in South Dakota, 1929–1941, p. 45. South Dakota State Historic Preservation Office, history.sd.gov.

14. Ibid., 46.

15. South Dakota State Planning Board, *Progress Report #1*, 15 Feb. 1935, State Archives.

16. South Dakota State Planning Board, *Progress Report #6*, 22 June 1935, State Archives.

17. *Argus-Leader*, 26 Feb. 1935.

18. Ibid., 29, 30 Apr. 1935.

19. *Daily Journal*, 4 Mar. 1935.

20. *Argus-Leader*, 22 June 1934.

21. Thomas Biolsi, "New Deal Visions v. Local Political Culture: The Agony of the South Dakota State Planning Board, 1934–1939," in Lauck, Miller, and Simmons, eds., *The Plains Political Tradition*, vol. 2 (Pierre: South Dakota Historical Society Press, 2014), 82, 83, 91.

22. Neil M. Maher, *Nature's New Deal* (New York: Oxford University Press, 2008), 19.

23. Kenneth E. Hendrickson, Jr., "The Civilian Conservation Corps in South Dakota," *South Dakota History* 11 (winter 1980): 2, 13.

24. Ibid., 6–7.

25. Hendrickson, "The CCC," 3–4.

26. R. Alton Lee, "The Civilian Conservation Corps in Kansas," *Journal of the West* 44 (fall 2005): 69.

27. *Daily Journal*, 14, 26 Apr. 1933.

28. Ibid., 3 May 1933.

29. Hendrickson, "The CCC," 4–5.

30. Ibid., 5.

31. *Daily Journal*, 26 May 1933.

32. Dorothy Schwieder, *Growing Up with the Town* (Iowa City: University of Iowa Press, 2002), 70.

33. Lee, "CCC in Kansas," 69–70.

34. Leuchtenburg, *Franklin D. Roosevelt*, 172; Maher, Nature's New Deal, 67; "cattle" quote from Stock, *Main Street in Crisis*, 24.

35. RG 35, entry 115, NA.

36. Hendrickson, "The CCC," 7–8.

37. Ibid., 9–11.

38. *Daily Journal*, 16 Sept. 1933.

39. Ibid., 15 May 1934.

40. Harry H. Woodring to Robert Fechner, 23 Apr. 1934, RG 35, entry 115, NA.

41. RG 35, entry 115, NA.

42. RG 69, box 275, NA.

43. *Daily Journal*, 6, 8 Jan. 1934.

44. Ibid., 22 Jan. 1935.

45. Ibid., 19 Mar. 1935. *See also* Julin, *Marvelous Hundred Square Miles*, 162–63.

46. *Daily Journal*, 19 Mar. 1935.

47. Ibid., 12 Aug. 1935.

48. RG 35, entry 9, NA.

49. Hendrickson, "The CCC," 16.

50. Ibid., 16–17.

51. Betty and Ernest K. Lindley, *A New Deal for Youth* (New York: Viking, 1938), 10–11.

52. Maher, *Nature's New Deal*, 43–44.

53. Ibid., 19–20.

5 Berry's Second Term and the Second New Deal

1. Quoted in Dubofsky, ed., *The New Deal*, 201–2.

2. Herbert M. Cass to Aubrey Williams, 17 July 1934, RG 69, box 272, NA.

3. T. J. Edmonds to Aubrey Williams, 4 Aug. 1934, RG 69, box 273, NA.

4. *Argus-Leader*, 2, 15 Aug. 1934.

5. T. J. Edmonds to Harry L. Hopkins, 14 Sept. 1934, RG 69, box 273, NA.

6. Ibid.

7. *Daily Journal*, 11 May 1934.

8. Ibid., Telephone conversation of Mr. Hopkins and Governor Tom Berry, 14 May 1934, RG 69, box 273, NA.

9. H. G. Burrell to Palmer Larson, 25 Oct. 1934, ibid.

10. *Argus-Leader*, 11 Feb., 30 Mar. 1934.

11. Cecil, "Income Tax," 157.

12. William C. Pratt, "Another South Dakota; or, The Road Not Taken: The Left and the Shaping of South Dakota Political Culture," in Lauck, Miller and Simmons, eds., *Plains Political Tradition*, 117–18.

13. O'Rourke, "South Dakota Politics," 236.

14. *Daily Journal*, 27 Oct., 9 Nov. 1934.

15. *Argus-Leader*, 19 Sept. 1934.

16. Ibid., 26 Sept. 1934.

17. Ibid., 23 Oct. 1934.

18. *Daily Journal*, 2 Nov. 1934.

19. Schell, *South Dakota History*, 295.

20. *Daily Journal*, 2, 7, 8 Nov. 1934.

21. Cecil, "Income Tax," 157–60.

22. *Daily Journal*, 8 Jan. 1935.

23. Cecil, "Income Tax," 161–63; O'Rourke, "New Deal Years," 249–53.

24. O'Rourke, "New Deal Years," 254.

25. Ibid.; Tom Berry to Harry L. Hopkins, 31 Dec. 1934.

26. Pierce Atwater to Harry L. Hopkins, 14 Jan. 1935, RG 69, box 273, NA.

27. Atwater to Hopkins, 15 Feb. 1935, box 272, ibid.

28. Atwater to Hopkins, 26 Jan. 1935, box 273, ibid.

29. *See* Eduard Lindeman, "Social Workers in the Depression," *The Nation* 138 (Mar. 1938): 274–75, for a brief account of this profession in the 1930s.

30. *Daily Journal*, 25 Mar. 1935.

31. Ibid., 7 May 1935.

32. Ibid., 11 Feb. 1935.

33. Ibid., 22 Mar. 1935.

34. Ibid., 9 Apr. 1935.

35. Ibid., 25 Mar. 1935.

36. Ibid., 27 Mar. 1935.

37. Ibid., 4 Dec. 1934. Rose, *Put to Work*, 95, cites a FERA study showing average monthly grants during this transition in South Dakota dropped from $15 to $6.

38. *Daily Journal*, 20, 23 Mar. 1935.

39. Jeff Singleton, *The American Dole* (Westport, Conn.: Greenwood Press, 2000), 132.

40. *Daily Journal*, 22 Jan. 1935; Stock, *Main Street in Crisis*, 33.

41. Salutos, *American Farmer*, 208–9.

42. Ibid., 210–18.

43. "Development and Growth of the REA Electrification Program in South Dakota," Bulletin # 75, Business Research Bureau, University of South Dakota (June 1962): 19.

44. Salutos, *American Farmer*, 119–20.

45. WPA Division of Social Research, "Effects of the Works Program on Rural Relief" (USGPO: Research Monograph XIII, 1938).

46. Ibid., xviii.

47. Ibid., 6, 17, 20, 43, 44, 49.

48. *Daily Journal*, 12 Apr. 1935.

49. Ibid., 18 Apr. 1935.

50. Ibid., 29 Apr. 1935.

51. Ibid., 26 Apr. 1935.

52. *Argus-Leader*, 27 Mar. 1935.

53. 301 U.S. 548.

54. *Daily Journal*, 21 Oct. 1935.

55. *Argus-Leader*, 15 Mar. 1934.

56. M. A. Kennedy to L. L. Eaker, 26 Aug. 1935, RG 69, box 2550, NA.

57. *Daily Journal*, 24 June 1935.

58. FERA transition to WPA, letter of 15 July 1935, RG 69, box 2549, NA.

59. "They'd Rather Live on Relief," *The Nation* 141 (7 Aug. 1935): 144; Daniel M. Kidney, "Harvest and Relief," *Survey Graphic* 29 (Sept. 1935): 420.

60. Kidney, "Harvest and Relief," 423.

61. Hubert Kelley, "Good Men Plowed Under," *American Magazine* 120 (Nov. 1935): 134.

62. *Daily Journal*, 23, 24 July 1935.

63. *Argus-Leader*, 22, 24, 27, 30 July 1935.

64. Ibid., 30 Aug. 1935.

65. Kidney, "Harvest and Relief," 420.

66. *Argus-Leader*, 23 Sept. 1935.

67. Ibid., 16 Sept. 1935.

68. Ibid., 27 July, 10 Aug. 1935.

69. Ibid., 28 Aug., 5, 7 Sept. 1935.

70. Ibid., 17, 25, 27 Sept. 1935.

71. Ibid., 30, 31 Oct. 1935.

72. Kennedy to Corrington Gill, 3 Jan. 1935; Kennedy to Tom Berry, 13 Jan. 1935, both in RG 69, box 2549, NA.

73. E. B. G. Longree to Nels Anderson, 20 Mar. 1936, RG 69, box 2552, NA.

74. R. Alton Lee, "Drought and Depression on the Great Plains: The Kansas Transition from New Deal Work Relief to Old Age Pensions," *Heritage of the Great Plains* 39 (spring/summer 2006): 12. *See also* Chad Alan Goldberg, "Contesting the Status of Relief Workers during the New Deal," *Social Science History* 29 (fall 2005).

75. RG 69, box 2549, NA.

76. Berry to Hopkins, 3 June 1936, ibid.

77. Singleton, *American Dole*, 178–79. For the conservative coalition, *see* James T. Patterson, *Congressional Conservatism and the New Deal* (Lexington: University of Kentucky Press, 1967).

78. *Daily Journal*, 1 Mar. 1935.

79. Linda Gordon, *Pitied But Not Entitled* (New York: Free Press, 1994), 193–94.

80. Ibid., 206–7, 209.

81. Dowdell to Woodward, 25 July 1935, ibid.

82. Dowdell to Woodward, 20 Aug. 1935, ibid.

83. Dowdell to Woodward, 7 Sept. 1935, ibid.

84. Ibid.

85. Woodward to Dowdell, 12, 18 Oct. 1935.

86. RG 69, box 274, NA.

87. RG 69, box 275, NA.

6 A New Deal for Minorities and Youth

1. *Daily Journal*, 3 July 1933.

2. Jason A. Heppler, "The American Indian Movement and South Dakota Politics," in Lauck, Miller, and Simmons, eds., *Plains Political Tradition*, vol. 1, 268.

3. Indians was the term used in the contemporary documents, so I shall use it here.

4. Gibson, *American Indian*, 501, 506.

5. *New York Times*, 7 Nov. 1922.

6. Statistics from Gibson, *American Indian*, 536.

7. Ibid., 349–50.

8. *Daily Journal*, 24 Feb. 1934.

9. Gibson, *American Indian*, 539.

10. *Daily Journal*, 20 Feb. 1934.

11. Ibid., 24 May 1932.

12. Ibid., 3, 5 Mar. 1934.

13. Ibid., 3 Mar. 1934.

14. Wolff and Cash, comps., "South Dakotans Remember," 255–57.

15. Ibid., 98.

16. Ibid., 102.

17. *Daily Journal*, 3 Mar. 1934.

18. Teresa M. Houser, "A Pivotal Decision: The Yankton Sioux and the Indian Reorganization Act of 1934," *South Dakota History* 42 (summer 2012): 95–96.

19. Ibid., 114–15.

20. Rolland Dewing, "Depression on South Dakota's Indian Reservation: The SDERA Survey of 1935," *South Dakota History* 21 (spring 1991): 84–87.

21. Ibid., 88–89.

22. Ibid., 89–90.

23. Ibid., 90–93.

24. Ibid., 94–96.

25. Roger Bromert, "The Sioux and the Indian-CCC," *South Dakota History* 8 (winter 1978): 344; Donald L. Parman, "The Indian and the Civilian Conservation Corps," in Roger L. Nichols, ed., *The American Indian Past and Present* (New York: Wiley & Sons, 2nd ed., 1981): 225. This is

abridged from Parman's article with the same title in *Pacific Historical Review* 40 (Feb. 1971).

26. Douglas Brinkley, *Rightful Heritage: Franklin D. Roosevelt and the Land of America* (New York: Harper, 2016): 261.

27. Parman, "The Indian and the CCC," 227.

28. Bromert, "The Sioux and the Indian-CCC," 345–47.

29. Richmond L. Clow, "Tribal Populations in Transition: Sioux Reservations and Federal Policy, 1934–1965," *South Dakota History* 19 (fall 1989): 374–75.

30. Inspection reports, Pine Ridge, RG 75, NA, KC.

31. *Daily Journal*, 11 Feb. 1937.

32. W. L. Eales to Harry L. Hopkins 23, 24 Aug. 1933, RG 69, box 272, NA.

33. Roger Bromert, "Sioux Rehabilitation Colonies: Experiments in Self-Sufficiency, 1936–1942," *South Dakota History* 14 (spring 1984): 32–33.

34. Houser, "A Pivotal Decision," 117.

35. *Daily Journal*, 6, 9 Apr. 1934; Harry F. Thompson, ed., *A New South Dakota History* (Sioux Falls: Center for Western Studies, 2005), 525.

36. Bromert, "Rehabilitation Colonies," 32–35; for a summary of Collier's plans, *see* "A New Deal for the American Indian," *Literary Digest* 117 (Apr. 1934): 21.

37. *Daily Journal*, 3 July 1933.

38. Bromert, "The Sioux and the Indian-CCC," 349–51.

39. Ibid., 347–48.

40. Ibid., 352–53.

41. Parman, "The Indian and the CCC," 233.

42. Bromert, "The Sioux and the Indian-CCC," 354–55.

43. Kennedy to Hopkins, 6 Aug. 1936, RG 69, box 225, NA.

44. William Zimmerman to Hopkins, 24 Nov. 1936; Thad Holt to Zimmerman, 2 Dec. 1936, both ibid.

45. M. A. Kennedy to F. C. Harrington, 23 Sept. 1936, RG 69, box 2549, NA.

46. Clow, "Tribal Populations," 371–72.

47. Ibid.

48. Ibid., 374.

49. *Daily Journal*, 16 Apr. 1935.

50. Bromert, "The Sioux and the Indian-CCC," 36–37.

51. Ibid., 37–38.

52. Ibid., 39–40; Grant, *Down and Out*, 1.

53. Bromert, "Rehabilitation Colonies," 40.

54. Parman, "The Indian and the CCC," 234, 236.

55. Walter A. Person, "Federal Relief through the Works Progress Administration, with Special Reference to South Dakota" (M.A. thesis: University of South Dakota, 1939): 43, quoting a U.S. Government manual issued by the National Emergency Council.

56. Kenneth E. Hendrickson, Jr., "The National Youth Administration in South Dakota, 1935–1943," *South Dakota History* 9 (Spring 1979): 136–37.

57. Ibid., 139.

58. Ibid., 135.

59. Person, "Federal Relief," 45–46.

60. Hendrickson, "NYA," 140.

61. Ibid., 135–36.

62. Ibid., 138–39.

63. Lindley and Lindley, *A New Deal*, 26–27.

64. Person, "Federal Relief," 49.

65. Ibid., 142–43.

66. Ibid., 143.

67. News clipping, RG 75, Pine Ridge WPA, NA, KC.

68. Person, "Federal Relief," 52.

7 Developing the Black Hills

1. Elizabeth Evenson Williams, *Emil Loriks* (Sioux Falls: Center for Western Studies, 1987), 154.

2. Black, *Roosevelt*, 311–13.

3. Joseph H. Cash, *Working the Homestake* (Ames: Iowa State University Press, 1973), is a sympathetic study of the company.

4. *Daily Journal*, 8, 6, 30 Sept. 1933.

5. Ibid., 30 Aug. 1933.

6. Ibid., 18 July, 4 Nov. 1935.

7. Duane Smith, *Staking a Claim in History* (Walnut Creek, Ca: Homestake Mining Company, 2001), 111; *Daily Journal*, 17 Jan. 1935.

8. Oyos, *Family Farmers' Advocate*, 63.

9. *Daily Journal*, 2 Feb. 1934.

10. Williams, *Emil Loriks*, 45–49.

11. Ibid., 52; Studs Terkel, *Hard Times* (New York: Avon Books, 1970), 264.

12. *Daily Journal*, 8, 12, 13 Feb. 1935.

13. Oyos, *Family Farmers' Advocate*, 64–67.

14. *Daily Journal*, 19 Jan. 1935; Williams, *Emil Loriks*, 50–51.

15. *Daily Journal*, 18 July, 4 Nov. 1935.

16. Fite, *Peter Norbeck*, 75–79; Julin, *Marvelous Hundred Square Miles*, 42–44, 118–21.

17. Julin, *Marvelous Hundred Square Miles*, 108–9.

18. Ibid., 136.

19. Ibid., 146–48.

20. Shelby Lee, "Traveling the Sunshine State: The Growth of Tourism in South Dakota, 1914–1939," *South Dakota History* 19 (fall 1989): 200.

21. *Daily Journal*, 1 July 1930.

22. Lee, "Traveling," 209.

23. Ibid., 154–55.

24. Ibid., 165.

25. Ibid., 105–7.

26. *Daily Journal*, 5, 10 June 1933.

27. Ibid., 11 July 1935.

28. Ibid., 29 Oct. 1934.

29. *Daily Journal*, 13 July 1934.

30. Ibid., 19 Nov. 1934; *see* ibid., 7 Mar. 1935 for the licenses.

31. *Argus-Leader*, 18 Aug. 1934.

32. Ibid., 14 Sept. 1934.

33. Ibid., 29 Dec. 1934.

34. James Cracco, "History of the South Dakota Highway Department, 1917–1941" (M.A. thesis: University of South Dakota, 1970): 61–73.

35. *Argus-Leader*, 15 Aug. 1935.

36. *Daily Journal*, 13 Jan., 4 Aug., 10 Sept. 1936, 21 June 1938.

37. Schwieder, *Growing Up*, 68, 135.

38. Julin, *Marvelous Hundred Square Miles*, 125–33.

39. *Daily Journal*, 4 Jan. 1936.

40. James Marten, "We Always Looked Forward to the Hunters Coming: The Culture of Pheasant Hunting in South Dakota," *South Dakota History* 29 (summer 1999): 88–91.

8 Republicans Administer the WPA in South Dakota

1. Philip A. Grant, Jr., "Presidential Politics in South Dakota, 1936," *South Dakota History* 3 (fall 1992): 269.

2. *Argus-Leader*, 6 Dec. 1935.

3. Cecil, "Income Tax," 164–65.

4. O'Rourke, "New Deal Years," 258.

5. *Daily Journal*, 10 Jan. 1936.

6. *Argus-Leader*, 27 June 1936. *See also* R. Alton Lee, "[Not] a Thin Dime: Kansas Relief Politics in the Campaign of 1936," *The Historian* 67 (fall 2005).

7. Grant, Jr., "Presidential Politics," 262.

8. Oyos, *Family Farmers' Advocate*, 69–70; O'Rourke, "New Deal Years," 266–69.

9. John E. Miller, "The Failure to Realign: The 1936 Election in South Dakota," *Journal of the West* 41 (fall 2002): 23–27. *See also* Arthur M. Schlesinger, Jr., *The Politics of Upheaval* (Boston: Houghton Mifflin, 1960): 639.

10. *Argus-Leader*, 27 Oct. 1936.

11. Ibid., 29 Oct. 1936.

12. Ibid., 15 Feb. 1936.

13. M. A. Kennedy to Harry L. Hopkins, 7 Oct. 1936; Aubrey Williams to Kennedy, 13 Oct. 1936, both in RG 69, box 2549, NA.

14. *Argus-Leader*, 9 Oct. 1936.

15. O'Rourke, "New Deal Years," 262.

16. *New York Times*, 30 Dec. 1936.

17. O'Rourke, "New Deal Years," 262.

18. *Argus-Leader*, 30 Dec. 1936.

19. Ibid., 20 Dec. 1936, 2 Oct. 1937; *New York Times*, 20 Dec. 1936.

20. Jon K. Lauck, John E. Miller and Edward Hogan, "Historical Musings: The Contours of South Dakota Political Culture," *South Dakota History* 34 (summer 2004): 173, claims that "among the reasons that Berry lost in 1936 was his failure to obtain the state's 'fair share' of federal relief funds." The citation for this statement was the Cecil article where he discusses the election of 1932 and the pages cited in the Miller article that present Jensen's charge that Berry failed "to obtain its share of relief funds."

21. Inda Avery, "Some South Dakotans' Opinions About the New Deal," *South Dakota History* 7 (summer 1977): 312.

22. *Argus-Leader*, 16 Nov. 1936.

23. Kennedy to Hopkins, 13 Nov. 1936; Williams to Berry, 9 Dec. 1936; Kennedy to Williams, 8 Dec. 1936, all in RG 69, box 2549, NA.

24. Huron to Hopkins, 11 Dec. 1936, ibid.

25. *Argus-Leader*, 28 Jan. 1937.

26. Tom Berry to Harry Hopkins, 10 May 1936; Williams to Berry, 20 May 1937, both in RG 69, box 2552, NA.

27. *Argus-Leader*, 5 Dec. 1935, 7 Oct. 1936, 8 Nov. 1937; Schell, *History of South Dakota*, 296.

28. O'Rourke, "New Deal Years," 263–65.

29. Cecil, "Income Tax," 165–66; Robinson, "Leslie Jensen," in Oyos, *Over a Century*, 135.

30. *Argus-Leader*, 20, 21 Jan. 1935.

31. Ibid., 29 Jan., 2–3 Feb. 1937.

32. Ibid., 29 Jan., 2, 3, 7, 17, 27 Feb. 1937.

33. Cecil, "Income Tax," 263–66.

34. *Argus-Leader*, 8, 25 Jan., 12 Feb. 1937; *Daily Journal*, 5 Mar. 1937.

35. Leslie Jensen to Franklin D. Roosevelt, 13 Feb. 1937, RG 35, entry 9, box 1, NA.

36. Ellery E. Kelley, WPA Division of Employment, Address at Mitchell Conference, 19–21 Sept. 1937, RG 69, box 2550, NA; *Argus-Leader*, 14 Feb. 1937.

37. *Argus-Leader*, 23 Mar., 12 Apr. 1937.

38. Ibid., 17 Mar. 1937.

39. Ibid., 8, 25 Jan., 12 Feb. 1937; *Daily Journal*, 5 Feb. 1937; *U.S. v. Darby*, 312 U.S. 100.

40. Jeff Shesol, *Supreme Power: Franklin Roosevelt vs. the Supreme Court* (New York: W. W. Norton, 2010), 294–96.

41. Melvyn I. Urofsky, *A March of Liberty* (New York: Alfred A. Knopf, 1988), 686–87.

42. Shesol, *Supreme Power*, 414.

43. *NLRB v. Jones and Laughlin Steel*, 301 U.S. 1 (1937) on the Wagner act; *Helvering v. Davis*, 301 U.S. 619 (1937) for Social Security, and *Wickard v. Filburn*, 317 U.S. 111 (1944) for the second AAA. G. Edward White, *The Constitution and the New Deal* (Harvard University Press, 2000), chapter 7, is excellent on the court-packing plan.

44. *Argus-Leader*, 22 June 1938.

45. Ibid., 21 July 1938.

46. Ibid., 22 June 1938.

47. Ibid., 3 Jan. 1939.

48. Ibid., 17 Aug. 1937.

49. Ibid., 14, 22 Apr., 9 Sept. 1937.

50. Ibid., 14 Sept. 1937.

51. Ibid., 6 Jan., 10 Mar. 1938.

52. Ibid., 19 Aug. 1938.

53. Ibid., 30 Sept. 1938.

54. Ibid., 21 Sept. 1938.

55. Ibid., 20 Oct. 1938.

56. E. J. B. Longrie to Fred Most, 13 Feb. 1937; Ervine Lavine to Harry L. Hopkins, 17 Feb. 1937, both in RG 69, box 2554, NA.

57. M. A. Kennedy to Harry L. Hopkins, 13 Mar. 1937, RG 69, box 2550, NA.

58. Kennedy to Hopkins, 9 Mar. 1937; Niles to Kennedy, 16 Mar. 1937, both in RG 69, box 2552, NA.

59. Kennedy to Gill, 23 Mar. 1937, RG 69, box 2550, NA.

60. Fred H. Hildebrandt to Harry L. Hopkins, 17 Sept. 1935; Laurence Westbrook to Fred H. Hildebrandt, 11 Oct. 1935, both in RG 69, box 2552, NA.

61. Hildebrandt to Hopkins, 12 Apr. 1937; Williams to Hildebrandt, 13 Apr. 1937, both in RG 69, box 2550, NA.

62. Lyle Ford to Earl Strathman, 10 Dec. 1937, ibid.

63. C. G. Steinbeck to E. A. Crockett, 7 Dec. 1937, ibid.

64. H. W. Apted to E. A. Crockett, 9 Dec. 1937, ibid.

65. Dow I. Sears to Leslie Jensen, 14 Dec. 1937, ibid.

66. Schwieder, *Growing Up*, 70, 132.

67. Kubek to Socoloff, 9 Jan. 1937; Hanson to Socoloff, 13 Jan. 1937, RG 69, box 2558, NA.

68. Kennedy to William Casimir Mayforth, 5 May 1938; William Warvelle Nelson to Mayforth, 11 May 1938, both ibid.

69. M. Lisle Reese, "The South Dakota Federal Writers Project: Memoirs of a State Director," *South Dakota History* 23 (spring 1993): 203–4.

70. Ibid., 207–12.

71. Ibid., 214; Kennedy to Woodward, 28 Dec. 1938, RG 69, box 2559, NA.

72. Kerper to Wilhelm, 28 Jan. 1938; Wilhelm to Anderson, 7 Feb. 1938; David K. Niles to Wilhelm, 23 Feb. 1938, all in RG 69, box 2553, NA.

73. Herbert Benjamin to David K. Niles, 25 Aug. 1938, RG 69, box 2554, NA; the WPA projects caused a shortage of harvest labor in Iowa, Kansas, Nebraska, and the Dakotas. *See* Kelley, "Good Men Plowed Under," 16–17, 130–36.

74. Herbert Benjamin to David K. Niles, 17 Sept. 1938, RG 69, box 2550, NA.

75. C. W. Anderson to George H. Field, 30 July 1938, RG 69, box 2552, NA.

76. Case to Hopkins, 18 July 1938; Niles to Case, 1 Aug. 1938, ibid.

77. Jensen to Williams, 18 Oct. 1938, RG 69, box 2550, NA.

78. Kennedy to Aubrey Williams, 21 Oct. 1938; Jensen to Williams, 28 Nov. 1938, ibid.

79. 10 Jan., 8 Feb. 1937.

80. *Pierre Daily Capital Journal*, 2 Feb. 1937.

81. Ibid., 7 Feb. 1937.

82. *Argus-Leader*, 15 Feb. 1937.

83. Chan Gurney to Mr. Whiting, 18 Mar. 1939; Kennedy to Howard Hunter, 25 July 1939, both in RG 69, box 2550, NA.

9 The Third New Deal and the Preparation for War

1. Wolff and Cash, "South Dakotans Remember," 239.

2. John W. Jeffries, "The 'New' New Deal," *Political Science Quarterly* 105 (fall 1990): 297.

3. Culver and Hyde, *American Dreamer*, 178–79.

4. Salutos, *American Farmer*, 262–63.

5. Ibid., 159–60.

6. Ibid., 161–65.

7. Ibid., 166–72.

8. *Argus-Leader*, 10, 17 Jan., 7, 10, 13, 14 Feb. 1938.

9. Ibid., 27 June 1938.

10. Ibid., 1 July 1938.

11. *Daily Journal*, 10 Jan. 1937.

12. Ibid., 8 Nov. 1938.

13. Ibid., 9, 14 Nov. 1938, 3 Jan. 1939.

14. Ibid., 17, 27 Jan. 1939.

15. Kennedy to Harrington, 14 Feb. 1939, RG 69, box 2550, NA.

16. Case to Fred Rauch, 30 Sept. 1939, RG 60, box 2552, NA.

17. Kennedy to Howard O. Hunter, 12 Dec. 1939, ibid.

18. *Argus-Leader*, 17, 29 Mar. 1939.

19. Nelson, *The Prairie Winnows Out Its Own*, 165, 174.

20. The *Daily Republic* in the Black Hills and the *Argus-Leader* in the east followed these events closely.

21. Berry to Harrington, 28 Oct. 1939, RG 69, box 2550, NA.

22. Steve J. Bucklin, "Fly-over Country? A Glimpse of South Dakota Through Its Aviation Industry," *South Dakota History* 45 (summer 2015): 114–17.

23. Ibid., 118–22. Janet R. Daly Bednarek, *America's Airports* (College Station: Texas A & M University Press, 2001): 97–99.

24. *Daily Journal*, 15, 20 Feb., 6, 19 Apr. 1938.

25. Ibid., 20 Feb. 1937.

26. Bucklin, "Fly-over," 120–21.

27. These activities and letters are in RG 69, box 2550, NA; *Daily Journal*, 31 July, 12 Oct. 1940.

28. *Daily Journal*, 5 Feb. 1940.

29. Ibid., 16 Oct. 1940.

30. Ibid., 4 Jan. 1940.

31. Ibid., 7 June 1941; David B. Miller, "Life Aboard 'Battleship X': The U.S.S. *South Dakota* in World War II," *South Dakota History* 23 (summer 1993).

32. *Daily Journal*, 9 Apr. 1940; *Statistical Abstract of the United States, 1941*, 200–201.

33. *Daily Journal*, 15 Mar., 5 Apr. 1940.

34. Ibid., 11, 15 Apr. 1940.

35. Ibid., 11 Apr., 24 May 1940.

36. Ibid., 18 Apr. 24 May 1940.

37. Ibid., 3 July 1940.

38. Vertical File, South Dakota State Archives, Pierre.

39. Ibid.

40. *Daily Journal*, 4 Sept. 1940.

41. R. Alton Lee, *Farmers vs. Wage Earners* (Lincoln: University of Nebraska Press, 2005), 214–15.

42. *Daily Journal*, 15 Mar. 1940, 8 Sept. 1941.

43. Ibid., 6 Sept. 1940.

44. Ibid., 14 Apr., 17 June, 22 Aug. 1941.

45. *See* Quincy Wright, "The Transfer of Destroyers to Great Britain," *American Journal of International Law* 34 (Oct. 1940).

46. *Daily Journal*, 29 Aug., 9 Sept., 15 Oct. 1940.

47. Ibid., 28 July, 14 Aug. 1941; Doris Kearns Goodwin, *No Ordinary Time* (New York: Simon and Schuster, 1994), 268.

48. Thomas Fleming, *The New Dealers' War* (New York: Basic Books, 2001), 82–83.

49. *New York Times*, 7 Dec. 1941, regular; 7 Dec. 1941, extra.

50. Stock, *Main Street in Crisis*, 206.

Conclusion

1. Avery, "Some South Dakotan's Opinions," 313. This experience is not unique to South Dakotans. Kansans endured the same trauma. *See* Thomas Frank, *What's the Matter with Kansas?* (New York: Henry Holt, 2004).

2. Quote from Miller, Lauck, and Hogan, "Historical Musings," 173.

3. O'Rourke, "New Deal Years," 269.

4. Lee, "'[Not] a Thin Dime, 478–79. For the overall picture of Kansas in the Great Depression, *see* Peter Fearon, *Kansas in the Great Depression* (Columbia: University of Missouri Press, 2007).

5. David B. Danbom, *Going It Alone* (St. Paul: Minnesota Historical Society Press, 2005): Conclusion.

6. D. Jerome Tweton, *The New Deal at the Grass Roots* (St. Paul: Minnesota Historical Society Press, 1988): Conclusion.

7. Hurt, *The Big Empty*, 123.

Bibliography

Avery, Inda. "Some South Dakotans' Opinions about the New Deal." *South Dakota History* 7 (summer 1977).

Bednarek, Janet R. Daly. *America's Airports: Airfield Development, 1918–1947*. College Station: Texas A & M University Press, 2001.

Bellush, Bernard. *The Failure of the NRA*. New York: W. W. Norton, 1975.

Black, Conrad. *Franklin Delano Roosevelt: Champion of Freedom*. New York: Public Affairs Press, 2003.

Bremer, William W. "Along the American Way: The New Deal's Work Relief Programs for the Unemployed." *Journal of American History* 62 (December 1975): 636–52.

Brinkley, Alan. *The End of Reform*. New York: Vintage Books, 1995.

——. *Voices of Protest*. New York: Vintage Books, 1983.

Brinkley, Douglas. *Rightful Heritage: Franklin D. Roosevelt and the Land of America*. New York: Harper, 2016.

Bromert, Roger. "The Sioux and the Indian-CCC." *South Dakota History* 8 (winter 1978): 340–56.

——. "Sioux Rehabilitation Colonies: Experiments in Self-Sufficiency, 1936–1942." *South Dakota History* 14 (spring 1984): 31–47.

Burns, James McGregor. *Roosevelt: The Lion and the Fox*. New York: Harcourt, Brace and World, 1956.

Carlson, Paul H., and Steve Porter. "South Dakota Congressmen and the Hundred Days of the New Deal." *South Dakota History* 8 (fall 1978): 327–39.

Cash, Joseph H. *Working the Homestake*. Ames: Iowa State University Press, 1973.

Cecil, Matthew. "Democratic Party Politics and the South Dakota Income Tax, 1933–1942." *South Dakota History* 26 (summer/fall 1986): 137–69.

Childs, Marquis W. "Main Street after Ten Years." *The New Republic* 73 (18 January 1933): 263–65.

Choate, Jean. "'Dear Mr. Gurney': D. B. Gurney's Campaign to Recover the Hog-Processing Tax for Farmers." *South Dakota History* 22 (winter 1992): 156–72.

Clem, Alan. *Prairie State Politics.* Washington, D.C.: Public Affairs Press, 1967.

Clow, Richmond. "Tribal Populations in Transition: Sioux Reservations and Federal Policy, 1934–1965." *South Dakota History* 19 (fall 1989): 361–91.

Cohen, Adam. *Nothing to Fear: FDR's Inner Circle and the Hundred Days That Created Modern America.* New York: Penguin, 2009.

Cracco, James. "History of the South Dakota Highway Department, 1919–1941." M.A. thesis, University of South Dakota, 1969.

Culver, John C., and John Hyde. *American Dreamer: A Life of Henry A. Wallace.* New York: W. W. Norton, 2000.

Danbom, David B. *Going It Alone: Fargo Grapples with the Great Depression.* St. Paul: Minnesota Historical Society Press, 2005.

——. *Born in the Country.* Baltimore: Johns Hopkins Press, 1995.

Dewing, Rolland. "Depression on South Dakota's Indian Reservations: The SDERA Survey of 1935." *South Dakota History* 21 (spring 1991): 84–96.

Dubofsky, Melvyn, ed. *The New Deal.* New York: Garland, 1992.

Egan, Timothy. *The Worst Hard Time.* Boston: Houghton Mifflin, 2006.

Farnham, Rebecca, and Irene Link. "Effects of the Work Program on Rural Relief." WPA, Division of Social Research, 1938.

Fite, Gilbert C. "Farmer Opinion and the Agricultural Adjustment Act, 1933." *Mississippi Valley Historical Review* 48 (March 1962): 656–73.

——. "John A. Simpson: The Southwest's Militant Farm Leader." *Mississippi Valley Historical Review* 35 (March 1949): 563–84.

——. "Peter Norbeck and the Defeat of the Nonpartisan League in South Dakota." *Mississippi Valley Historical Review* 33 (September 1946): 217–36.

——. *Peter Norbeck: Prairie Statesman.* Pierre: South Dakota State Historical Society Press, 2005.

——. *George N. Peek and the Fight for Farm Parity.* Norman: University of Oklahoma Press, 1954.

Fleming, Thomas. *The New Dealers' War: FDR and the War within World War II.* New York: Basic Books, 2001.

Frank, Thomas. *What's the Matter with Kansas? How Conservatives Won the Heart of America*. New York: Henry Holt, 2004.

Galbraith, John Kenneth. *The Great Crash*. Boston: Houghton Mifflin, 1954.

Gibson, Arrell Morgan. *The American Indian*. Boston: D. C. Heath, 1980.

Golay, Michael. *America 1933: The Great Depression, Lorena Hickok, Eleanor Roosevelt, and the Shaping of the New Deal*. New York: Free Press, 2013.

Goldberg, Chad Alan. "Contesting the Status of Relief Workers during the New Deal." *Social Science History* 29 (fall 2005): 337–71.

Goodwin, Doris Kearns. *No Ordinary Time: Franklin and Eleanor Roosevelt and the Home Front in World War II*. New York: Simon & Schuster, 1994.

Gordon, Linda. *Pitied But Not Entitled: Single Mothers and the History of Welfare*. New York: Free Press, 1994.

Gould, Lewis L. *The Most Exclusive Club: A History of the Modern United States Senate*. New York: Basic Books, 2005.

Graham, Otis L. "Historians and the New Deals." *Social Studies* 54 (April 1963): 133–40.

Grant, Michael Johnston. *Down and Out on the Family Farm: Rural Rehabilitation in the Great Plains*. Lincoln: University of Nebraska Press, 2002.

Grant, Philip A., Jr. "Presidential Politics in South Dakota, 1936." *South Dakota History* 3 (fall 1992): 261–75.

Grattan, C. Hartley. "Who is on Relief?" *Scribners Magazine* 97 (June 1935): 24–30.

Handy-Marchello, Barbara. *Women of the Northern Plains: Gender and Settlement on the Homestead Frontier, 1870–1930*. St. Paul: Minnesota Historical Society Press, 2005.

Hendrickson, Kenneth E., Jr. "The Civilian Conservation Corps in South Dakota." *South Dakota History* 11 (winter 1980): 1–20.

———. "The National Youth Administration in South Dakota, 1935–1943." *South Dakota History* 9 (spring 1979): 131–51.

Hooks, Gregory M. "A New Deal for Farmers and Social Scientists: The Politics of Rural Sociology in the Depression Era." *Rural Sociology* 48 (1983): 386–405.

Houser, Teresa M. "A Pivotal Decision: The Yankton Sioux and the Indian Reorganization Act of 1934." *South Dakota History* 42 (summer 2012): 95–125.

Howard, Christopher. "Sowing the Seeds of Welfare: The Transformation of Mothers' Pensions, 1900–1940." *Journal of Public Policy* 4 (1992): 188–227.

Hurt, R. Douglas. *The Big Empty: The Great Plains in the Twentieth Century*. Tucson: University of Arizona, 2011.

Jeffries, John W. "The 'New' New Deal: FDR and American Liberalism, 1937–1945." *Political Science Quarterly* 105 (fall 1990): 397–418.

Johnson, Hugh. *The Blue Eagle from Egg to Earth*. New York: Doubleday, 1935.

Johnson, Lyle R. "Decade of Drought." *South Dakota History* 43 (fall 2013).

Johnson, William R. "National Farm Organizations and the Reshaping of Agricultural Policy in 1932." *Agricultural History* 37 (January 1963): 35–42.

Jones, John Finbar, and John Middlemist Herrick. *Citizens in Service: Volunteers in Social Welfare during the Depression, 1929–1941*. East Lansing: Michigan State University Press, 1976.

Julin, Suzanne Barta. *A Marvelous Hundred Square Miles: Black Hills Tourism, 1880–1941*. Pierre: South Dakota State Historical Society Press, 2009.

Kelley, Hubert. "Good Men Plowed Under." *American Magazine* 120 (November 1935): 16–17, 130–36.

Kennedy, David M. *Freedom from Fear:The American People in Depression and War, 1929–1945*. New York: Oxford University Press, 2001.

Kidney, Daniel M. "Harvest and Relief." *Survey Graphic* 24 (September 1935): 420–25, 461, 464.

Kirkendall, Richard S. "Howard Tolley and Agricultural Planning in the 1930s." *Agricultural History* 39 (October 1964): 25–33.

Kumlein, W. F. "A Graphic Summary of the Relief Situation in South Dakota (1930–1935)." Bulletin #310, Agricultural Experiment Station. Brookings, S.Dak. May 1937.

Lambert, C. Roger. "The Drought Cattle Purchase, 1934–1935." *Agricultural History* 45 (April 1971): 85–93.

——. "Slaughter of the Innocents: The Public Protests to AAA Killing of Little Pigs." *Midwest Quarterly* 14 (April 1933): 247–56.

——. "Want and Plenty: The Federal Surplus Relief Corporation and the AAA." *Agricultural History* 46 (July 1972): 390–99.

——, and Kevin F. Mykill. "Federal Food for the Hungry: 1930–1940." In R. Alton Lee, ed., *Agricultural Legacies*. Vermillion: University of South Dakota Press, 1986: 89–104.

Landis, Paul H. "Rural Relief in South Dakota." FERA Division of Research and Statistics, Bulletin #289, June 1934.

Lauck, Jon K., John E. Miller, and Donald C. Simmons, Jr., eds. *The Plains Political Tradition: Essays on South Dakota Political Culture*. Pierre: South Dakota State Historical Society, vol. 1: 2011, vol. 2: 2014.

Lee, R. Alton. "The Civilian Conservation Corps in Kansas." *Journal of the West* 44 (fall 2005): 69–73.

——. "Drought and Depression on the Great Plains." *Heritage of the Great Plains* 39 (spring/summer 2006): 5–29.

——. *A History of Regulatory Taxation.* Lexington: University of Kentucky Press, 1973.

——. "[Not] a Thin Dime: Kansas Relief Politics in the Campaign of 1936." *The Historian* 67 (fall 2005): 474–488.

——. *Farmers vs. Wage Earners: A History of Organized Labor in Kansas, 1860–1960.* Lincoln: University of Nebraska Press, 2005.

——. *Principle over Party.* Pierre: South Dakota State Historical Society Press, 2011.

Lee, Shelby. "Traveling the Sunshine State: The Growth of Tourism in South Dakota, 1914–1939." *South Dakota History* 19 (fall 1989): 194–223.

Leuchtenberg, William E. *Franklin D. Roosevelt and the New Deal.* New York: Harper and Row, 1963.

Lindeman, Eduard. "Social Workers in the Depression." *The Nation* 138 (7 March 1938): 274–75.

Lindley, Betty, and Ernest K. Lindley. *A New Deal for Youth: The Story of the National Youth Administration.* New York: Viking Press, 1938.

Lowitt, Richard, and Maurine Beasley, eds. *One Third of a Nation: Lorena Hickok Reports on the Great Depression.* Urbana: University of Illinois Press, 1981.

Lubbow, Roy. *The Struggle for Social Security, 1900–1935.* University of Pittsburgh Press, 1986.

Maher, Neil M. *Nature's New Deal: The Civilian Conservation Corps and the Roots of the American Environmental Movement.* New York: Oxford University Press, 2008.

Mangus, A. R. *Changing Aspects of Rural Relief.* WPA research monograph 14. New York: Da Capo Press, 1971.

Marten, James A. "'We Always Looked Forward to the Hunters Coming': The Culture of Pheasant Hunting in South Dakota." *South Dakota History* 29 (summer 1999): 88–112.

Matthews, Allan. "Agrarian Radicals: The United Farmers League of South Dakota." *South Dakota History* 3 (fall 1973): 408–21.

May, Irwin M., Jr. "Cotton and Cattle: The FSRC and Emergency Work Relief." *Agricultural History* 46 (July 1972): 401–13.

Miller, David B. "Life aboard 'Battleship X': The U.S.S. *South Dakota* in World War II." *South Dakota History* 23 (summer 1993): 142–65.

Miller, John E. "The Failure to Realign: The 1936 Election in South Dakota." *Journal of the West* 41 (fall 2002): 2–29.

——. "Restrained, Respectable Radicals: The South Dakota Farm Holiday." *Agricultural History* 59 (July 1985): 429–47.

——, Jon Lauck, and Edward Hogan. "Historical Musings: The Contours of South Dakota Political Culture." *South Dakota History* 34 (summer 2004): 158–78.

Nelson, Paula M. *The Prairie Winnows Out Its Own: The West River Country of South Dakota in the Years and Depression and Dust.* Iowa City: University of Iowa Press, 1996.

"A New Deal for the American Indian." *Literary Digest* 117 (April 1934): 21.

O'Connor, Debra. "Union in His Blood." *Sioux Falls Argus-Leader*, 20 October 1981.

O'Rouke, Paul A. "South Dakota Politics during the New Deal Years." *South Dakota History* 1 (summer 1971): 231–71.

Oyos, Lynwood E. "Labor's House Divided: The Morrell Strike of 1935–1937." *South Dakota History* 18 (spring/summer 1988): 67–88.

——. *Over a Century of Leadership: South Dakota Territorial and State Governors.* Sioux Falls, S.Dak.: Center for Western Studies, 1987.

——. *The Family Farmers' Advocate: The South Dakota Farmers Union, 1914–2000.* Sioux Falls, S.Dak.: Center for Western Studies, 2000.

Parman, Donald L. "The Indian and the Civilian Conservation Corps." *Pacific Historical Review* 40 (February 1971): 39–56.

Patterson, James T. *The New Deal and the States: Federalism in Transition.* Princeton University Press, 1969.

Perisco, Joseph E. *Franklin and Lucy: Mrs. Rutherfurd and the Other Remarkable Women in Roosevelt's Life.* New York: Random House, 2008.

Perkins, Val L. "The AAA and the Politics of Agriculture: Agricultural Policy Formulation in the Fall of 1933." *Agricultural History* 39 (October 1965): 220–29.

Person, Walter A. "Federal Relief through the Works Progress Administration, with Special Reference to South Dakota." M.A. thesis: University of South Dakota, 1939.

Popper, Deborah Epstein, and Frank J. Popper. "Dust to Dust: A Daring Proposal for Dealing with an Inevitable Disaster." *Planning* 12 (December 1987).

Pratt, William C. "Rethinking the Farm Revolt of the 1930s." *Great Plains Quarterly* 8 (summer 1988): 131–44.

——. "Rural Radicalism on the Northern Plains, 1912–1950." *Montana: The Magazine of Western History* 42 (winter 1992): 43–55.

Reese, M. Lisle. "The South Dakota Federal Writers' Project: Memoirs of a State Director." *South Dakota History* 23 (spring 1993): 203–4.

Riley, Linda. "Farm Women's Roles in the Agricultural Development of South Dakota." *South Dakota History* 13 (spring/summer 1985): 85–121.

Rose, Nancy E. *Put to Work: Relief Programs in the Great Depression.* New York: Monthly Review Press, 1994.

Rosenman, Alvin. "Old Age Assistance." *American Academy of Political Sciences* 202 (March 1939): 53.

Salutos, Theodore. *The American Farmer and the New Deal.* Ames: Iowa State University Press, 1982.

Schaels, Amity. *The Forgotten Man.* New York: HarperCollins, 2007.

Schell, Herbert S. *History of South Dakota.* Lincoln: University of Nebraska Press, 1969.

Schlesinger, Arthur M., Jr. *The Coming of the New Deal.* Boston: Houghton Mifflin, 1959.

——. *The Politics of Upheaval.* Boston: Houghton Mifflin, 1960.

——, and Fred L. Israel, eds. *History of American Presidential Elections: 1789–2001.* New York: Chelsea House, 1978.

Schwieder, Dorothy. "South Dakota Farm Women and the Great Depression." *Journal of the West* 24 (October 1985): 6–18.

——, and Dorothy Hubbard. *Growing Up with the Town: Family and Community on the Great Plains.* Iowa City: University of Iowa Press, 2002.

Sherwood, Robert E. *Roosevelt and Hopkins: An Intimate History.* New York: Harper & Brothers, 1950.

Shesol, Jeff. *Supreme Power: Franklin Roosevelt vs. the Supreme Court.* New York: W. W. Norton, 2010.

Shover, John L. "The Communist Party and the Midwest Crisis of 1933." *Journal of American History* 51 (September 1964): 248–66.

——. *Cornbelt Rebellion: The Farmers' Holiday Association.* Urbana: University of Illinois Press, 1965.

——. "Depression Letters from American Farmers." *Agricultural History* 36 (July 1962): 163–68.

——. "The Penny-Auction Rebellion." *American West* 2 (Fall 1965): 64–72.

——. "Populism in the Nineteen-Thirties: The Battle for the AAA." *Agricultural History* 39 (January 1965): 17–24.

Singleton, Jeff. *The American Dole: Unemployment Relief and the Welfare State in the Great Depression*. Westport, Conn.: Greenwood Press, 2000.

Socolsky, George E. "The Political Burden of Relief." *Atlantic Monthly* 158 (September 1936): 331–40.

Soffar, Allan J. "The Forest Shelterbelt Project, 1934–1944." *Journal of the West* 14 (July 1975): 95–107.

Sparkes, Boyden. "The New Deal for Transients." *Saturday Evening Post* 208 (19 October 1935): 23, 90–95.

Stock, Catherine McNicol. *Main Street in Crisis: The Great Depression and the Old Middle Class on the Northern Plains*. Chapel Hill: University of North Carolina Press, 1992.

Stolberg , Benjamin, and Warren Jay Vinton. "The New Deal vs. Recovery." *The American Mercury* 33 (December 1934): 385–97.

Swain, Martha H. "The Forgotten Woman: Ellen S. Woodward and Women's Relief in the New Deal." *Prologue* 15 (winter 1983): 201–13.

Terkel, Studs. *Hard Times*. New York: Avon Books, 1970.

"They'd Rather Live on Relief." *The Nation* 141 (7 August 1937): 144.

Thompson, Harry F., ed. *A New South Dakota History*. Sioux Falls, S.Dak.: Center for Western Studies, 2005.

Tweton, D. Jerome. *The New Deal at the Grass Roots: Programs for the People in Otter Tail County, Minnesota*. St. Paul: Minnesota Historical Society Press, 1988.

Urofsky, Melvin I. *A March of Liberty: A Constitutional History of the United States*. New York: Alfred A. Knopf, 1988.

Watkins, T. H. *The Hungry Years*. New York: Henry Holt, 1999.

White, G. Edward. *The Constitution and the New Deal*. Harvard University Press, 2000.

Williams, Elizabeth E. *Emil Loriks: Builder of a New Economic Order*. Sioux Falls, S.Dak.: Center for Western Studies, 1987.

Williams, Elizabeth Evenson. "W. R. Ronald: Prairie Editor and an AAA Architect." *South Dakota History* 1 (fall 1974): 272–92.

Wilson, Joan Hoff. *Herbert Hoover: Forgotten Progressive*. Prospect Heights, Ill.: Waveland Press, 1975.

Wolff, Gerald W., and Joseph H. Cash, comps. "South Dakotans Remember the Great Depression." *South Dakota History* 19 (summer 1989): 224–58.

Wright, Quincy. "The Transfer of Destroyers to Great Britain." *American Journal of International Law* 34 (October 1940): 14.

Index